SCIENCE COMICS

DOGS
From Predator to Protector

DOGS
From Predator to Protector

ANDY HIRSCH

:01

First Second

New York

For all the dogs. Who's a good dog?
Yes-you-are, yes-you-are!

First Second

Copyright © 2017 by Andy Hirsch

Drawn in Manga Studio EX 5. Colored in Adobe Photoshop CS5. Lettered with Comicrazy font from Comicraft.

Published by First Second
First Second is an imprint of Roaring Brook Press,
a division of Holtzbrinck Publishing Holdings Limited Partnership
120 Broadway, New York, NY 10271
All rights reserved

Library of Congress Control Number: 2016961597

Paperback ISBN: 978-1-62672-768-7
Hardcover ISBN: 978-1-62672-767-0

Our books may be purchased in bulk for promotional, educational, or business use. Please
contact your local bookseller or the Macmillan Corporate and Premium Sales Department
at (800) 221-7945 ext. 5442 or by e-mail at MacmillanSpecialMarkets@macmillan.com.

FIRST
EDITION

First edition 2017
Series editor: Dave Roman
Book design by John Green

Printed in China by Toppan Leefung Printing Ltd., Dongguan City, Guangdong Province
Paperback: 10 9 8 7 6
Hardcover: 10 9 8 7 6 5 4 3 2

In a few moments, you will meet a dog named Rudy, a scraggly, friendly little guy with four legs who loves balls and his human, who excels at meeting new dogs and people, and who, interestingly enough, dabbles in time travel. With Rudy as your guide, you will gain access to a journey of evolution, genetics, and, ultimately, the inner world of the dog, a world that most people don't know.

Did that last sentence surprise you? After all, people know dogs! Surely you've met a dog. Or many dogs! There's a good chance that a dog lives with your family and maybe even sleeps in your bed. Heck, you might even live with a dog named Rudy! And dogs are not new. Maybe your parents, grandparents, and great-grandparents grew up with dogs weaving in and out of their legs, helping out on a farm, or licking them awake in the morning. Dogs have lived alongside us humans for many thousands of years as our companions and even our fellow workers.

But it wasn't until very recently that humans really started to *understand* dogs. It all started when different scientific fields started putting dogs under a scientific microscope. Instead of viewing dogs as a species we already understood, researchers began to ask scientific, testable questions about dogs: Where did they come from? Why do dogs bark? Why do they sniff

butts? And why do we keep dogs—and not wolves—as pets? It turns out lots and lots of scientists have been working really hard to find the answers to these questions. And Rudy has made it his sole purpose in life to share the secret world of the dog with you.

For example, the dog of your parents' day was thought to be a wolf in dog's clothing, vying for control over people and needing to be kept in line. Although some people perpetuate this myth today, we now know that the dog of today is distantly removed from this wolf ancestor. Instead, dogs are not trying to control us, and most disputes between dogs and humans arise from miscommunication—we don't understand where they are coming from and why they do what they do. Scientists have helped unpack these tricky questions so that dogs and people can live their best lives together.

Perhaps you have heard that for a dog to bond with you, it's best to bring him or her into your home as a puppy? Research published at the turn of the twenty-first century flipped this idea on its head. Instead, because of their evolutionary history alongside us, dogs of all ages, not just puppies, are ready to bond with humans. Not only can old dogs learn new tricks, but dogs of all ages can make great family members.

You are born in the Age of the Dog, and for this, we have to admit, we

are a bit jealous. Oh, hi. We are Julie and Mia, two researchers who study the science of dog behavior, cognition, learning, and welfare. We also study working dogs and the dog-human relationship. (Phew! We are busy!) Like your parents, we grew up in an era that was high on dog love but low on dog understanding. While love is a big part of the equation, it works most effectively in conjunction with its best friend, *understanding*. It is understanding of what dogs want and why they do what they do that helps us provide dogs with happy, healthy lives. It is understanding that helps us see dogs on their terms and not as miniature humans wearing dog costumes meeting each other in weird ways. (Yes, we are talking about butt sniffing again, a normal part of how dogs greet one another.) We hope you enjoy this journey with Rudy—we certainly did!

Julie Hecht and Mia Cobb (who happens to live with a dog named Rudy),
canine scientists,
Do You Believe in Dog? blog,
The Graduate Center, CUNY, USA & Monash University, Australia

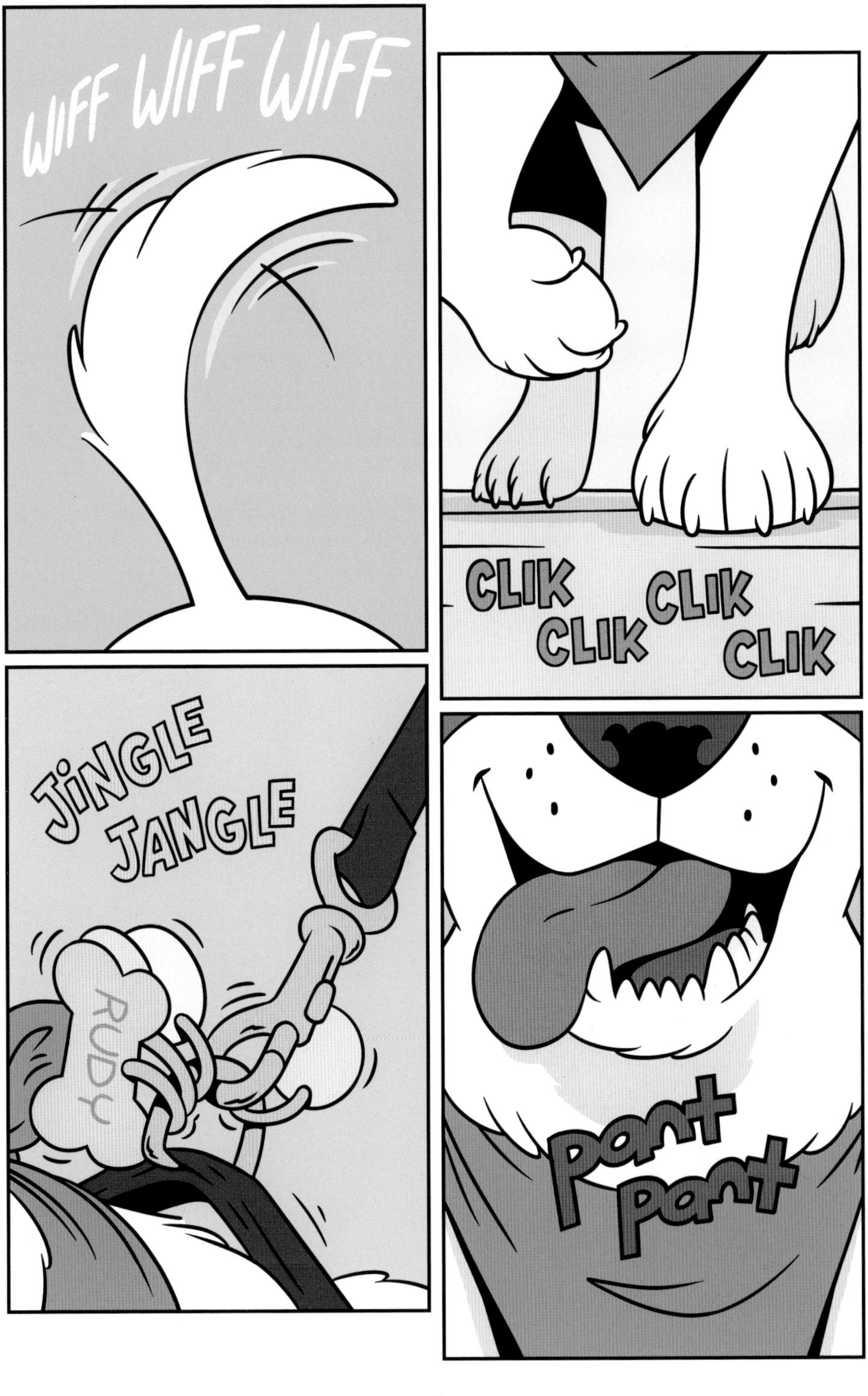
WIFF WIFF WIFF
CLIK CLIK CLIK CLIK
JINGLE JANGLE
RUDY
pant pant

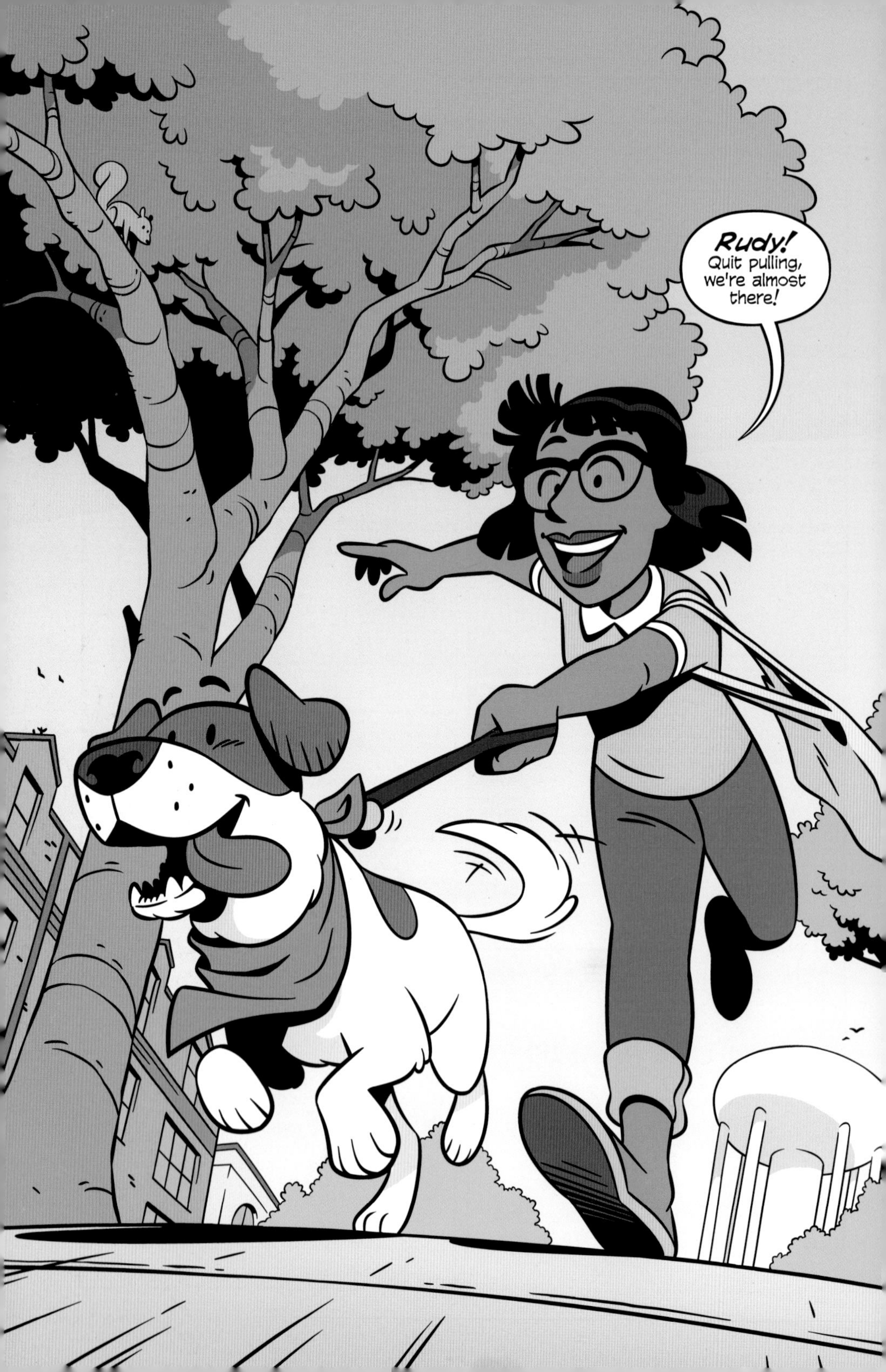
Rudy! Quit pulling, we're almost there!

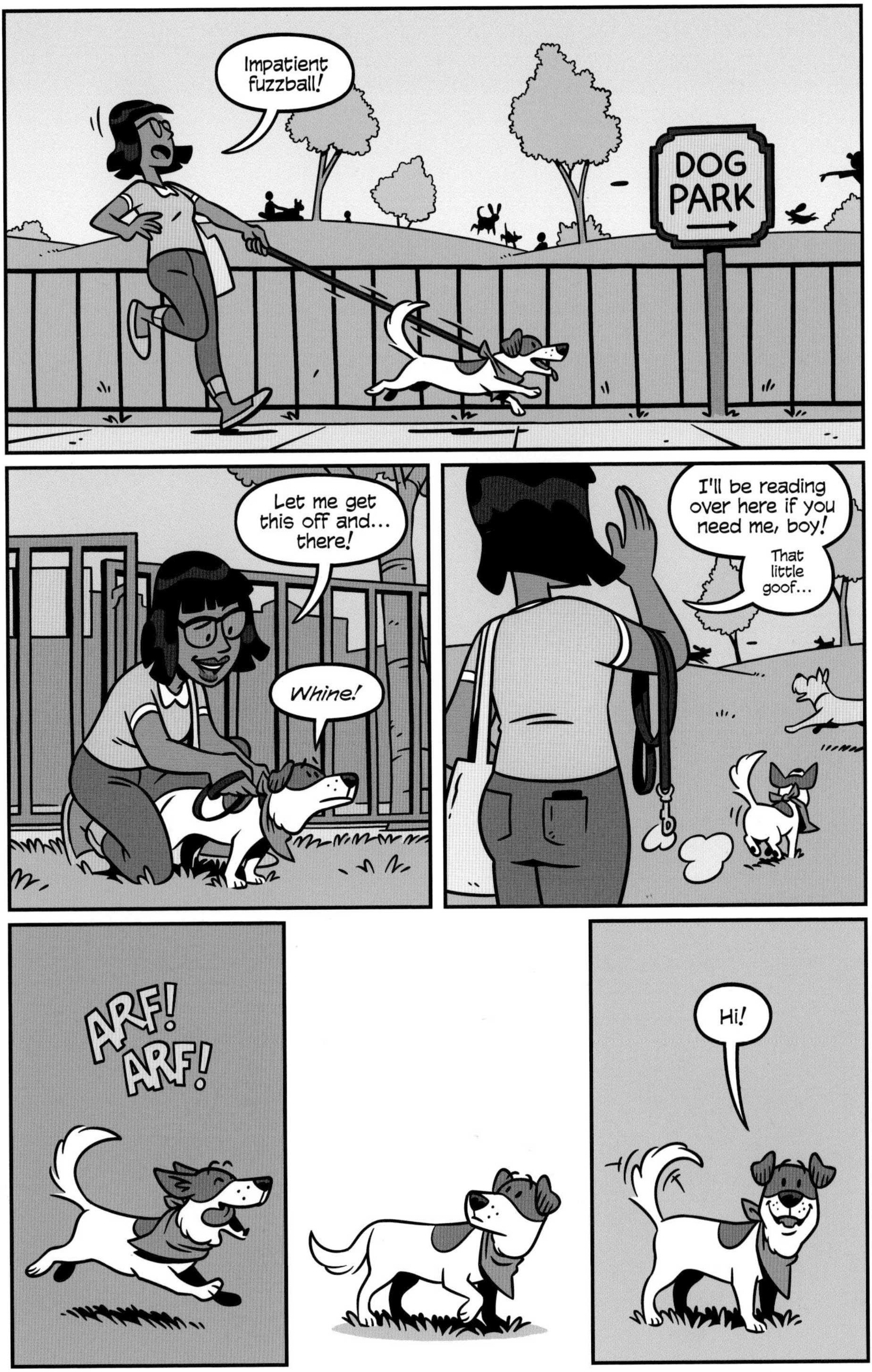
Impatient fuzzball!
DOG PARK
Let me get this off and... there!
Whine!
I'll be reading over here if you need me, boy!
That little goof...
ARF! ARF!
Hi!

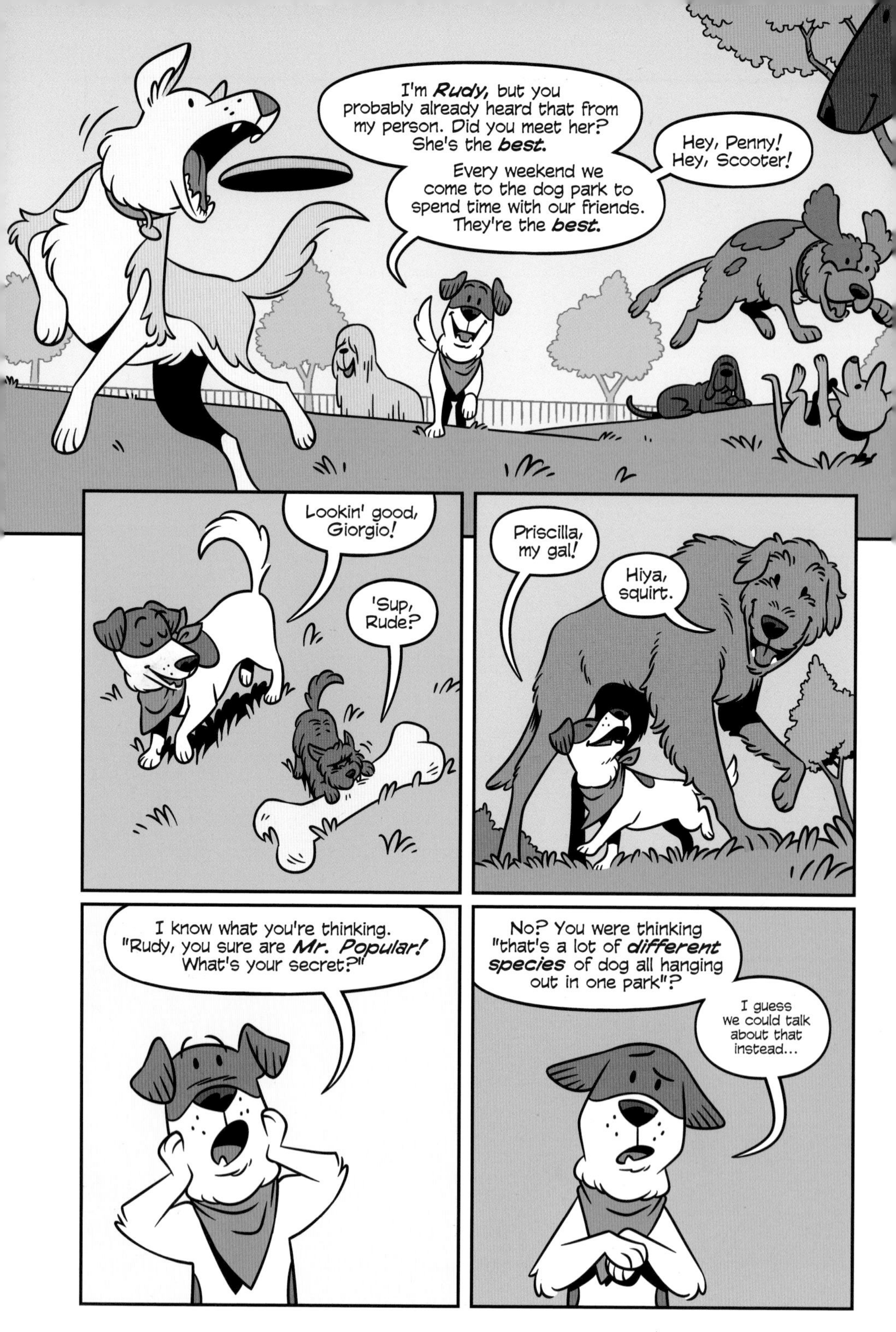

I'm *Rudy,* but you probably already heard that from my person. Did you meet her? She's the *best.*
Every weekend we come to the dog park to spend time with our friends. They're the *best.*
Hey, Penny! Hey, Scooter!
Lookin' good, Giorgio!
'Sup, Rude?
Priscilla, my gal!
Hiya, squirt.
I know what you're thinking. "Rudy, you sure are *Mr. Popular!* What's your secret?"
No? You were thinking "that's a lot of *different species* of dog all hanging out in one park"?
I guess we could talk about that instead...

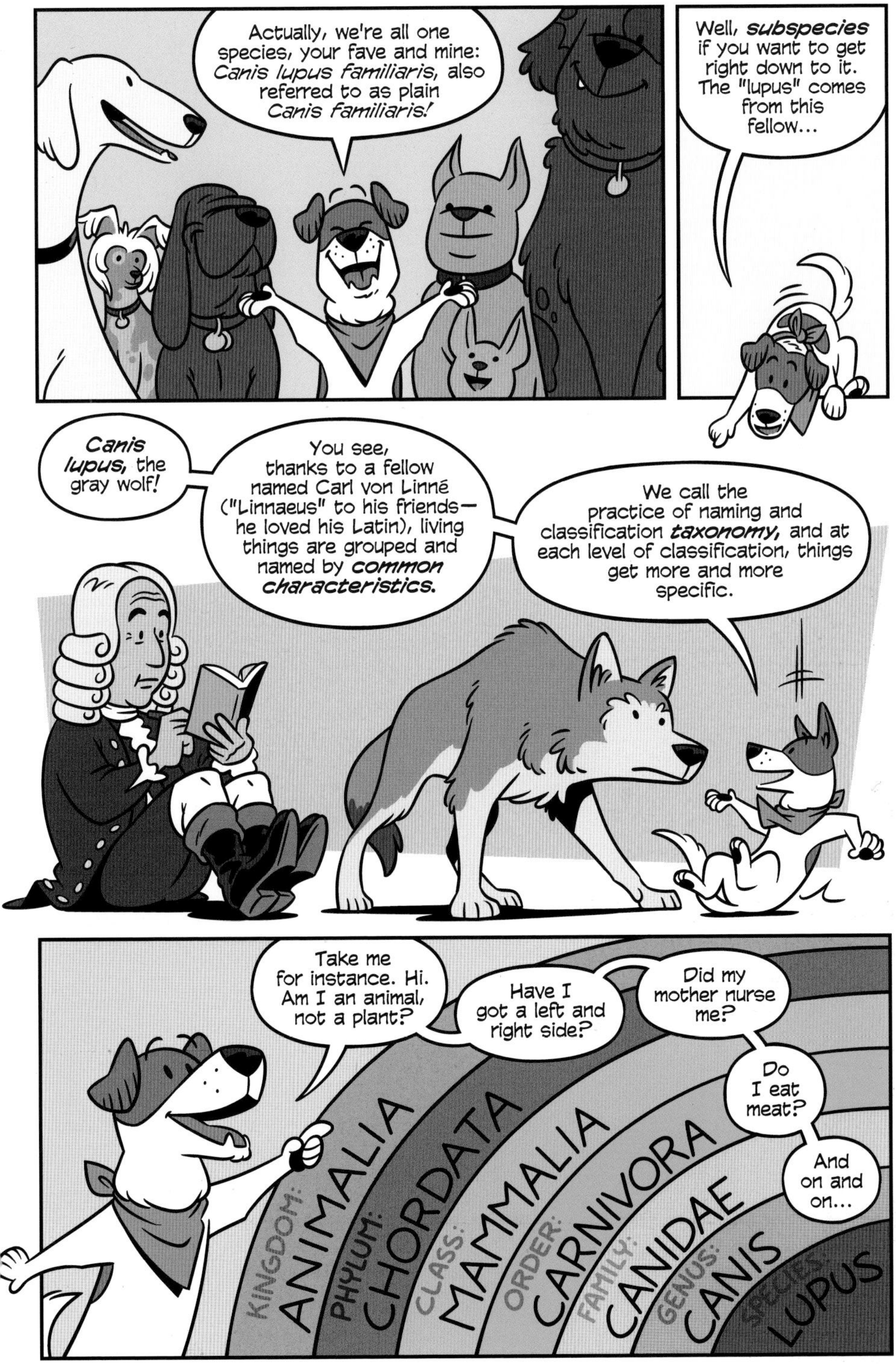
Actually, we're all one species, your fave and mine: *Canis lupus familiaris,* also referred to as plain *Canis familiaris!*
Well, ***subspecies*** if you want to get right down to it. The "lupus" comes from this fellow...
Canis lupus, the gray wolf!
You see, thanks to a fellow named Carl von Linné ("Linnaeus" to his friends— he loved his Latin), living things are grouped and named by ***common characteristics.***
We call the practice of naming and classification ***taxonomy,*** and at each level of classification, things get more and more specific.
Take me for instance. Hi. Am I an animal, not a plant?
Have I got a left and right side?
Did my mother nurse me?
Do I eat meat?
And on and on...
KINGDOM: ANIMALIA
PHYLUM: CHORDATA
CLASS: MAMMALIA
ORDER: CARNIVORA
FAMILY: CANIDAE
GENUS: CANIS
SPECIES: LUPUS

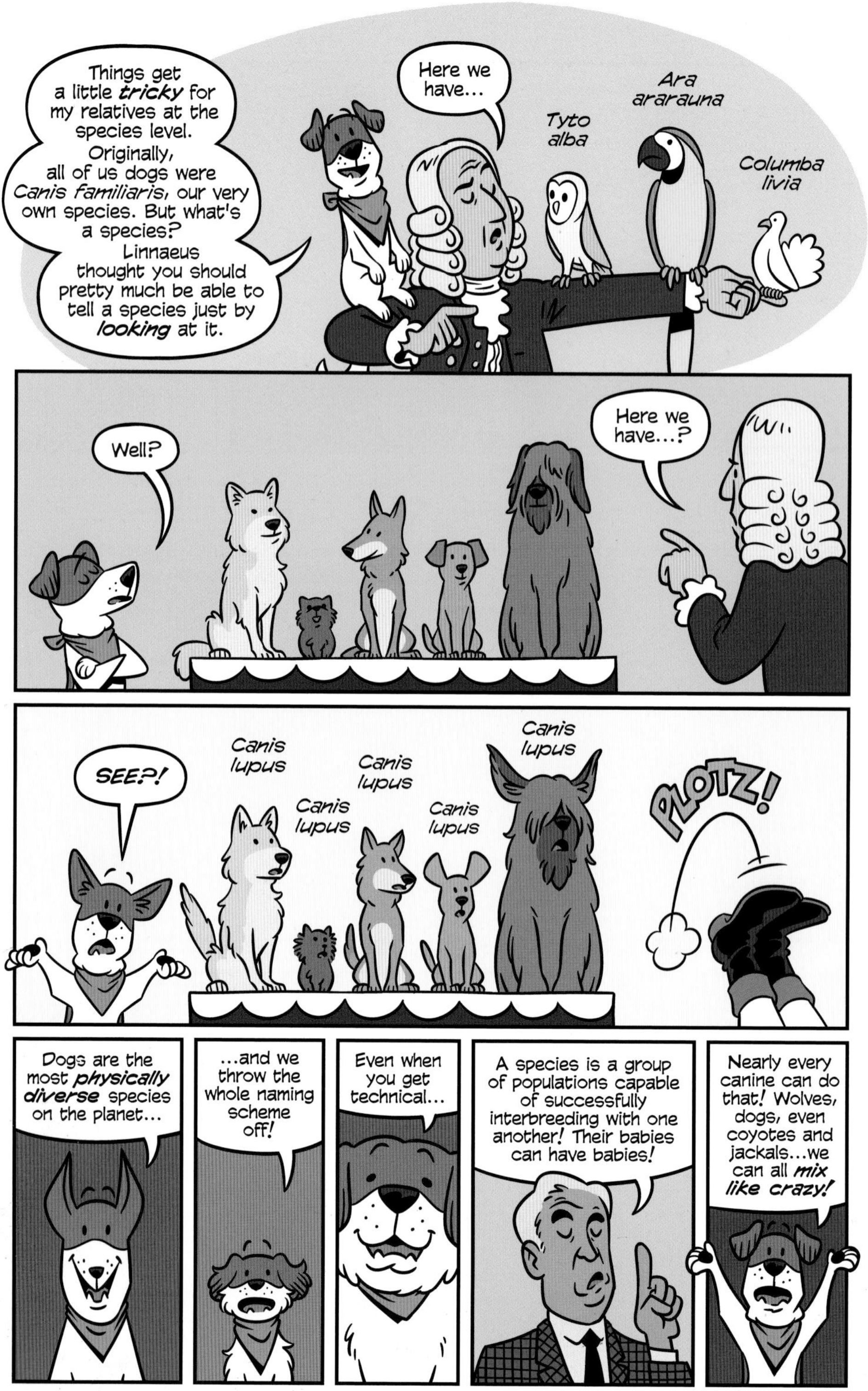
Things get a little *tricky* for my relatives at the species level.
Originally, all of us dogs were *Canis familiaris*, our very own species. But what's a species?
Linnaeus thought you should pretty much be able to tell a species just by *looking* at it.
Here we have...
Tyto alba
Ara ararauna
Columba livia
Well?
Here we have...?
SEE?!
Canis lupus
Canis lupus
Canis lupus
Canis lupus
Canis lupus
PLOTZ!
Dogs are the most *physically diverse* species on the planet...
...and we throw the whole naming scheme off!
Even when you get technical...
A species is a group of populations capable of successfully interbreeding with one another! Their babies can have babies!
Nearly every canine can do that! Wolves, dogs, even coyotes and jackals...we can all *mix like crazy!*

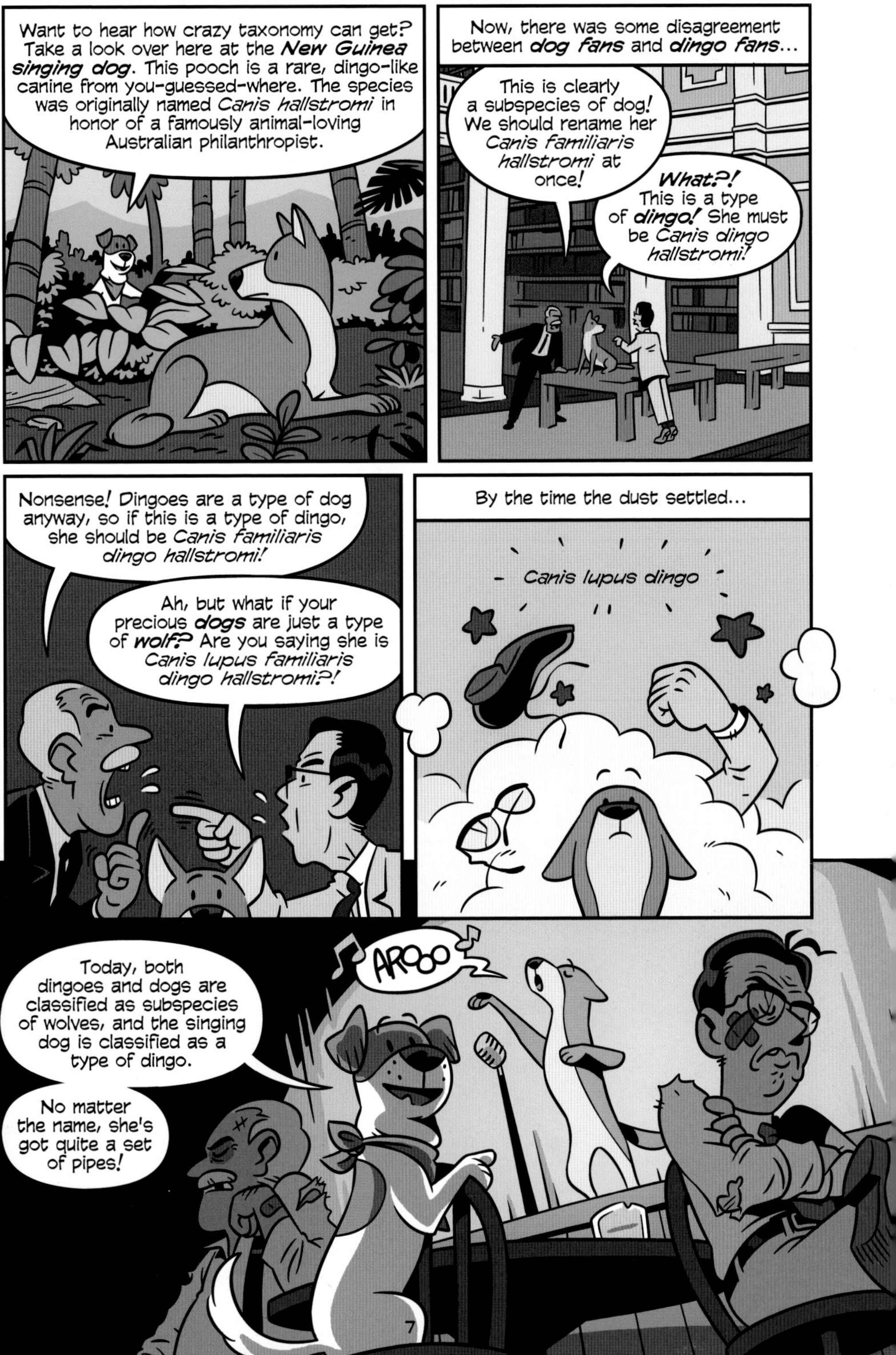
Want to hear how crazy taxonomy can get? Take a look over here at the New Guinea singing dog. This pooch is a rare, dingo-like canine from you-guessed-where. The species was originally named Canis hallstromi in honor of a famously animal-loving Australian philanthropist.
Now, there was some disagreement between dog fans and dingo fans...
This is clearly a subspecies of dog! We should rename her Canis familiaris hallstromi at once!
What?! This is a type of dingo! She must be Canis dingo hallstromi!
Nonsense! Dingoes are a type of dog anyway, so if this is a type of dingo, she should be Canis familiaris dingo hallstromi!
Ah, but what if your precious dogs are just a type of wolf? Are you saying she is Canis lupus familiaris dingo hallstromi?!
By the time the dust settled...
Canis lupus dingo
AROOO
Today, both dingoes and dogs are classified as subspecies of wolves, and the singing dog is classified as a type of dingo.
No matter the name, she's got quite a set of pipes!

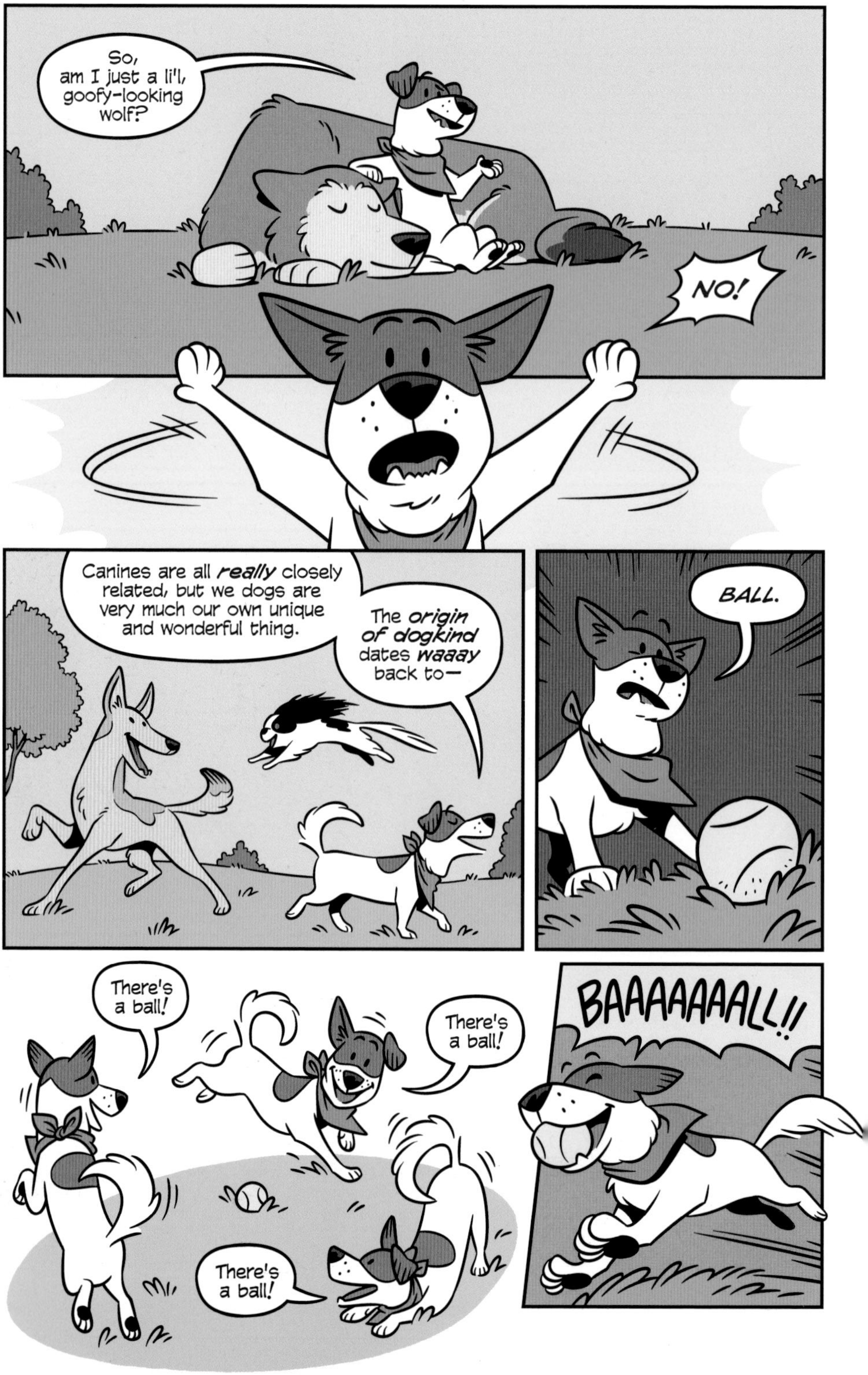
So, am I just a li'l, goofy-looking wolf?
NO!
Canines are all *really* closely related, but we dogs are very much our own unique and wonderful thing.
The *origin of dogkind* dates *waaay* back to—
BALL.
There's a ball!
There's a ball!
There's a ball!
BAAAAAAALL!!

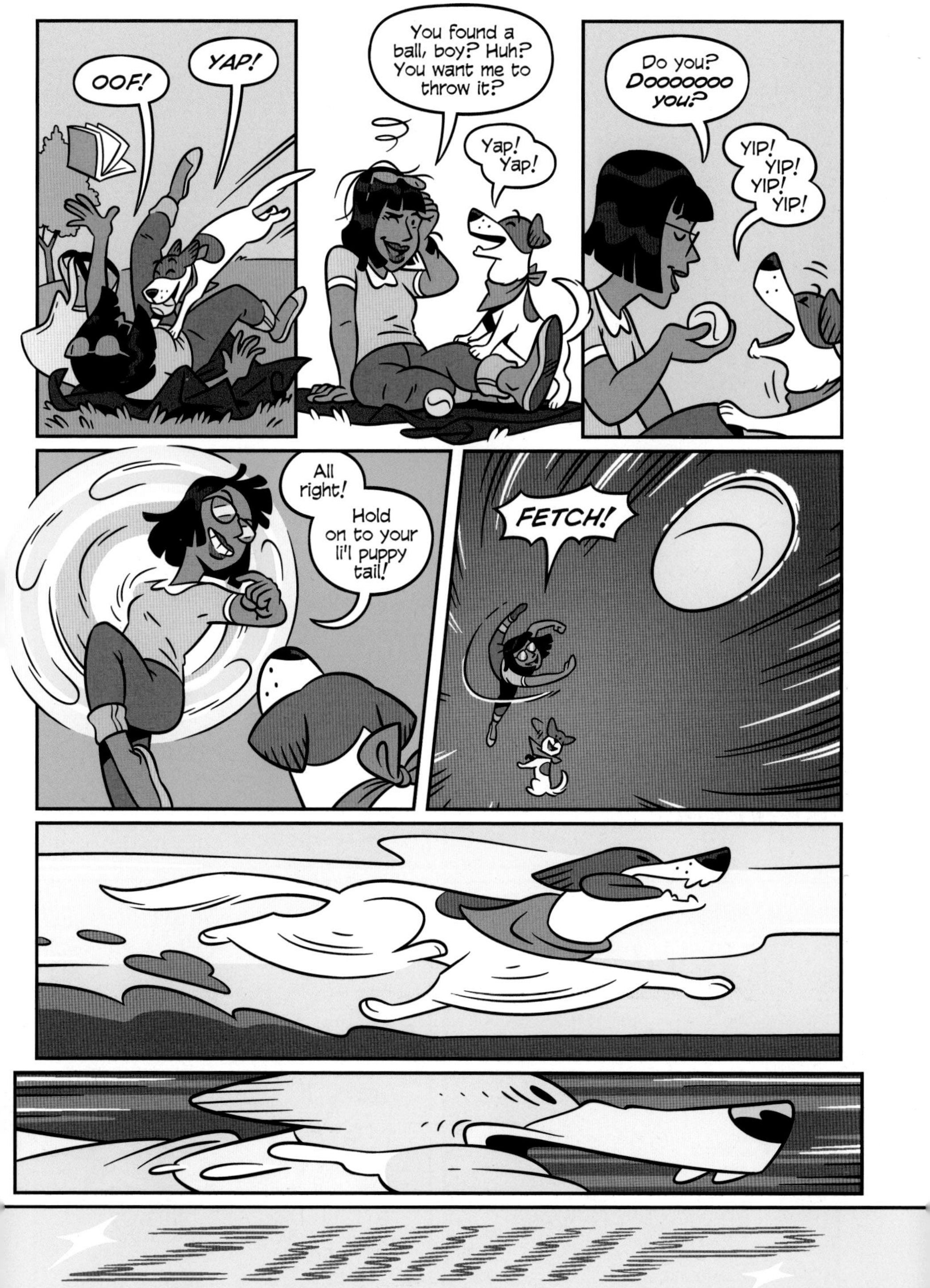
OOF!
YAP!
You found a ball, boy? Huh? You want me to throw it?
Yap! Yap!
Do you? Dooooooo you?
YIP! YIP! YIP! YIP!
All right!
Hold on to your li'l puppy tail!
FETCH!

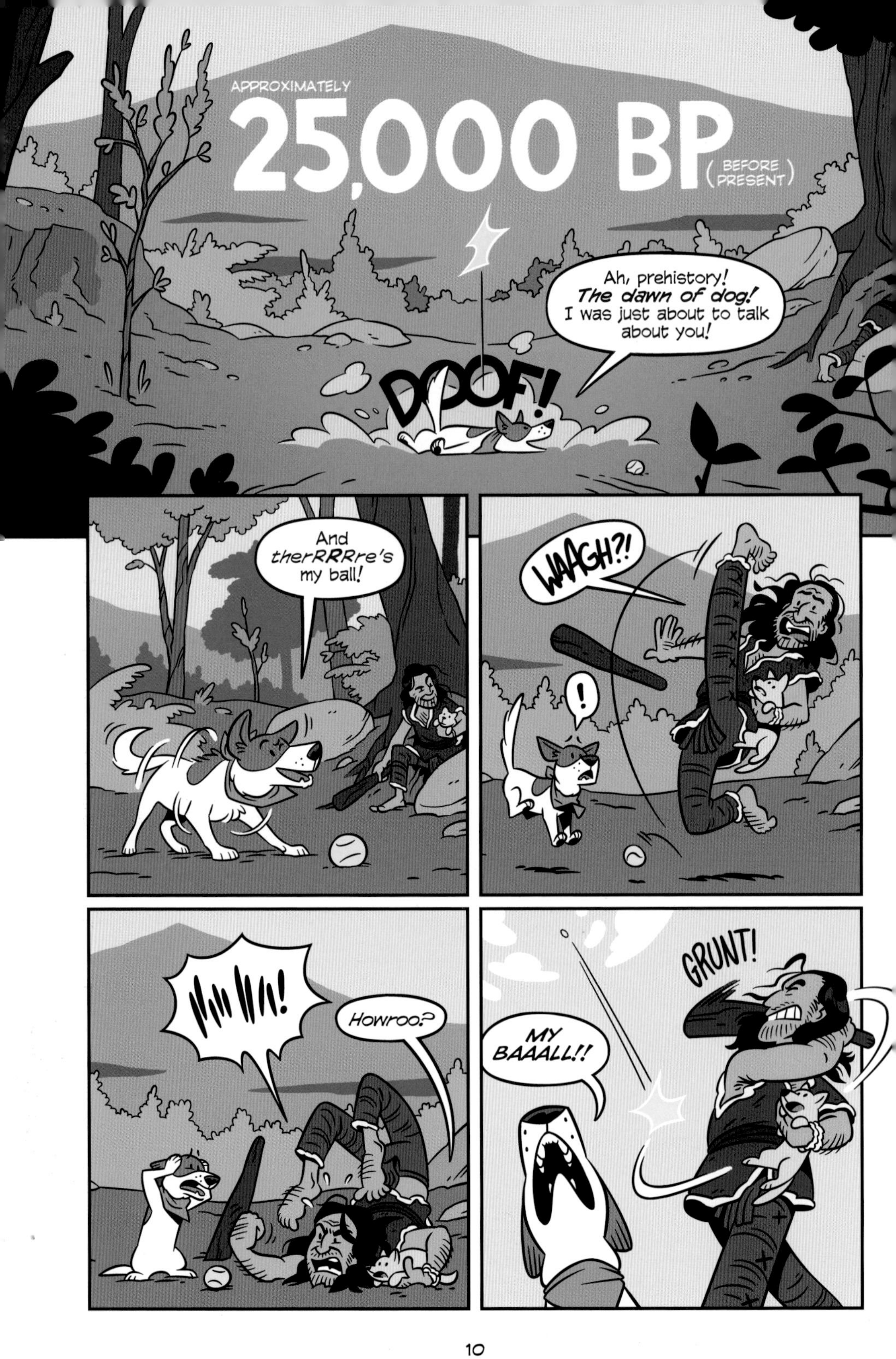

APPROXIMATELY
25,000 BP (BEFORE PRESENT)
Ah, prehistory! The dawn of dog! I was just about to talk about you!
DOOF!
And therRRRre's my ball!
WAAGH?!
!
Howroo?
GRUNT!
MY BAAALL!!

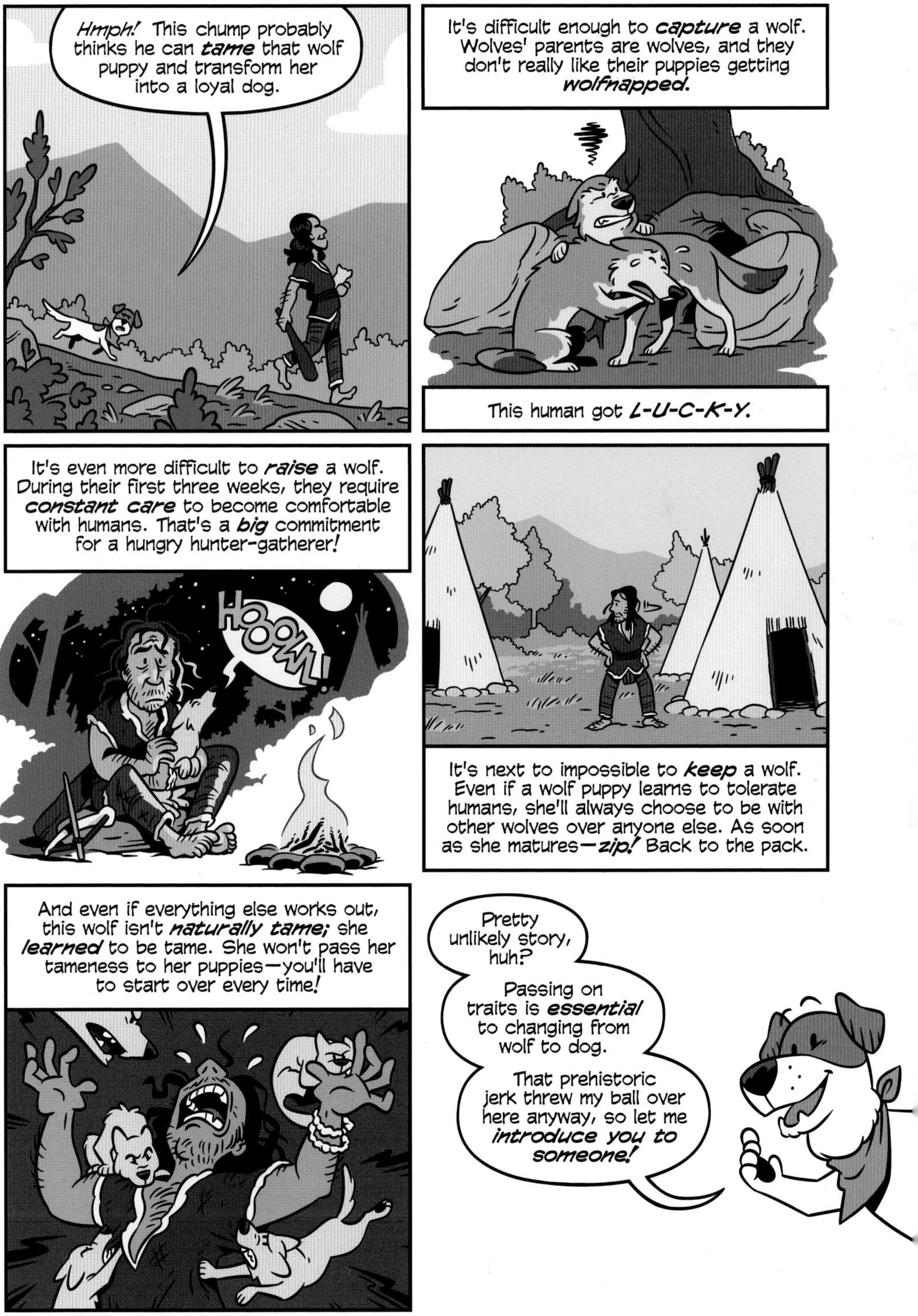
Hmph! This chump probably thinks he can tame that wolf puppy and transform her into a loyal dog.
It's difficult enough to capture a wolf. Wolves' parents are wolves, and they don't really like their puppies getting wolfnapped.
This human got L-U-C-K-Y.
It's even more difficult to raise a wolf. During their first three weeks, they require constant care to become comfortable with humans. That's a big commitment for a hungry hunter-gatherer!
HOOOWL!
It's next to impossible to keep a wolf. Even if a wolf puppy learns to tolerate humans, she'll always choose to be with other wolves over anyone else. As soon as she matures—zip! Back to the pack.
And even if everything else works out, this wolf isn't naturally tame; she learned to be tame. She won't pass her tameness to her puppies—you'll have to start over every time!
Pretty unlikely story, huh?
Passing on traits is essential to changing from wolf to dog.
That prehistoric jerk threw my ball over here anyway, so let me introduce you to someone!

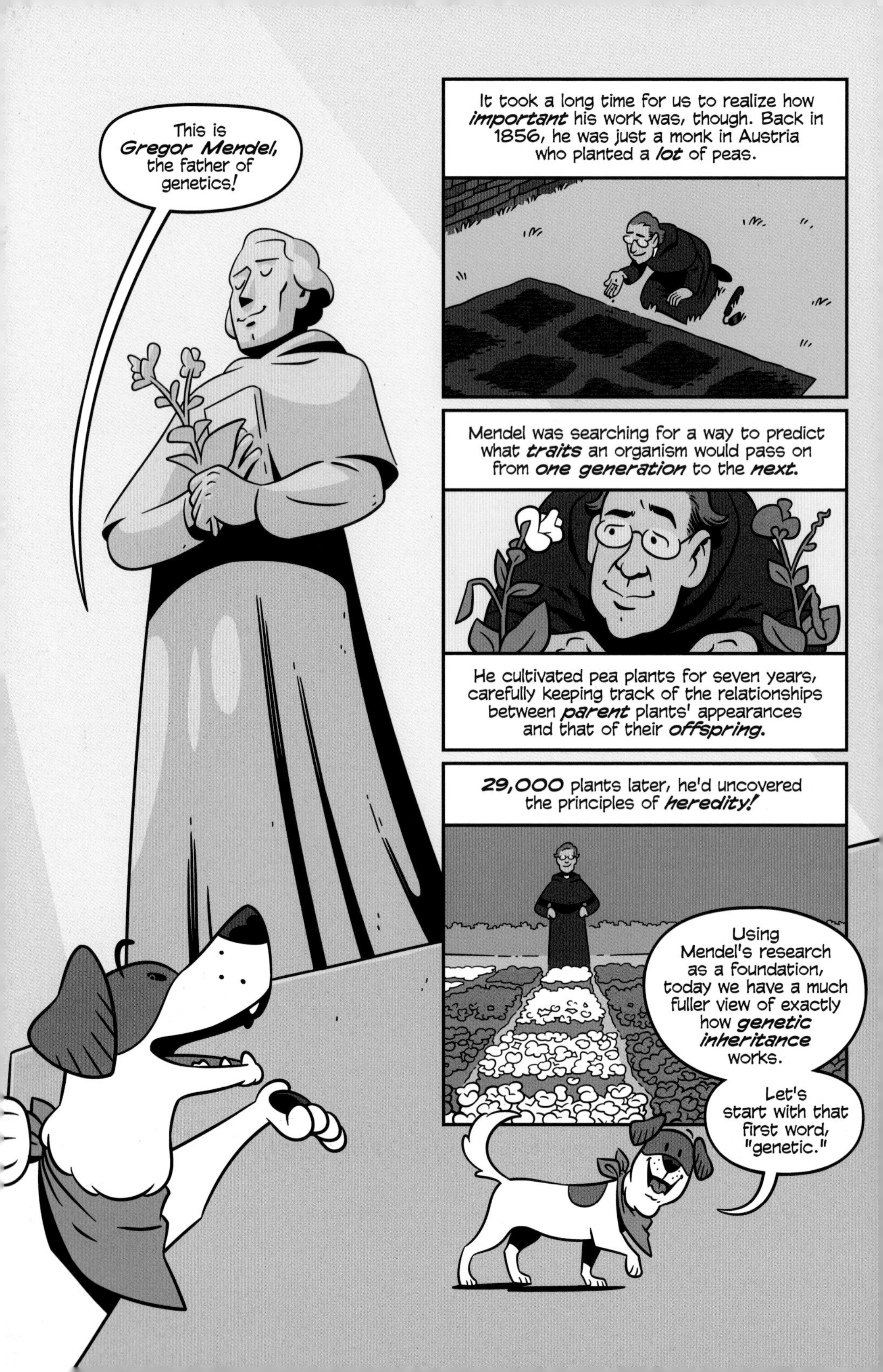

This is *Gregor Mendel,* the father of genetics!
It took a long time for us to realize how *important* his work was, though. Back in 1856, he was just a monk in Austria who planted a *lot* of peas.
Mendel was searching for a way to predict what *traits* an organism would pass on from *one generation* to the *next.*
He cultivated pea plants for seven years, carefully keeping track of the relationships between *parent* plants' appearances and that of their *offspring.*
29,000 plants later, he'd uncovered the principles of *heredity!*
Using Mendel's research as a foundation, today we have a much fuller view of exactly how *genetic inheritance* works.
Let's start with that first word, "genetic."

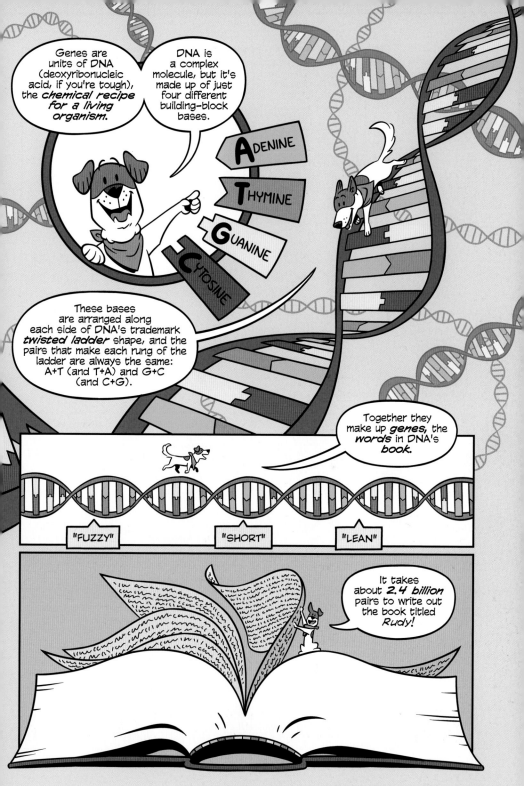

Genes are units of DNA (deoxyribonucleic acid, if you're tough), the *chemical recipe for a living organism.*

DNA is a complex molecule, but it's made up of just four different building-block bases.

ADENINE

THYMINE

GUANINE

CYTOSINE

These bases are arranged along each side of DNA's trademark *twisted ladder* shape, and the pairs that make each rung of the ladder are always the same: A+T (and T+A) and G+C (and C+G).

Together they make up *genes,* the *words* in DNA's *book.*

"FUZZY"

"SHORT"

"LEAN"

It takes about *2.4 billion* pairs to write out the book titled *Rudy!*

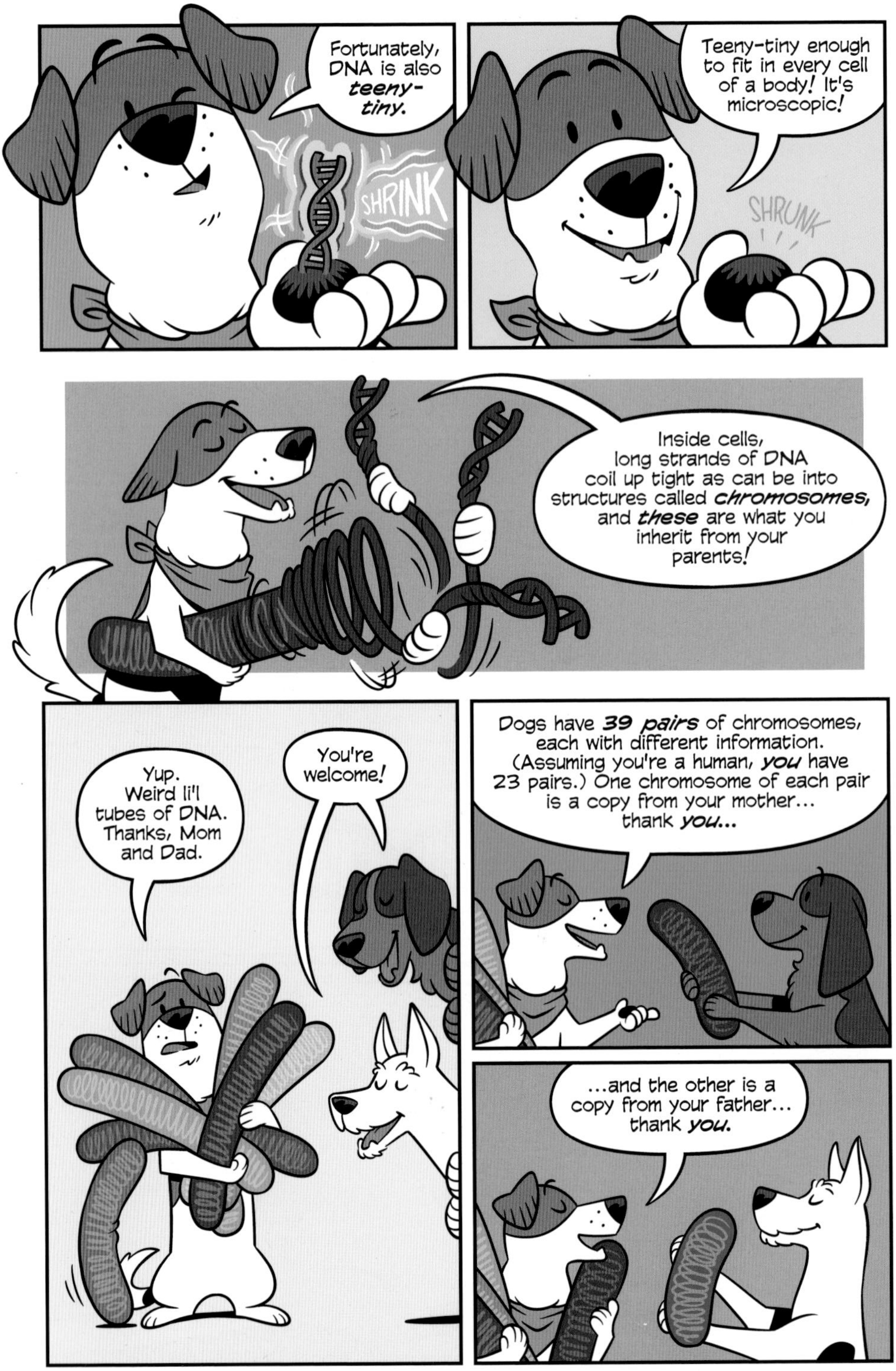
Fortunately, DNA is also *teeny-tiny.*
SHRINK
Teeny-tiny enough to fit in every cell of a body! It's microscopic!
SHRUNK
Inside cells, long strands of DNA coil up tight as can be into structures called *chromosomes,* and *these* are what you inherit from your parents!
Yup. Weird li'l tubes of DNA. Thanks, Mom and Dad.
You're welcome!
Dogs have **39 pairs** of chromosomes, each with different information. (Assuming you're a human, *you* have 23 pairs.) One chromosome of each pair is a copy from your mother... thank *you*...
...and the other is a copy from your father... thank *you.*

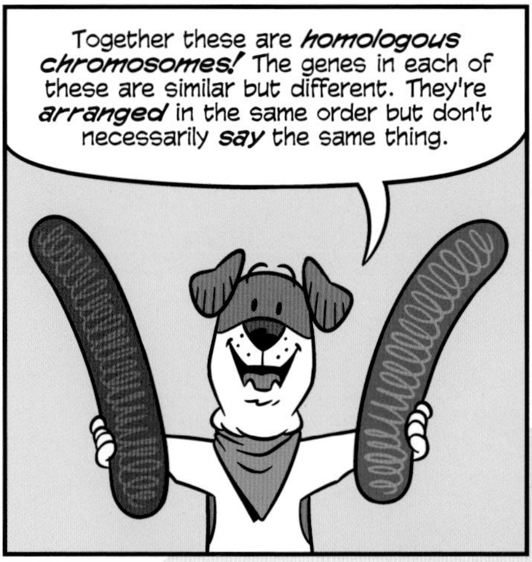
Together these are *homologous chromosomes!* The genes in each of these are similar but different. They're *arranged* in the same order but don't necessarily *say* the same thing.

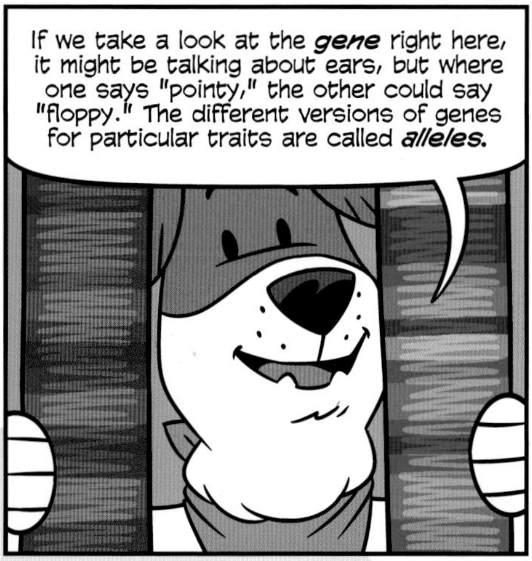
If we take a look at the *gene* right here, it might be talking about ears, but where one says "pointy," the other could say "floppy." The different versions of genes for particular traits are called *alleles.*

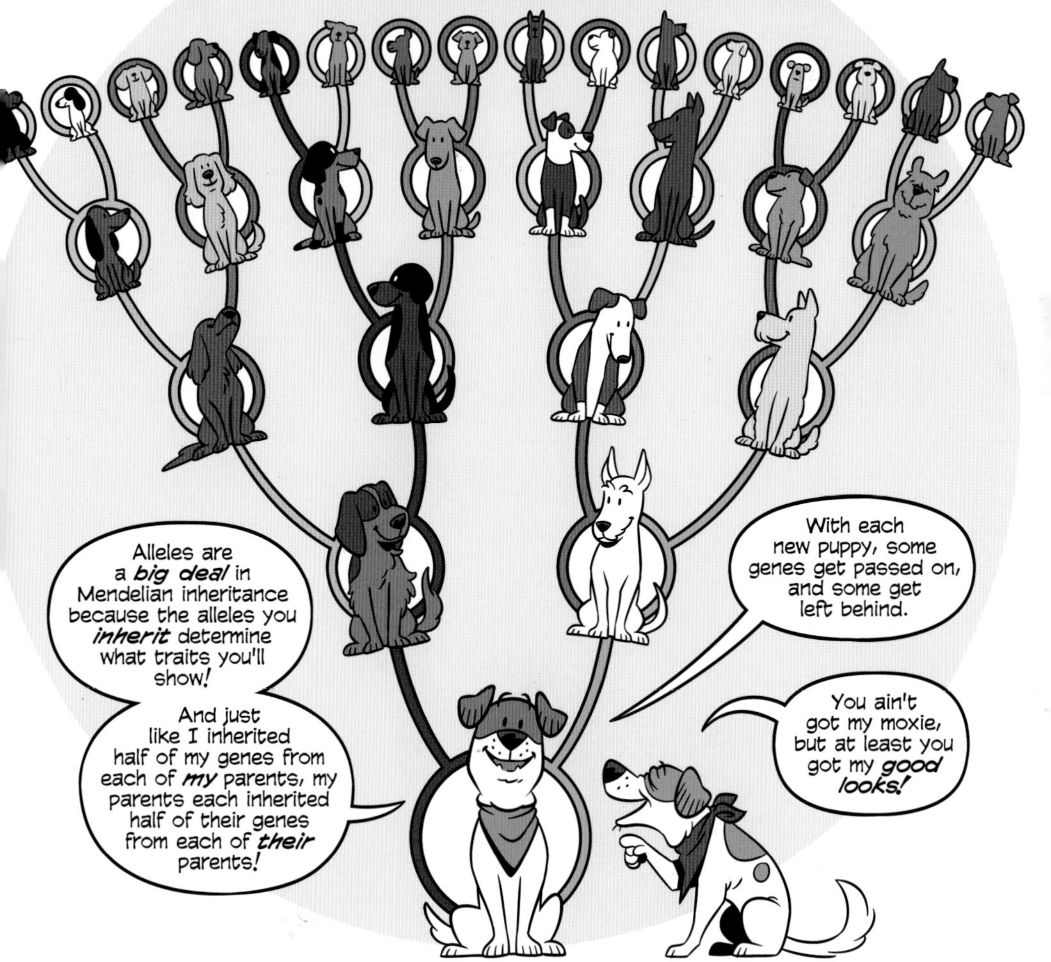
Alleles are a *big deal* in Mendelian inheritance because the alleles you *inherit* determine what traits you'll show!
And just like I inherited half of my genes from each of *my* parents, my parents each inherited half of their genes from each of *their* parents!
With each new puppy, some genes get passed on, and some get left behind.
You ain't got my moxie, but at least you got my *good looks!*

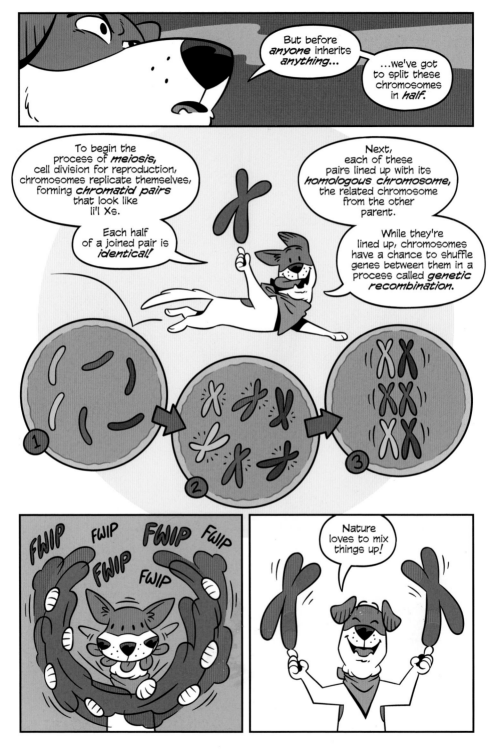

But before *anyone* inherits *anything*...

...we've got to split these chromosomes in *half*.

To begin the process of *meiosis*, cell division for reproduction, chromosomes replicate themselves, forming *chromatid pairs* that look like li'l Xs.

Each half of a joined pair is *identical!*

Next, each of these pairs lined up with its *homologous chromosome*, the related chromosome from the other parent.

While they're lined up, chromosomes have a chance to shuffle genes between them in a process called *genetic recombination.*

①
②
③

FWIP FWIP FWIP FWIP FWIP FWIP

Nature loves to mix things up!

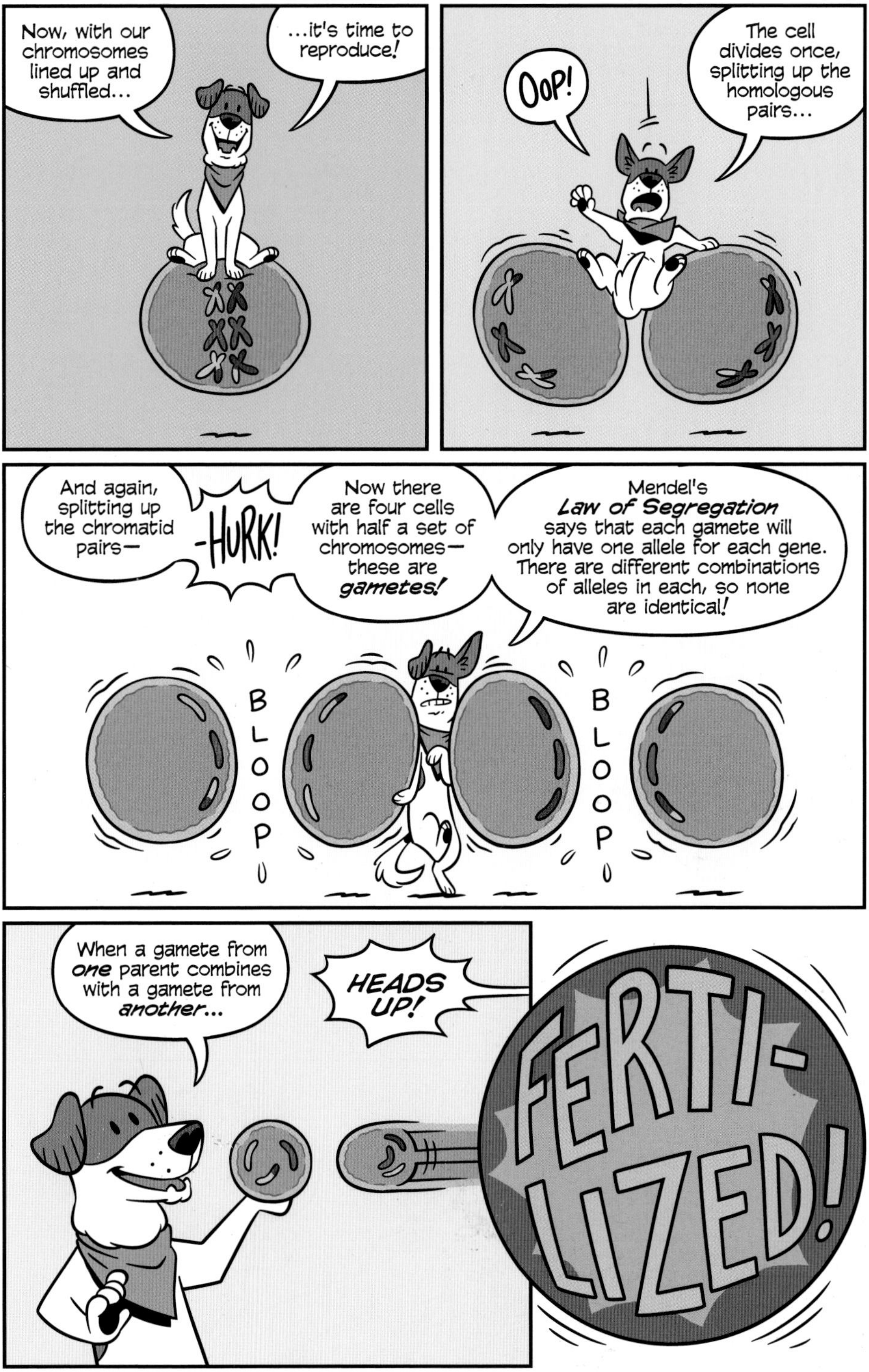

Now, with our chromosomes lined up and shuffled...
...it's time to reproduce!
OOP!
The cell divides once, splitting up the homologous pairs...
And again, splitting up the chromatid pairs—
-HURK!
Now there are four cells with half a set of chromosomes—these are *gametes!*
Mendel's ***Law of Segregation*** says that each gamete will only have one allele for each gene. There are different combinations of alleles in each, so none are identical!
BLOOP
BLOOP
When a gamete from ***one*** parent combines with a gamete from ***another...***
HEADS UP!
FERTI-LIZED!

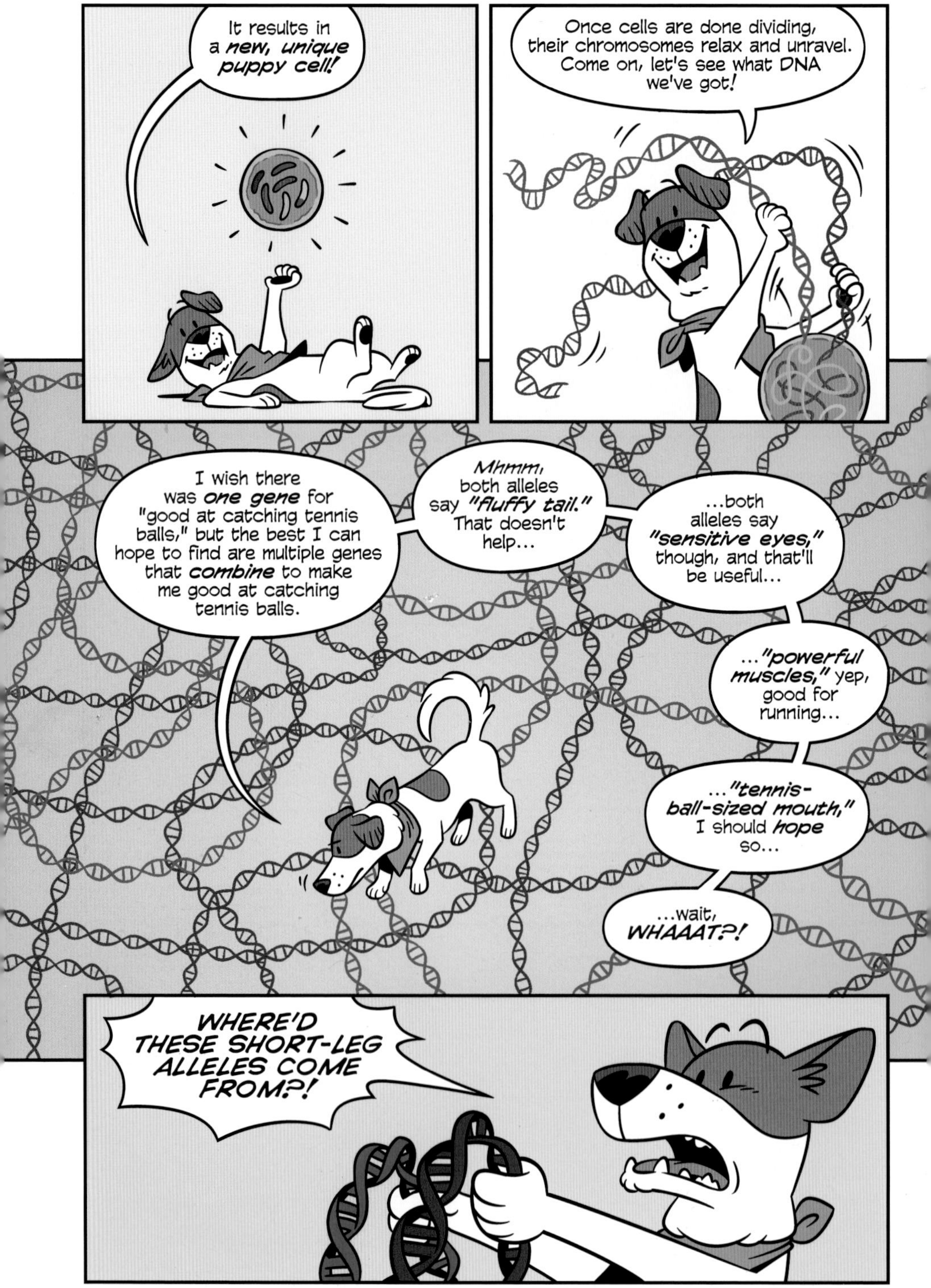
It results in a *new, unique puppy cell!*
Once cells are done dividing, their chromosomes relax and unravel. Come on, let's see what DNA we've got!
I wish there was *one gene* for "good at catching tennis balls," but the best I can hope to find are multiple genes that *combine* to make me good at catching tennis balls.
Mhmm, both alleles say *"fluffy tail."* That doesn't help...
...both alleles say *"sensitive eyes,"* though, and that'll be useful...
...*"powerful muscles,"* yep, good for running...
...*"tennis-ball-sized mouth,"* I should *hope* so...
...wait, *WHAAAT?!*
WHERE'D THESE SHORT-LEG ALLELES COME FROM?!

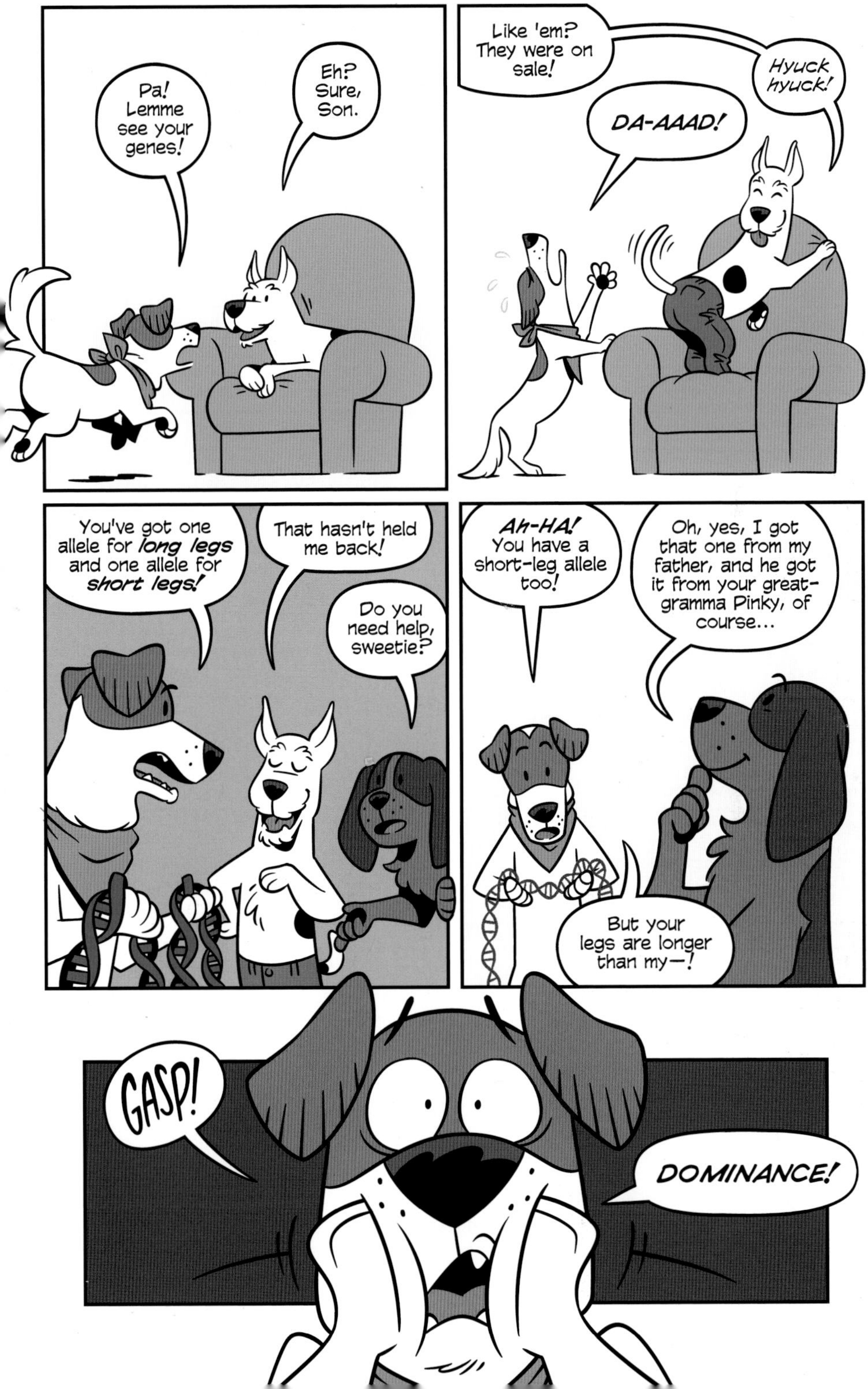

Pa! Lemme see your genes!
Eh? Sure, Son.
Like 'em? They were on sale!
Hyuck hyuck!
DA-AAAD!
You've got one allele for long legs and one allele for short legs!
That hasn't held me back!
Do you need help, sweetie?
Ah-HA! You have a short-leg allele too!
Oh, yes, I got that one from my father, and he got it from your great-gramma Pinky, of course...
But your legs are longer than my—!
GASP!
DOMINANCE!

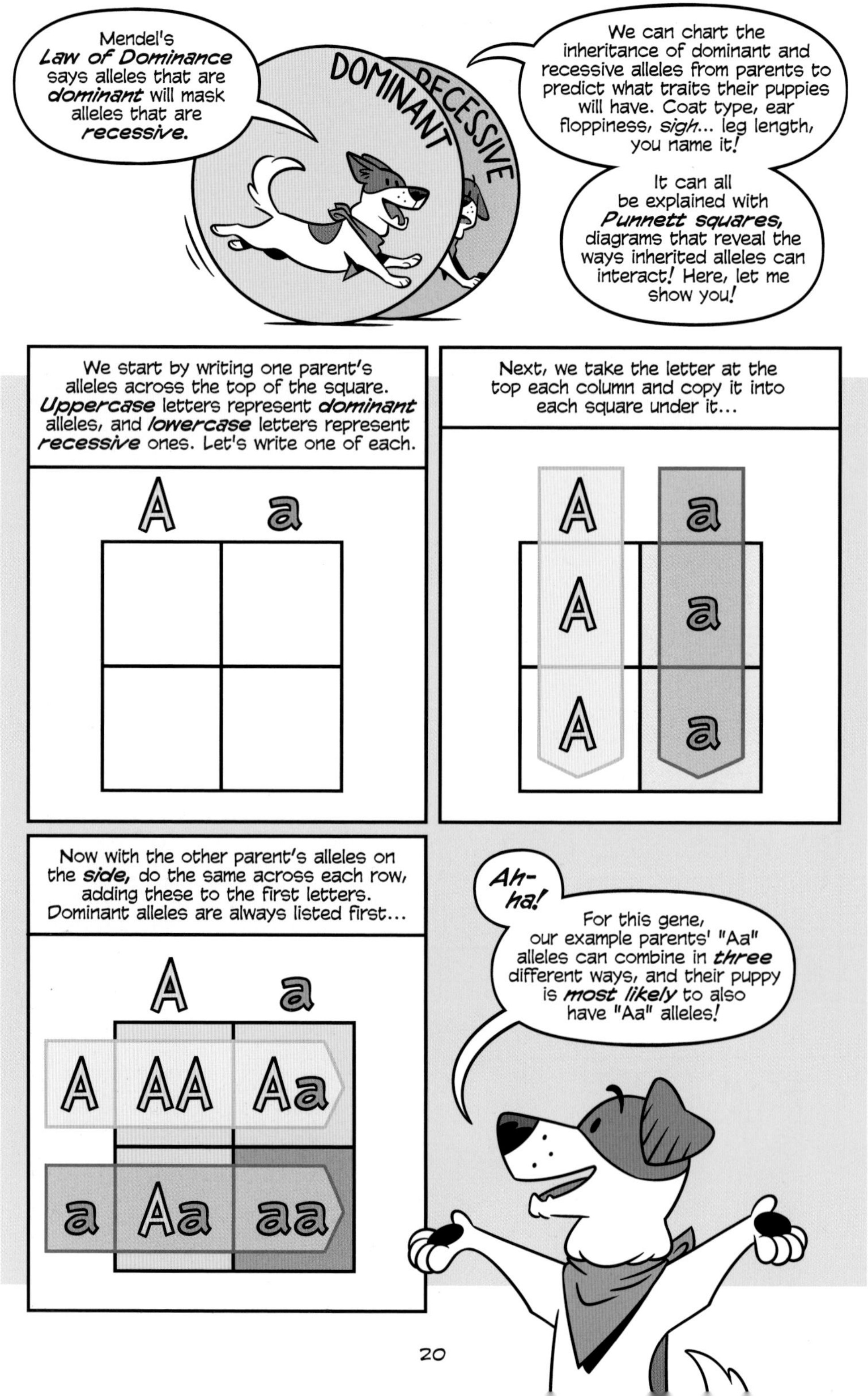

Mendel's *Law of Dominance* says alleles that are *dominant* will mask alleles that are *recessive.*
DOMINANT
RECESSIVE
We can chart the inheritance of dominant and recessive alleles from parents to predict what traits their puppies will have. Coat type, ear floppiness, *sigh*... leg length, you name it!
It can all be explained with *Punnett squares,* diagrams that reveal the ways inherited alleles can interact! Here, let me show you!
We start by writing one parent's alleles across the top of the square. *Uppercase* letters represent *dominant* alleles, and *lowercase* letters represent *recessive* ones. Let's write one of each.
A a
Next, we take the letter at the top each column and copy it into each square under it...
A a
A a
A a
Now with the other parent's alleles on the *side,* do the same across each row, adding these to the first letters. Dominant alleles are always listed first...
A a
A AA Aa
a Aa aa
Ah-ha!
For this gene, our example parents' "Aa" alleles can combine in *three* different ways, and their puppy is *most likely* to also have "Aa" alleles!

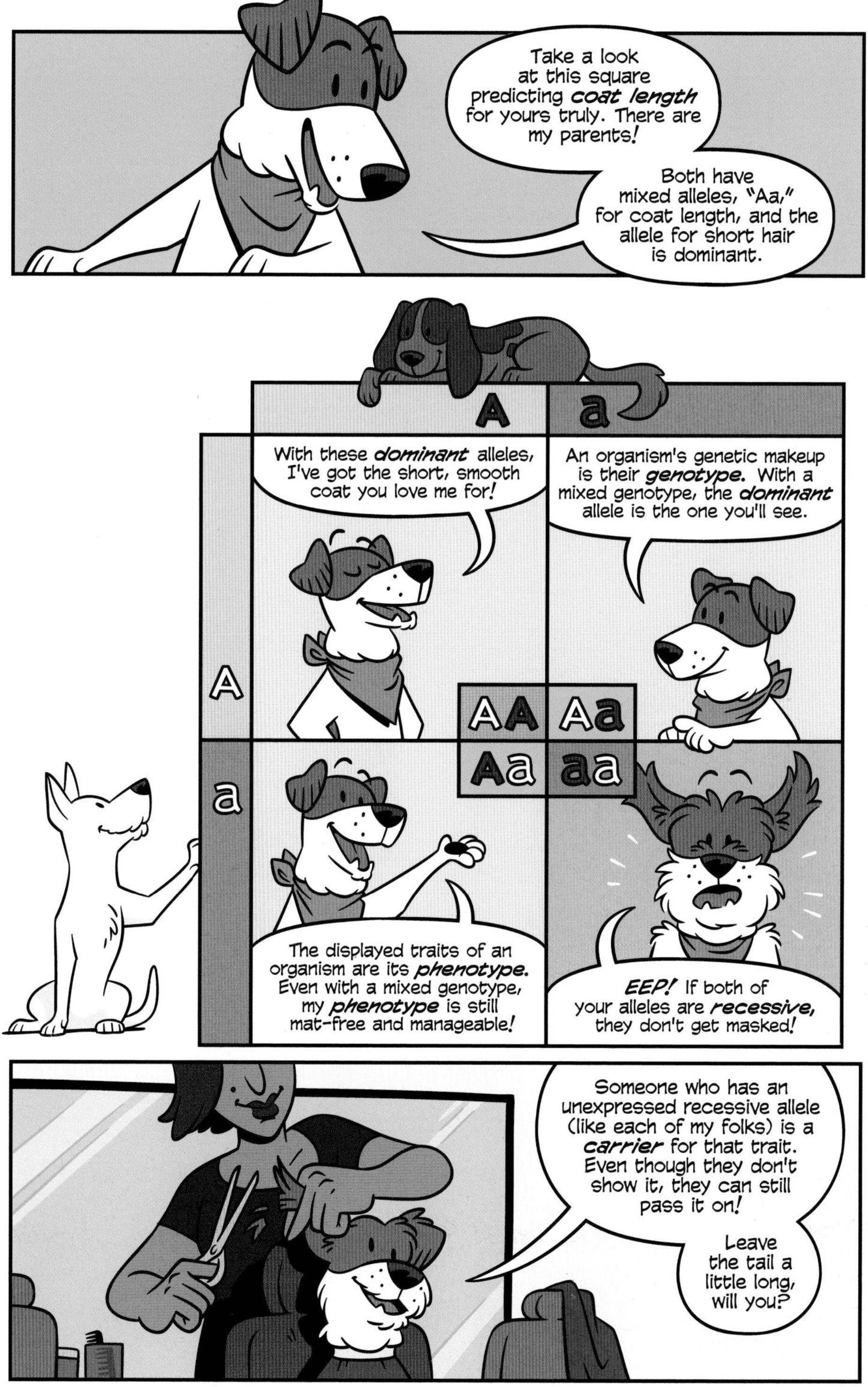

Take a look at this square predicting *coat length* for yours truly. There are my parents!
Both have mixed alleles, "Aa," for coat length, and the allele for short hair is dominant.
A
a
A
a
With these *dominant* alleles, I've got the short, smooth coat you love me for!
An organism's genetic makeup is their *genotype.* With a mixed genotype, the *dominant* allele is the one you'll see.
AA
Aa
Aa
aa
The displayed traits of an organism are its *phenotype.* Even with a mixed genotype, my *phenotype* is still mat-free and manageable!
EEP! If both of your alleles are *recessive,* they don't get masked!
Someone who has an unexpressed recessive allele (like each of my folks) is a *carrier* for that trait. Even though they don't show it, they can still pass it on!
Leave the tail a little long, will you?

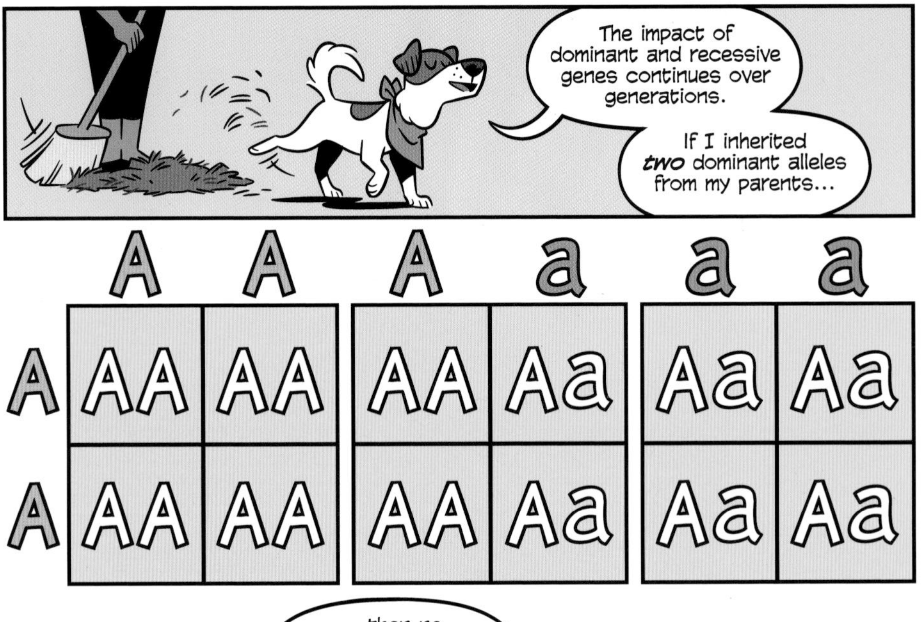
The impact of dominant and recessive genes continues over generations.
If I inherited *two* dominant alleles from my parents...

	A	A
A	AA	AA
A	AA	AA

	A	a
A	AA	Aa
A	AA	Aa

	a	a
A	Aa	Aa
A	Aa	Aa

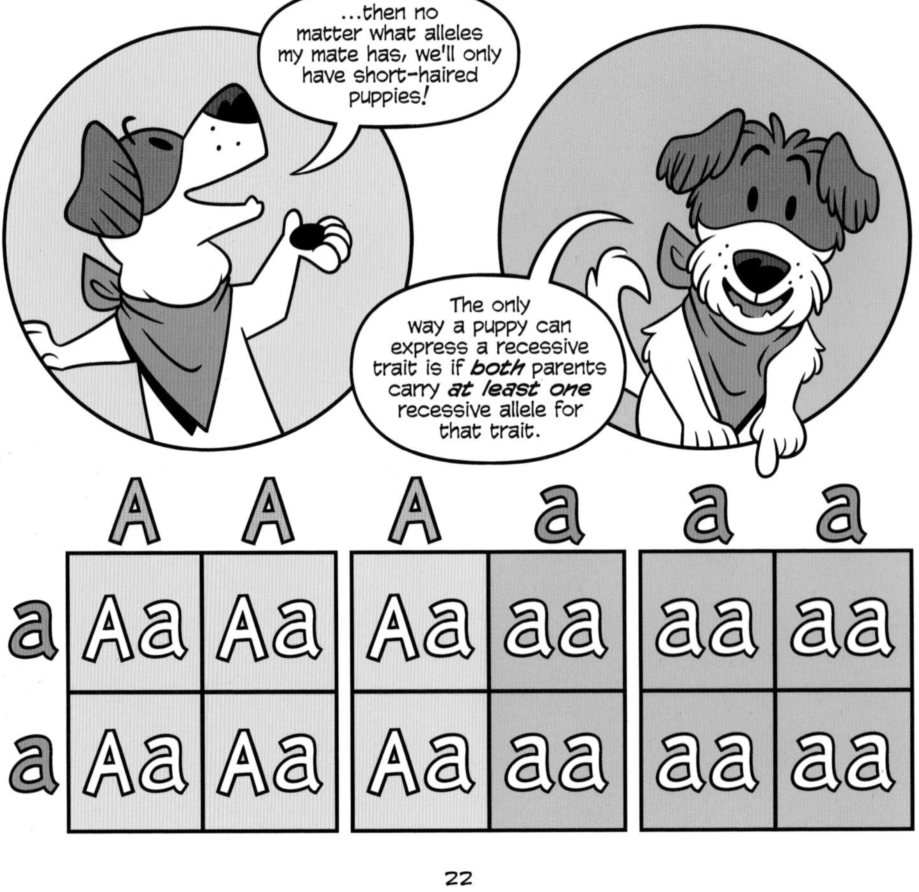
...then no matter what alleles my mate has, we'll only have short-haired puppies!
The only way a puppy can express a recessive trait is if *both* parents carry *at least one* recessive allele for that trait.

	A	A
a	Aa	Aa
a	Aa	Aa

	A	a
a	Aa	aa
a	Aa	aa

	a	a
a	aa	aa
a	aa	aa

That's an example of a trait with *complete dominance,* but it doesn't always work that way!

Which brings us back to the case of my short, short legs...

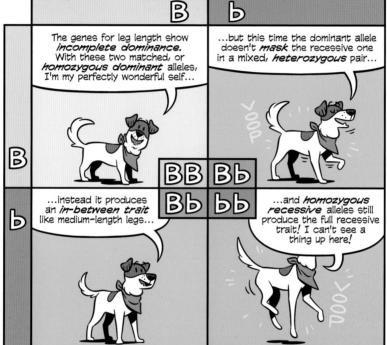

B | **b**

The genes for leg length show *incomplete dominance.* With these two matched, or *homozygous dominant* alleles, I'm my perfectly wonderful self...

...but this time the dominant allele doesn't *mask* the recessive one in a mixed, *heterozygous* pair...

...instead it produces an *in-between trait* like medium-length legs...

BB | Bb
Bb | bb

...and *homozygous recessive* alleles still produce the full recessive trait! I can't see a thing up here!

Alleles can even be *codominant,* meaning *both* traits are expressed. Your genes are a big, messy mix of all sorts of allelic interactions!

23

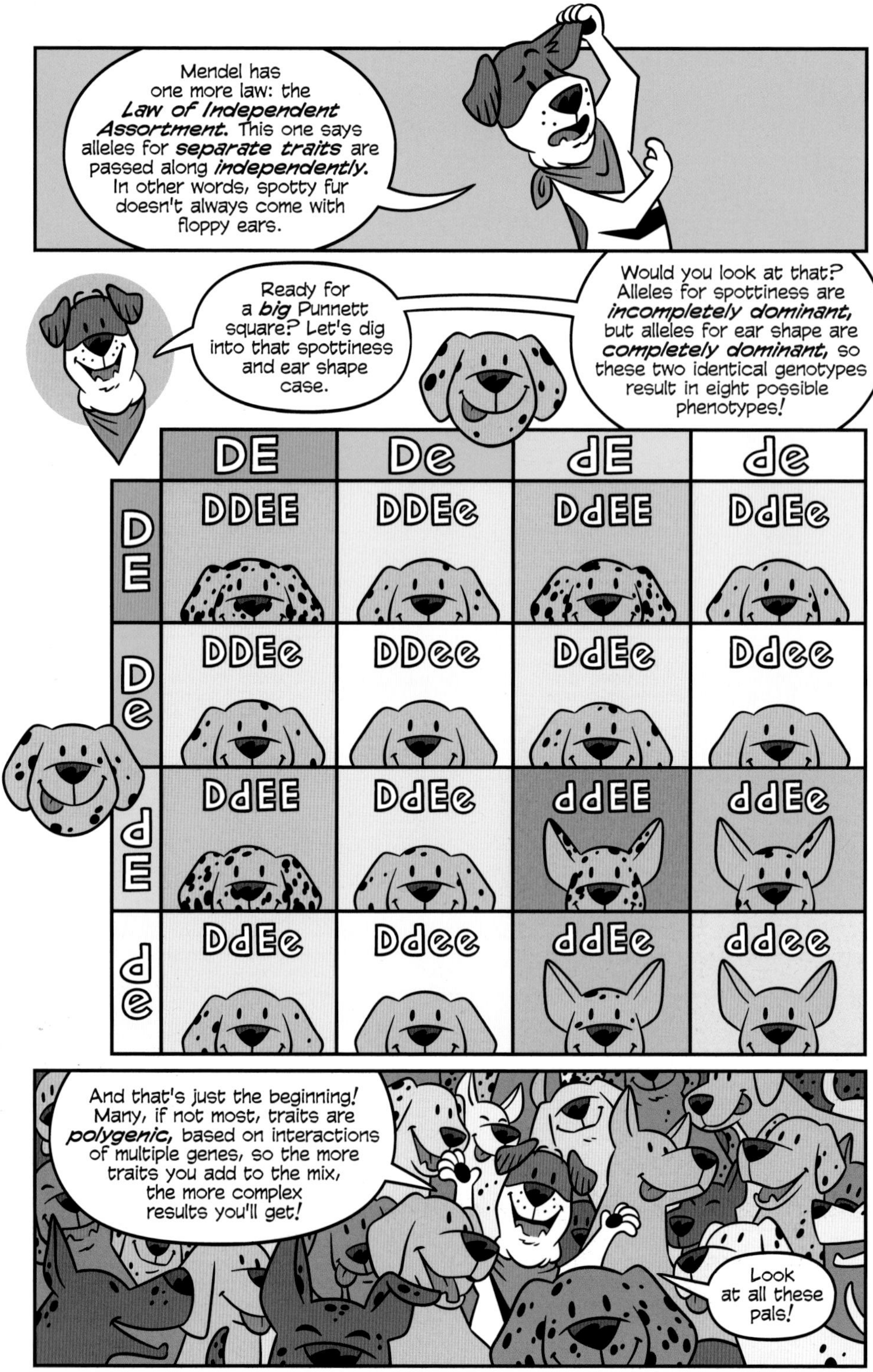

Mendel has one more law: the *Law of Independent Assortment.* This one says alleles for *separate traits* are passed along *independently.* In other words, spotty fur doesn't always come with floppy ears.
Ready for a *big* Punnett square? Let's dig into that spottiness and ear shape case.
Would you look at that? Alleles for spottiness are *incompletely dominant,* but alleles for ear shape are *completely dominant,* so these two identical genotypes result in eight possible phenotypes!
DE
De
dE
de
DE
DDEE
DDEe
DdEE
DdEe
De
DDEe
DDee
DdEe
Ddee
dE
DdEE
DdEe
ddEE
ddEe
de
DdEe
Ddee
ddEe
ddee
And that's just the beginning! Many, if not most, traits are *polygenic,* based on interactions of multiple genes, so the more traits you add to the mix, the more complex results you'll get!
Look at all these pals!

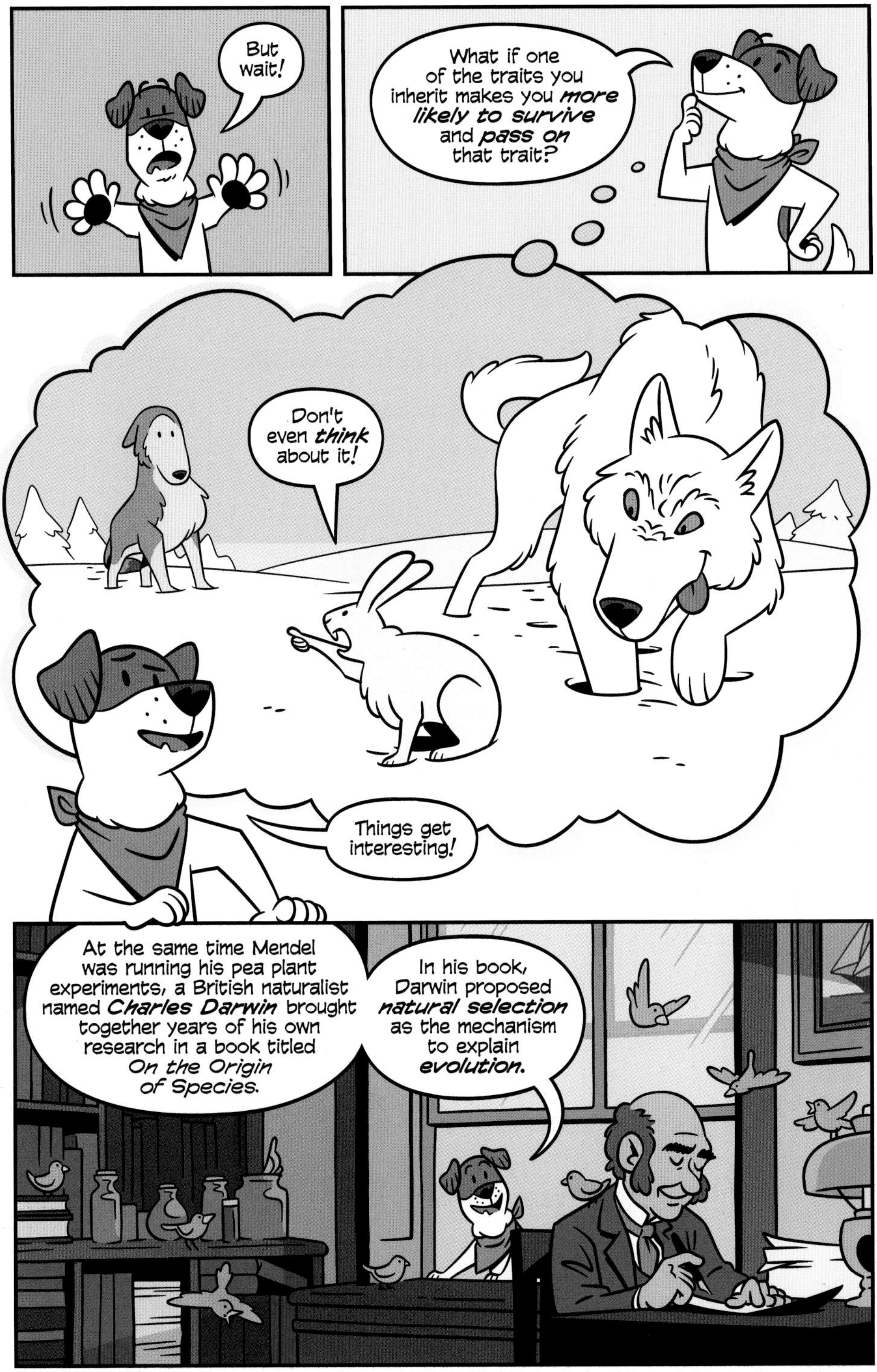

But wait!
What if one of the traits you inherit makes you ***more likely to survive*** and ***pass on*** that trait?
Don't even ***think*** about it!
Things get interesting!
At the same time Mendel was running his pea plant experiments, a British naturalist named ***Charles Darwin*** brought together years of his own research in a book titled *On the Origin of Species*.
In his book, Darwin proposed ***natural selection*** as the mechanism to explain ***evolution***.

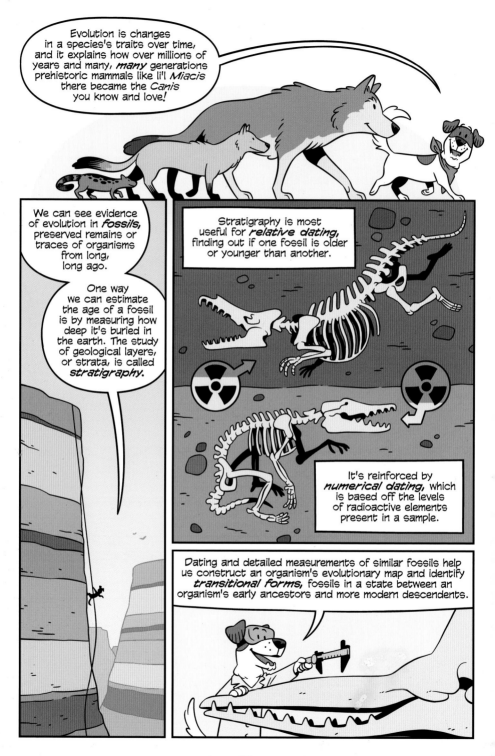

Evolution is changes in a species's traits over time, and it explains how over millions of years and many, *many* generations prehistoric mammals like li'l *Miacis* there became the *Canis* you know and love!

We can see evidence of evolution in *fossils*, preserved remains or traces of organisms from long, long ago.

One way we can estimate the age of a fossil is by measuring how deep it's buried in the earth. The study of geological layers, or strata, is called *stratigraphy*.

Stratigraphy is most useful for *relative dating*, finding out if one fossil is older or younger than another.

It's reinforced by *numerical dating*, which is based off the levels of radioactive elements present in a sample.

Dating and detailed measurements of similar fossils help us construct an organism's evolutionary map and identify *transitional forms*, fossils in a state between an organism's early ancestors and more modern descendents.

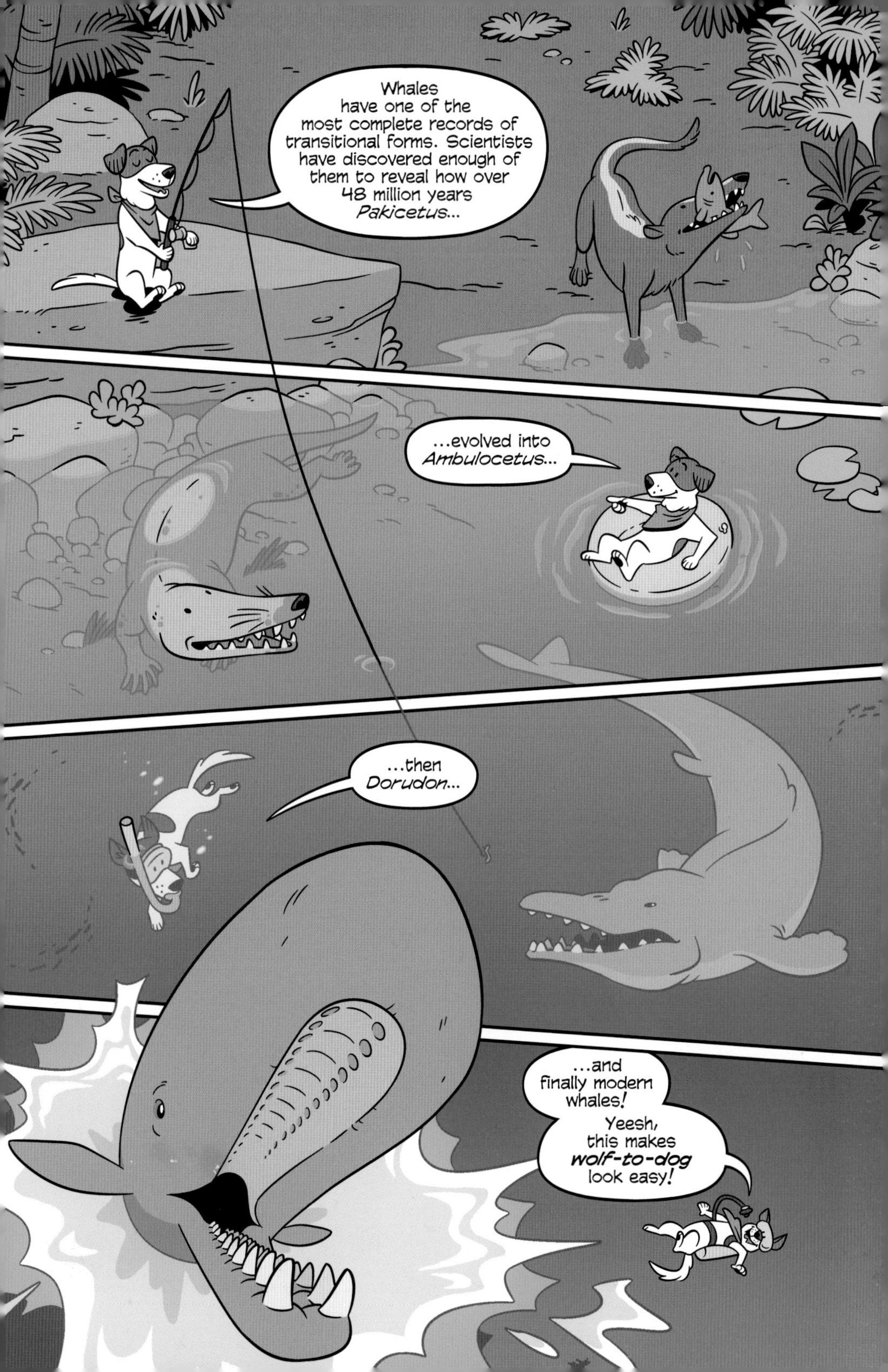

Whales have one of the most complete records of transitional forms. Scientists have discovered enough of them to reveal how over 48 million years *Pakicetus*...
...evolved into *Ambulocetus*...
...then *Dorudon*...
...and finally modern whales!
Yeesh, this makes ***wolf-to-dog*** look easy!

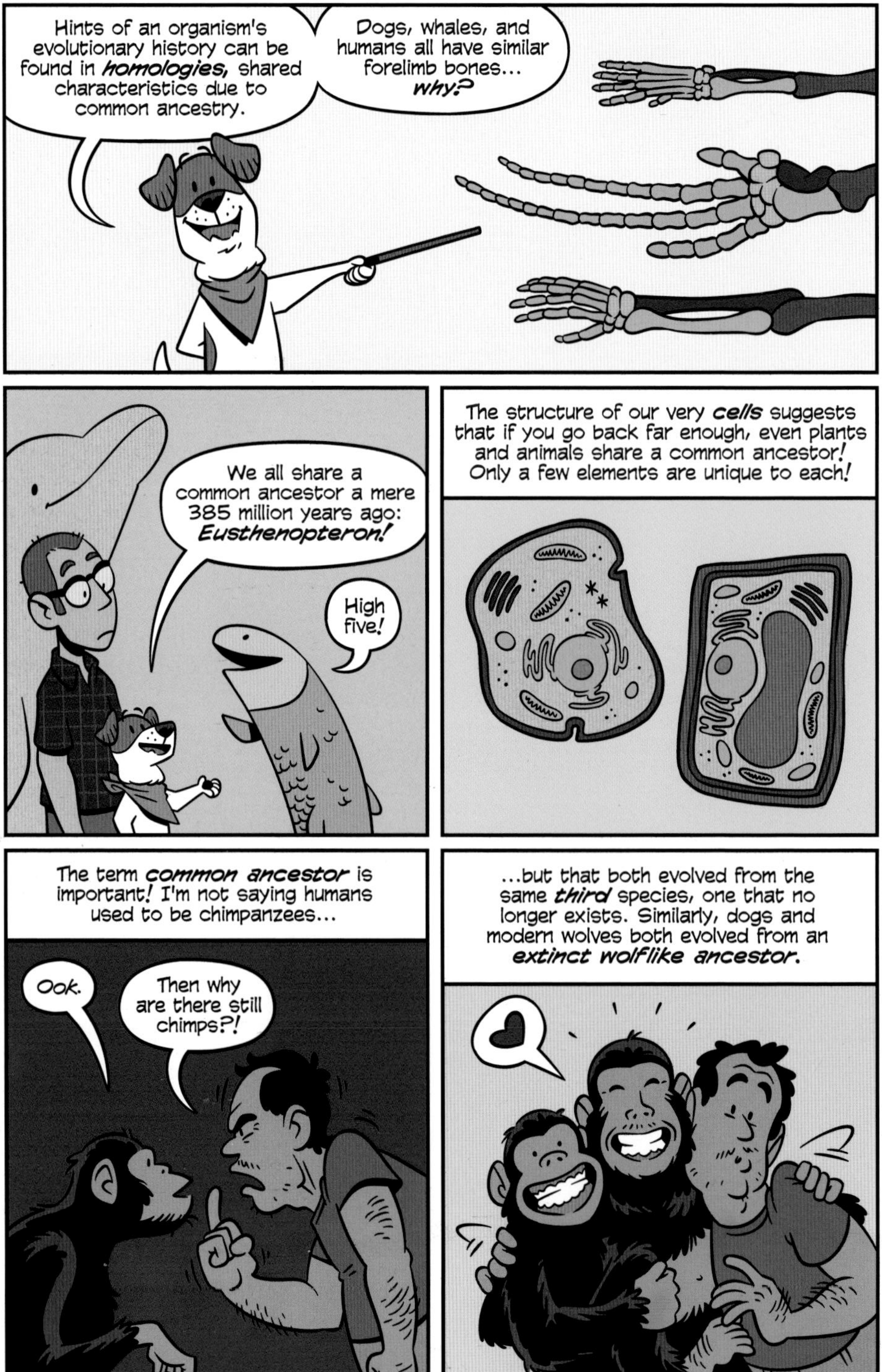
Hints of an organism's evolutionary history can be found in ***homologies,*** shared characteristics due to common ancestry.
Dogs, whales, and humans all have similar forelimb bones... ***why?***
We all share a common ancestor a mere 385 million years ago: ***Eusthenopteron!***
High five!
The structure of our very ***cells*** suggests that if you go back far enough, even plants and animals share a common ancestor! Only a few elements are unique to each!
The term ***common ancestor*** is important! I'm not saying humans used to be chimpanzees...
Ook.
Then why are there still chimps?!
...but that both evolved from the same ***third*** species, one that no longer exists. Similarly, dogs and modern wolves both evolved from an ***extinct wolflike ancestor.***

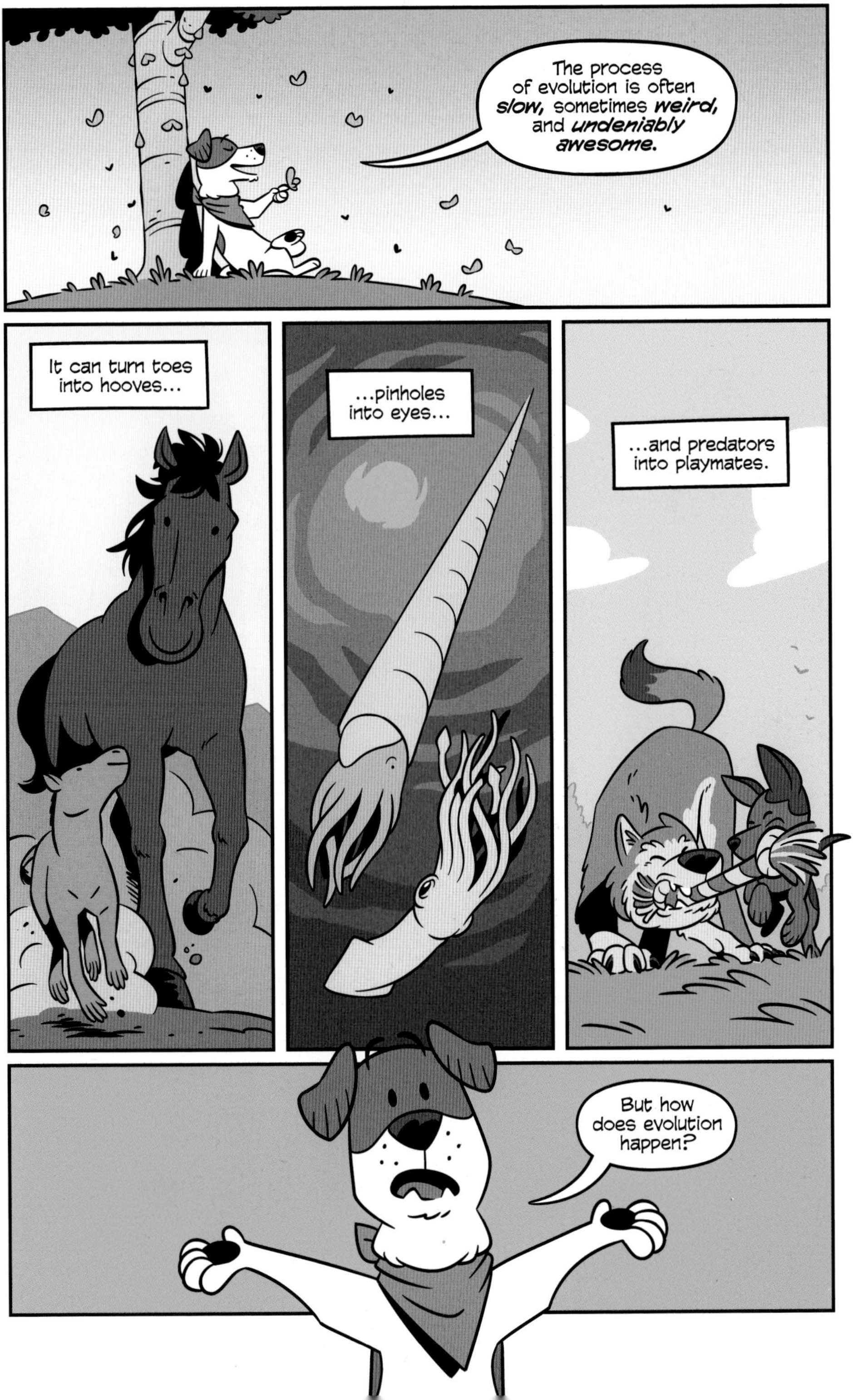
The process of evolution is often *slow,* sometimes ***weird,*** and ***undeniably awesome.***
It can turn toes into hooves...
...pinholes into eyes...
...and predators into playmates.
But how does evolution happen?

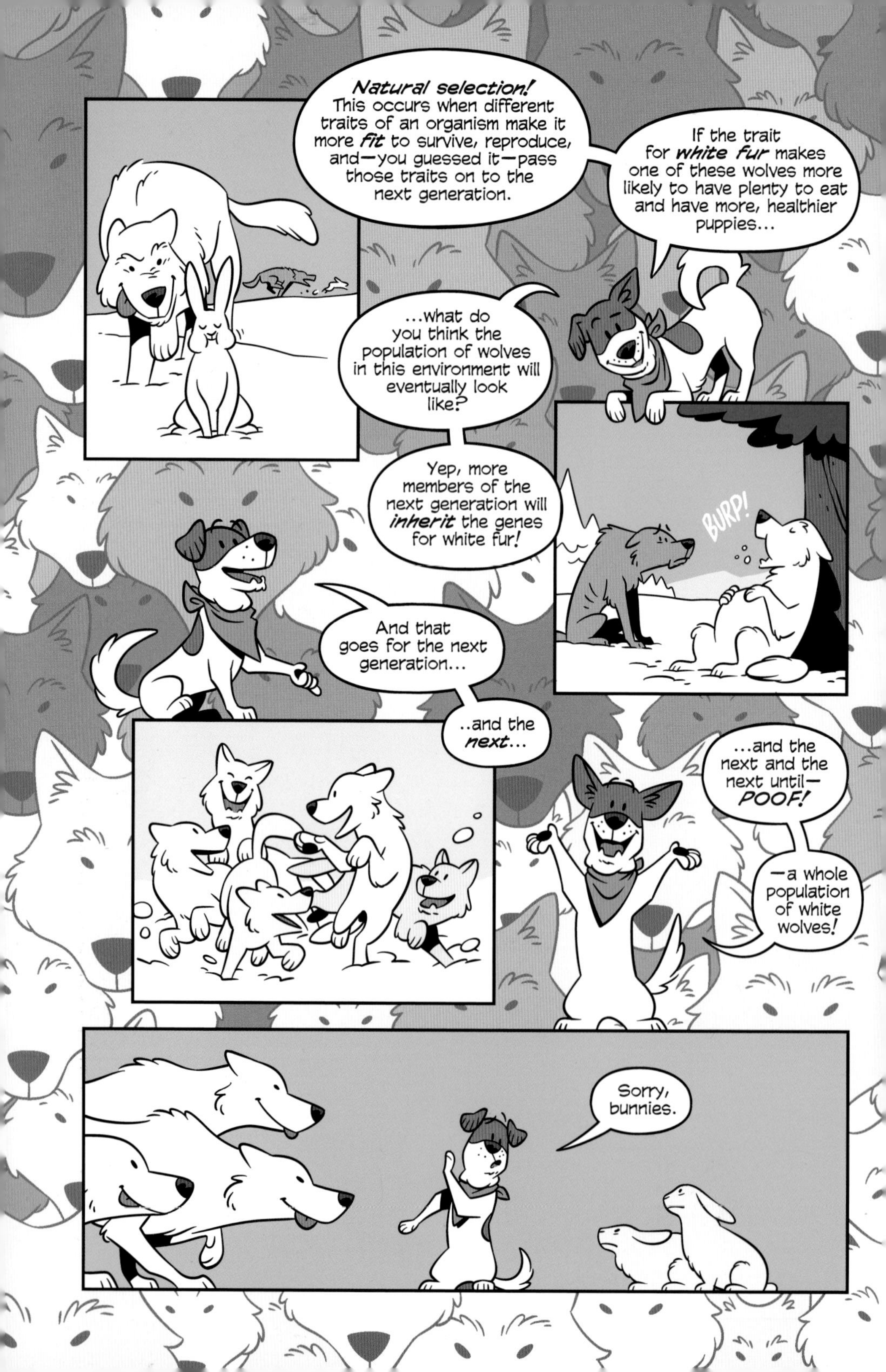

Natural selection! This occurs when different traits of an organism make it more *fit* to survive, reproduce, and—you guessed it—pass those traits on to the next generation.
If the trait for *white fur* makes one of these wolves more likely to have plenty to eat and have more, healthier puppies...
...what do you think the population of wolves in this environment will eventually look like?
Yep, more members of the next generation will *inherit* the genes for white fur!
BURP!
And that goes for the next generation...
..and the *next*...
...and the next and the next until—*POOF!*
—a whole population of white wolves!
Sorry, bunnies.

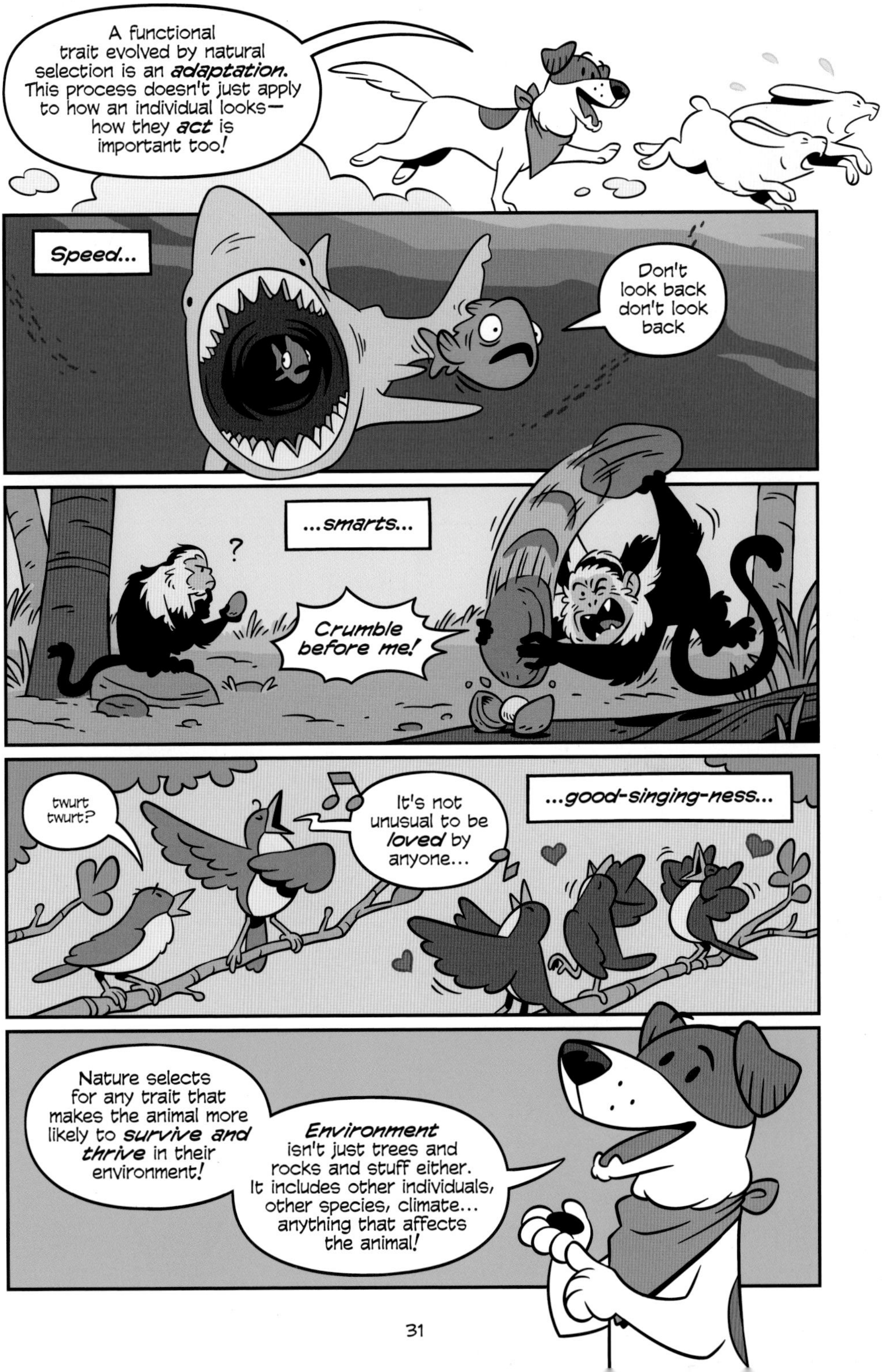

A functional trait evolved by natural selection is an ***adaptation.*** This process doesn't just apply to how an individual looks—how they ***act*** is important too!
Speed...
Don't look back don't look back
...smarts...
?
Crumble before me!
twurt twurt?
It's not unusual to be ***loved*** by anyone...
...good-singing-ness...
Nature selects for any trait that makes the animal more likely to ***survive and thrive*** in their environment!
Environment isn't just trees and rocks and stuff either. It includes other individuals, other species, climate... anything that affects the animal!

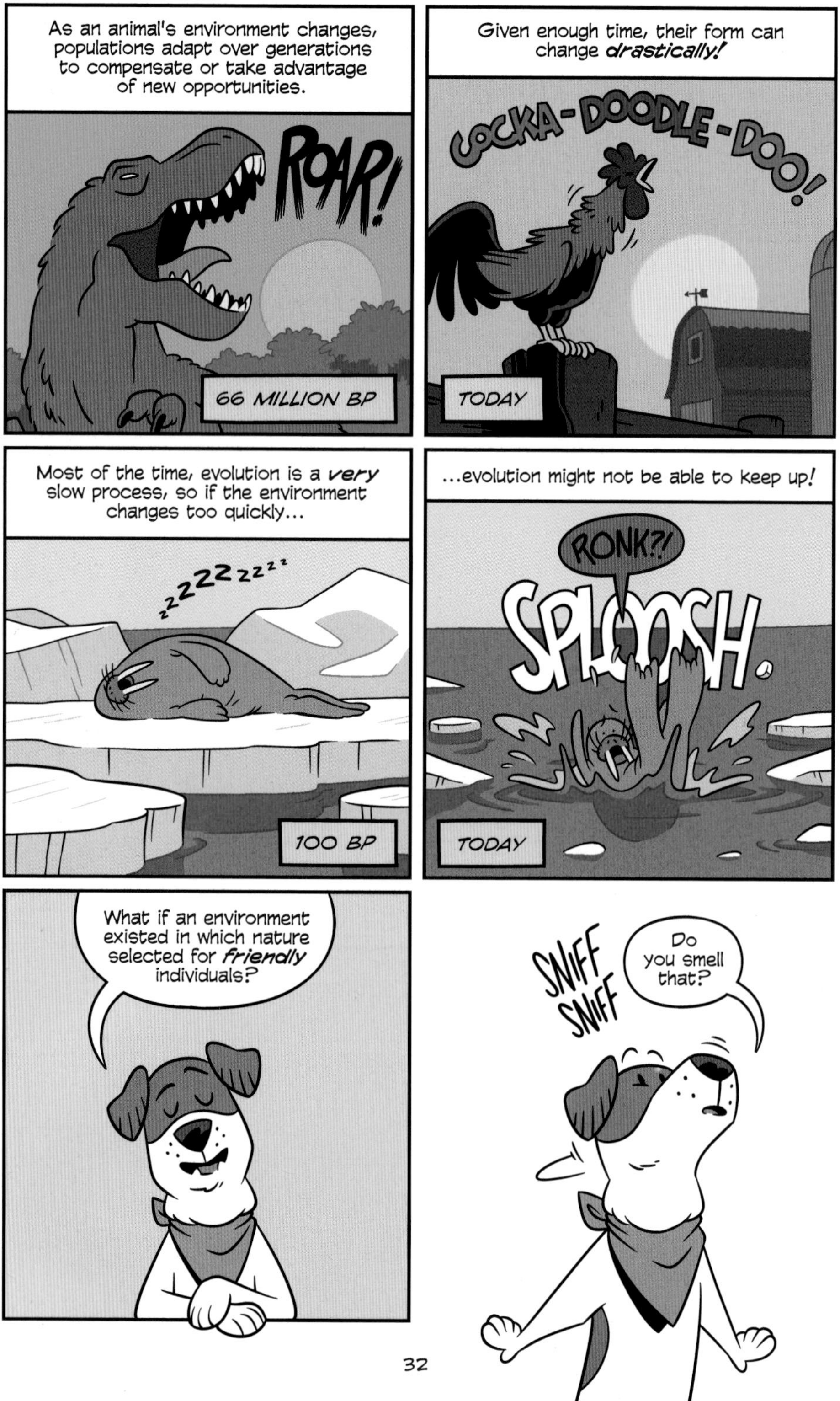
As an animal's environment changes, populations adapt over generations to compensate or take advantage of new opportunities.
ROAR!
66 MILLION BP
Given enough time, their form can change *drastically!*
COCKA-DOODLE-DOO!
TODAY
Most of the time, evolution is a *very* slow process, so if the environment changes too quickly...
zzZZZzzzz
100 BP
...evolution might not be able to keep up!
RONK?!
SPLOOSH
TODAY
What if an environment existed in which nature selected for *friendly* individuals?
SNIFF SNIFF
Do you smell that?

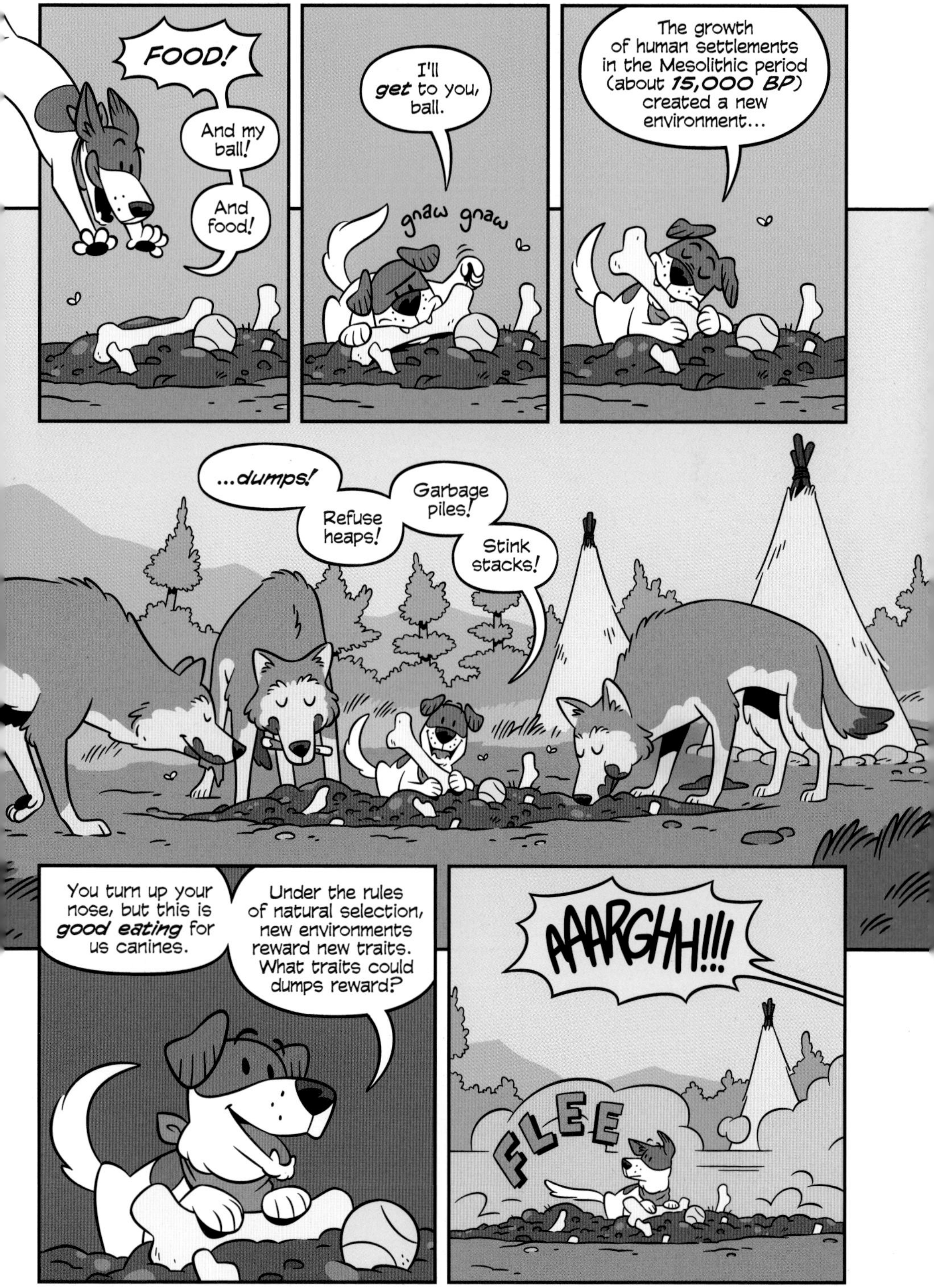
FOOD!
And my ball!
And food!
I'll get to you, ball.
gnaw gnaw
The growth of human settlements in the Mesolithic period (about 15,000 BP) created a new environment...
...dumps!
Refuse heaps!
Garbage piles!
Stink stacks!
You turn up your nose, but this is good eating for us canines.
Under the rules of natural selection, new environments reward new traits. What traits could dumps reward?
AAARGHH!!!!
FLEE

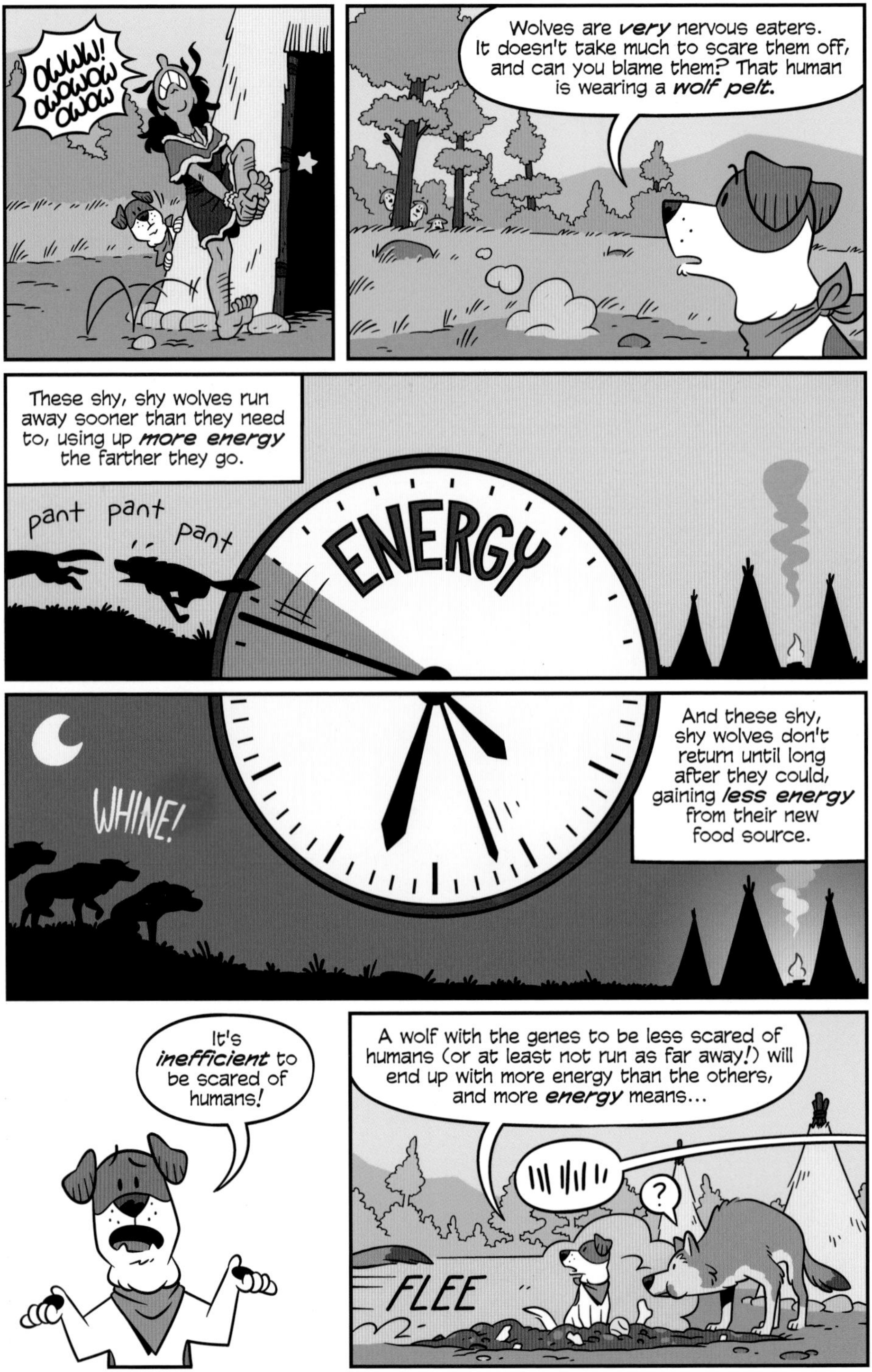
OWWW! OWOWOW OWOW
Wolves are very nervous eaters. It doesn't take much to scare them off, and can you blame them? That human is wearing a wolf pelt.
These shy, shy wolves run away sooner than they need to, using up more energy the farther they go.
pant pant pant
ENERGY
WHINE!
And these shy, shy wolves don't return until long after they could, gaining less energy from their new food source.
It's inefficient to be scared of humans!
A wolf with the genes to be less scared of humans (or at least not run as far away!) will end up with more energy than the others, and more energy means...
?
FLEE

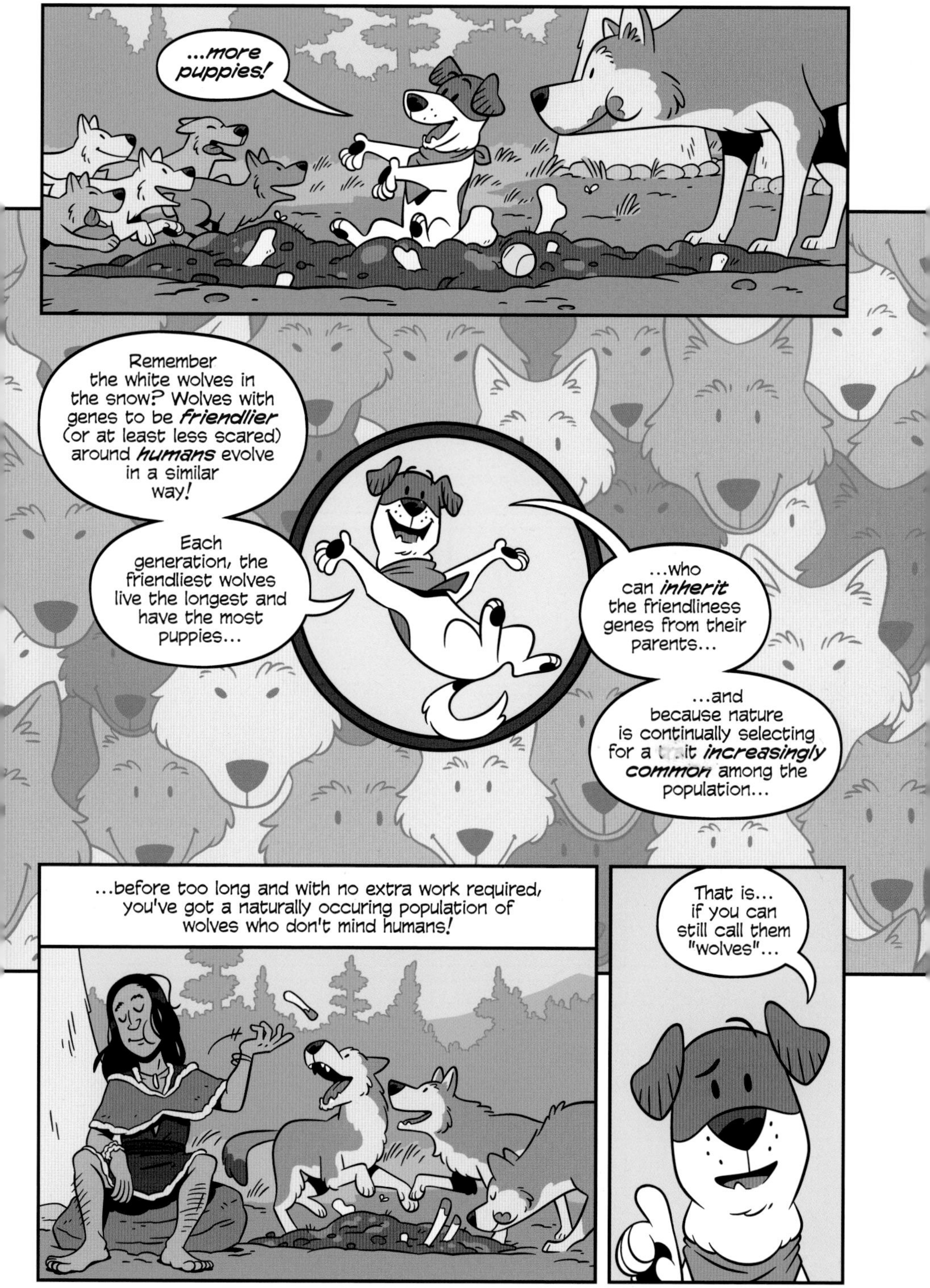
...more puppies!
Remember the white wolves in the snow? Wolves with genes to be *friendlier* (or at least less scared) around *humans* evolve in a similar way!
Each generation, the friendliest wolves live the longest and have the most puppies...
...who can *inherit* the friendliness genes from their parents...
...and because nature is continually selecting for a trait *increasingly common* among the population...
...before too long and with no extra work required, you've got a naturally occuring population of wolves who don't mind humans!
That is... if you can still call them "wolves"...

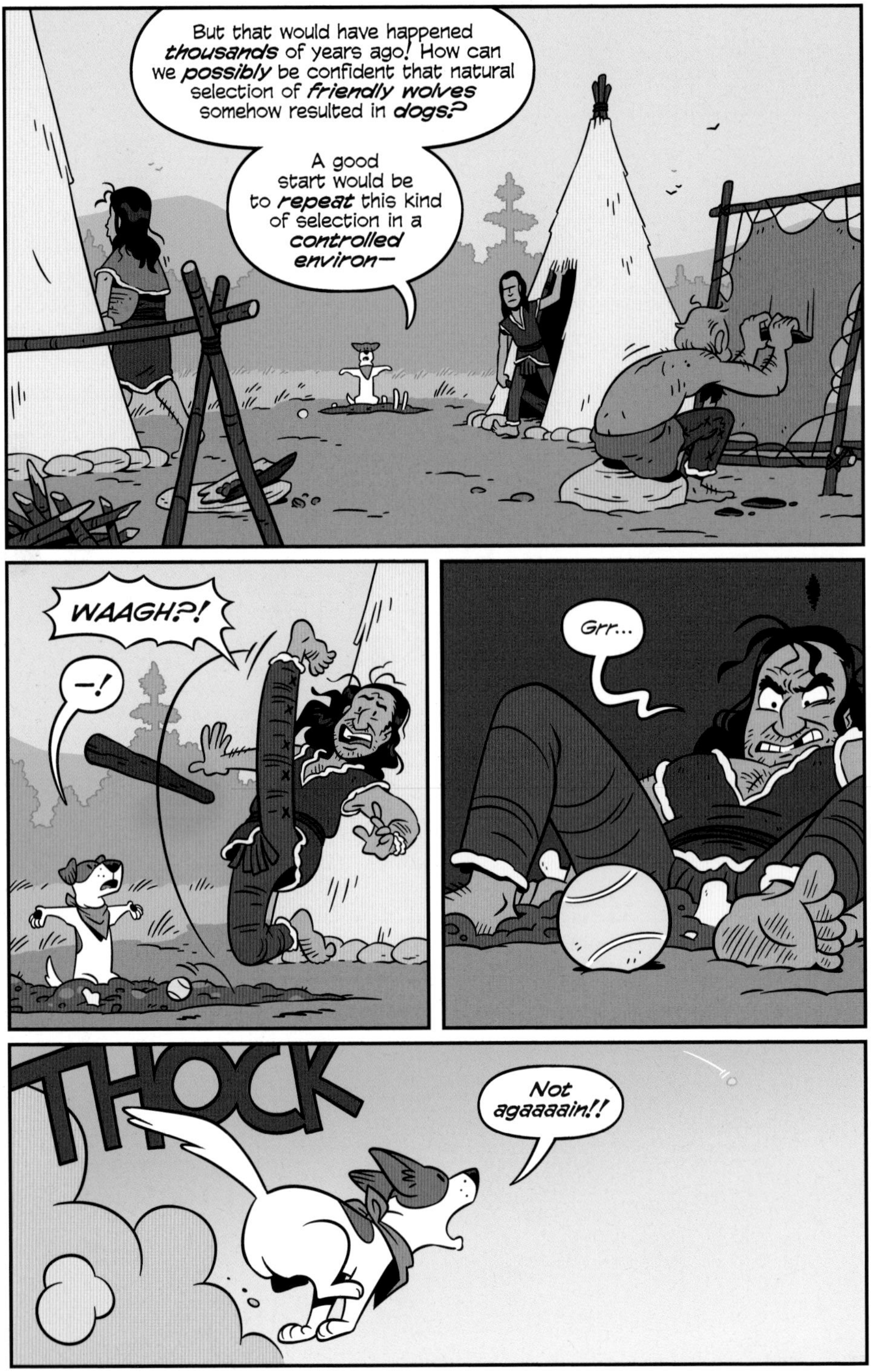
But that would have happened *thousands* of years ago! How can we *possibly* be confident that natural selection of *friendly wolves* somehow resulted in *dogs?*
A good start would be to *repeat* this kind of selection in a *controlled environ—*
WAAGH?!
—!
Grr...
THOCK
Not agaaaain!!

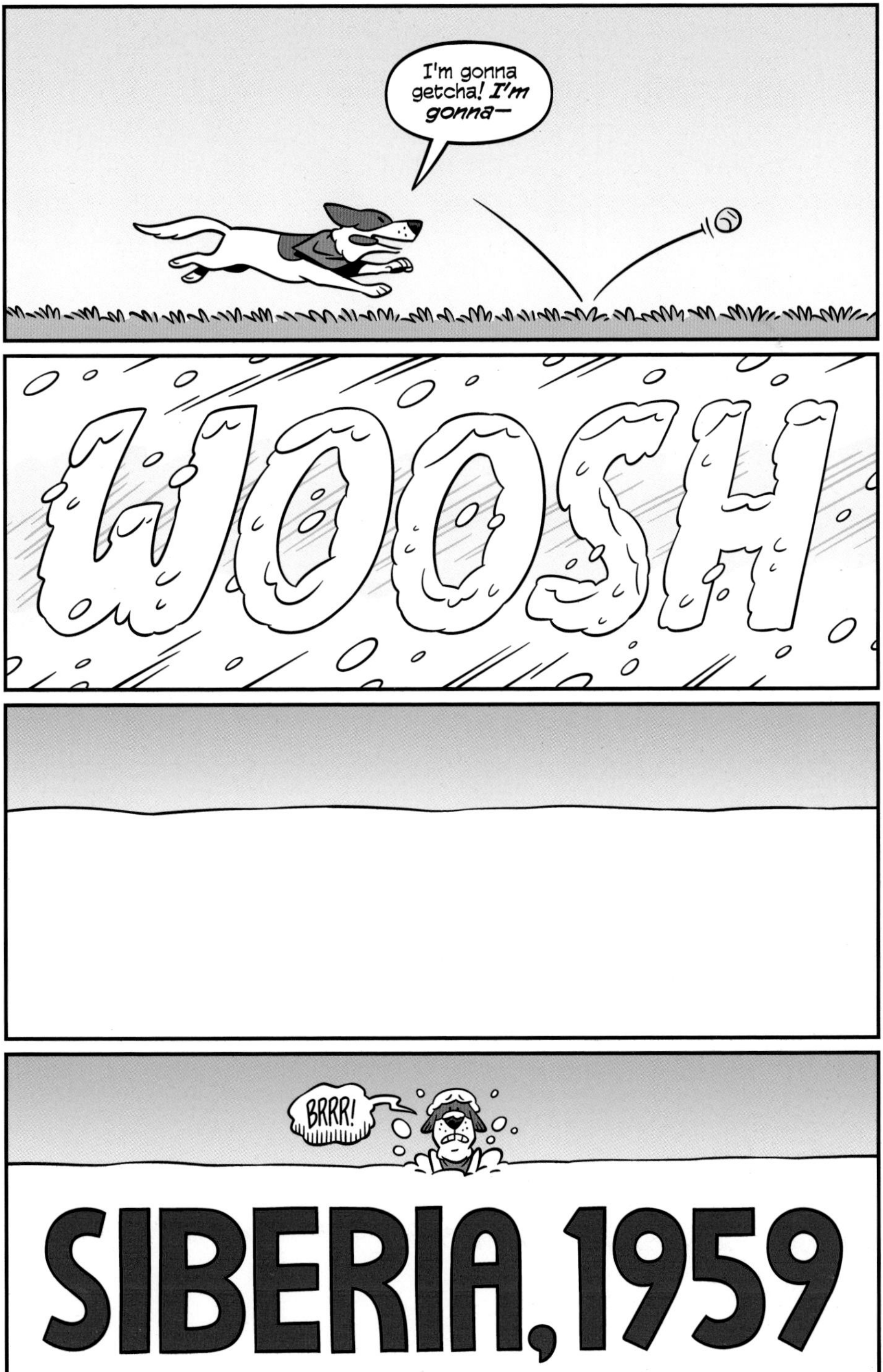
I'm gonna getcha! *I'm gonna—*
WOOSH
BRRR!
SIBERIA, 1959

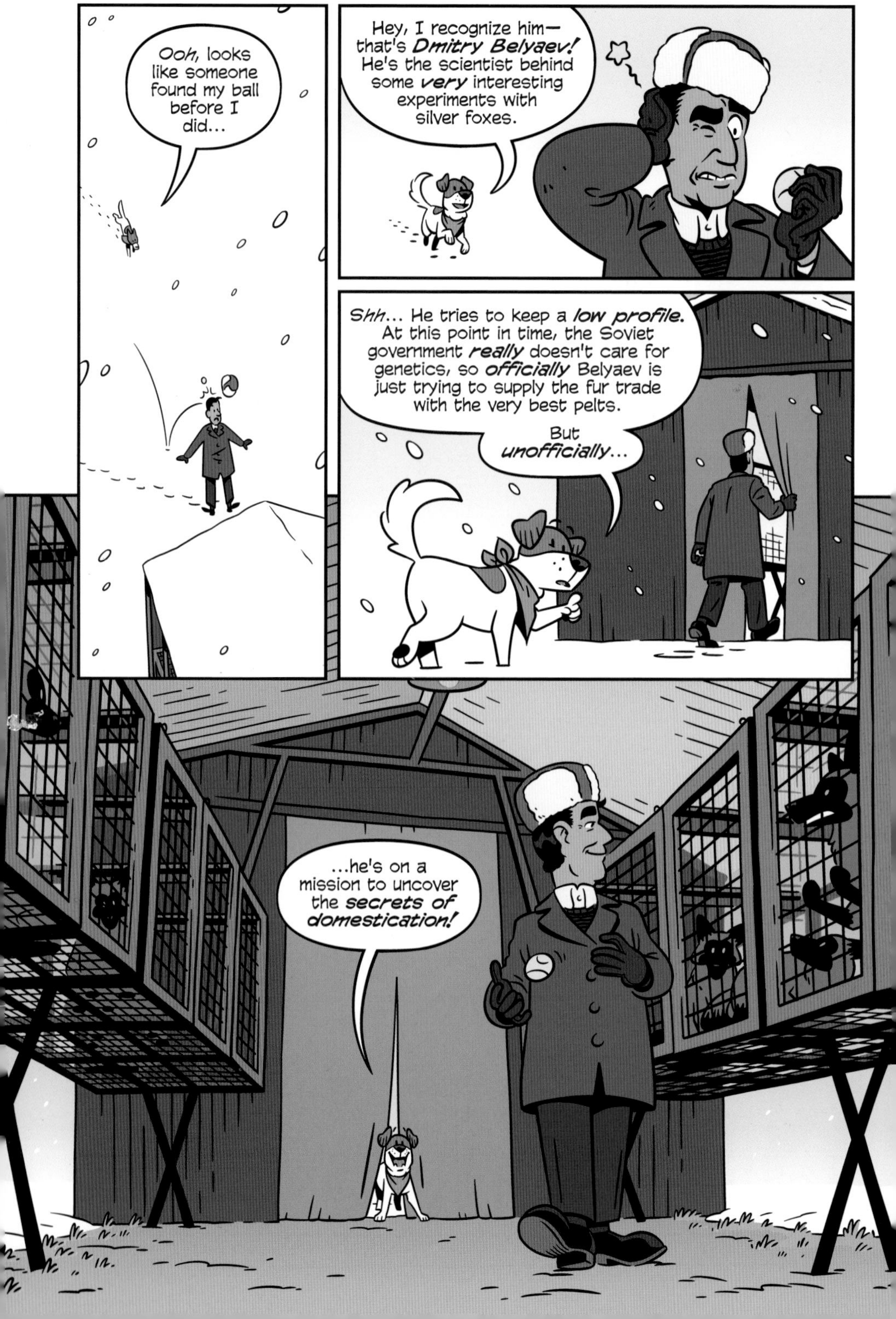
Ooh, looks like someone found my ball before I did...
Hey, I recognize him—that's Dmitry Belyaev! He's the scientist behind some very interesting experiments with silver foxes.
Shh... He tries to keep a low profile. At this point in time, the Soviet government really doesn't care for genetics, so officially Belyaev is just trying to supply the fur trade with the very best pelts.
But unofficially...
...he's on a mission to uncover the secrets of domestication!

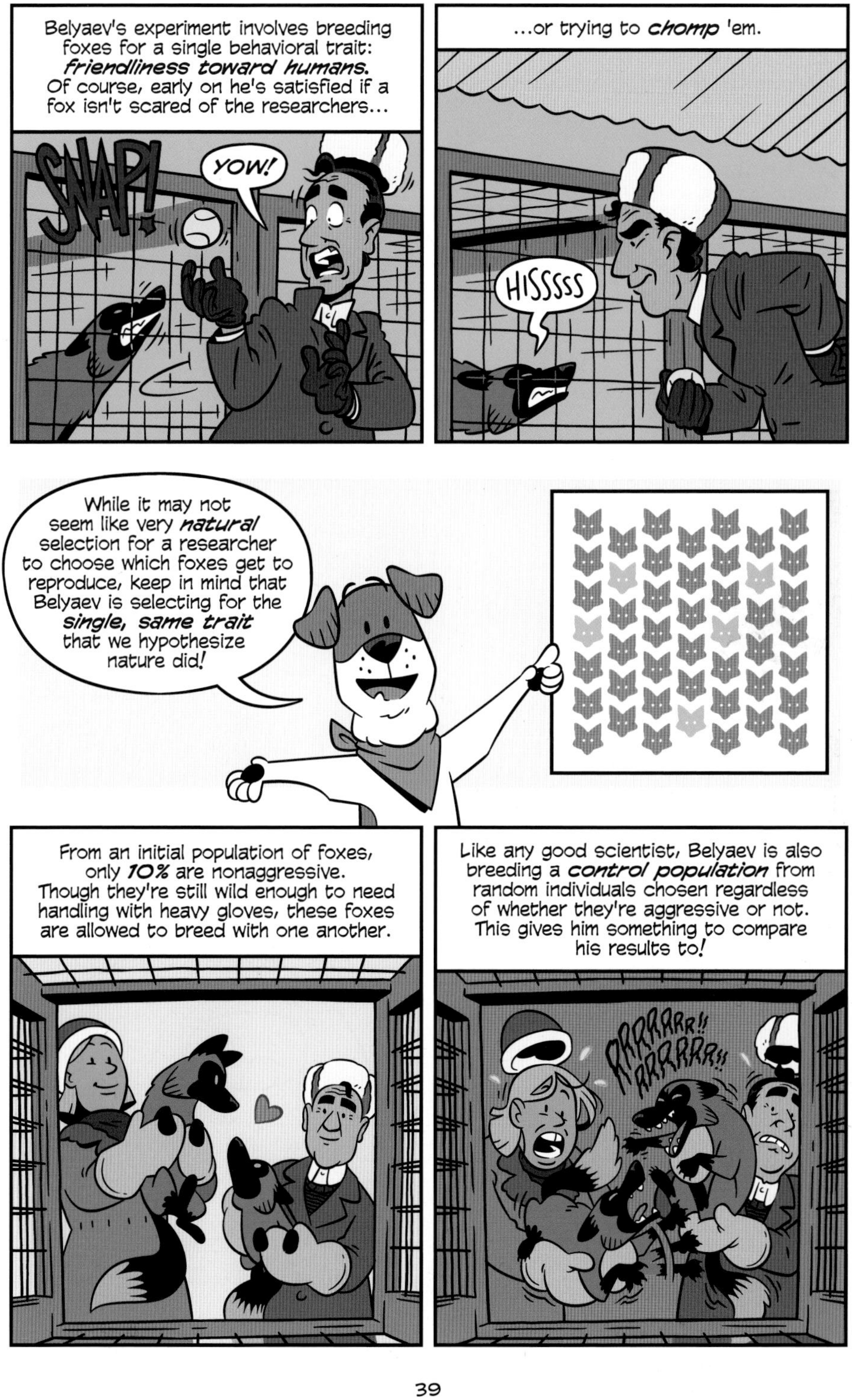
Belyaev's experiment involves breeding foxes for a single behavioral trait: *friendliness toward humans.* Of course, early on he's satisfied if a fox isn't scared of the researchers...
SNAP!
YOW!
...or trying to *chomp* 'em.
HISSSSS
While it may not seem like very *natural* selection for a researcher to choose which foxes get to reproduce, keep in mind that Belyaev is selecting for the *single, same trait* that we hypothesize nature did!
From an initial population of foxes, only *10%* are nonaggressive. Though they're still wild enough to need handling with heavy gloves, these foxes are allowed to breed with one another.
Like any good scientist, Belyaev is also breeding a *control population* from random individuals chosen regardless of whether they're aggressive or not. This gives him something to compare his results to!
RRRRRRR!!
RRRRRRR!!

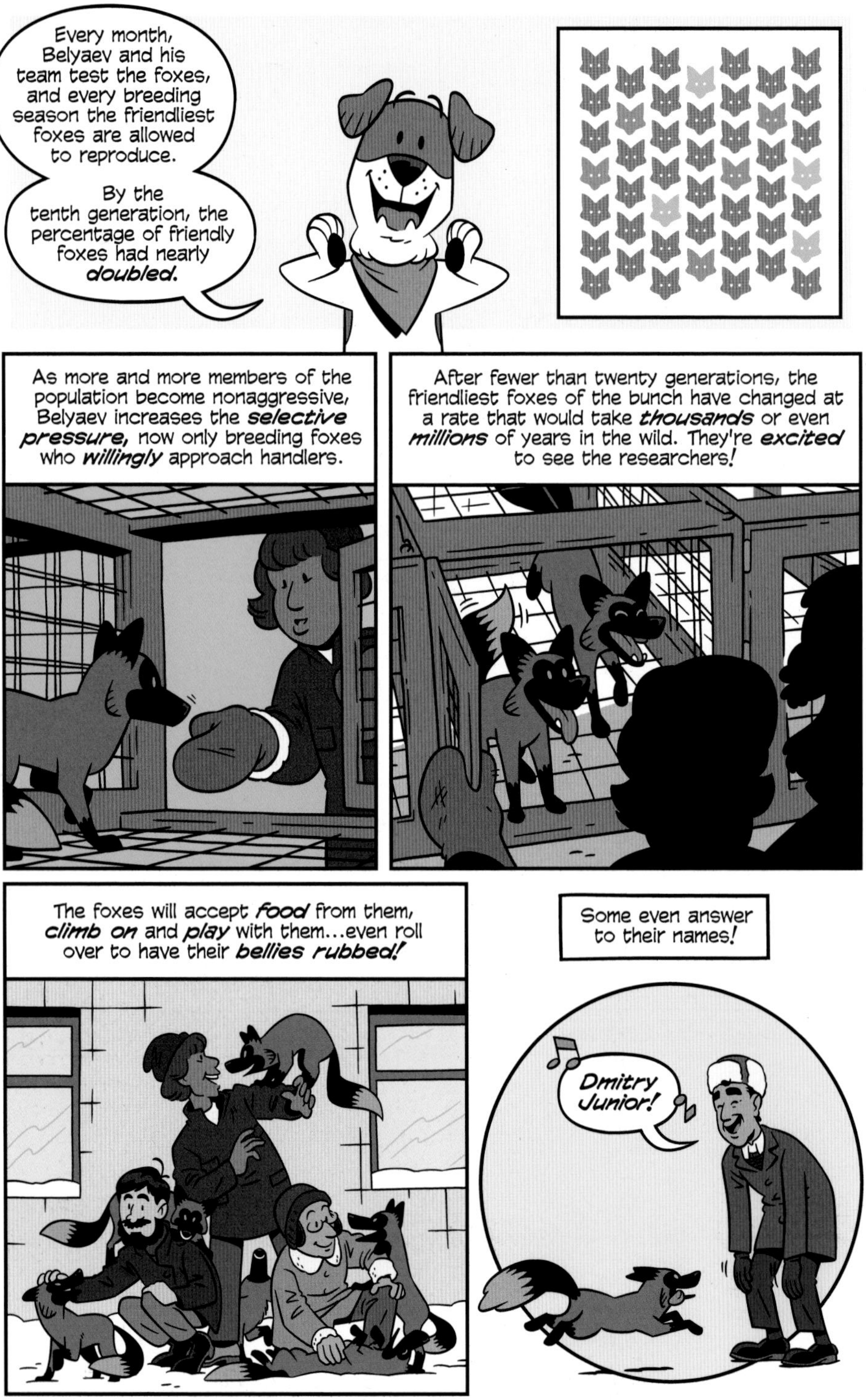
Every month, Belyaev and his team test the foxes, and every breeding season the friendliest foxes are allowed to reproduce.
By the tenth generation, the percentage of friendly foxes had nearly doubled.
As more and more members of the population become nonaggressive, Belyaev increases the selective pressure, now only breeding foxes who willingly approach handlers.
After fewer than twenty generations, the friendliest foxes of the bunch have changed at a rate that would take thousands or even millions of years in the wild. They're excited to see the researchers!
The foxes will accept food from them, climb on and play with them...even roll over to have their bellies rubbed!
Some even answer to their names!
Dmitry Junior!

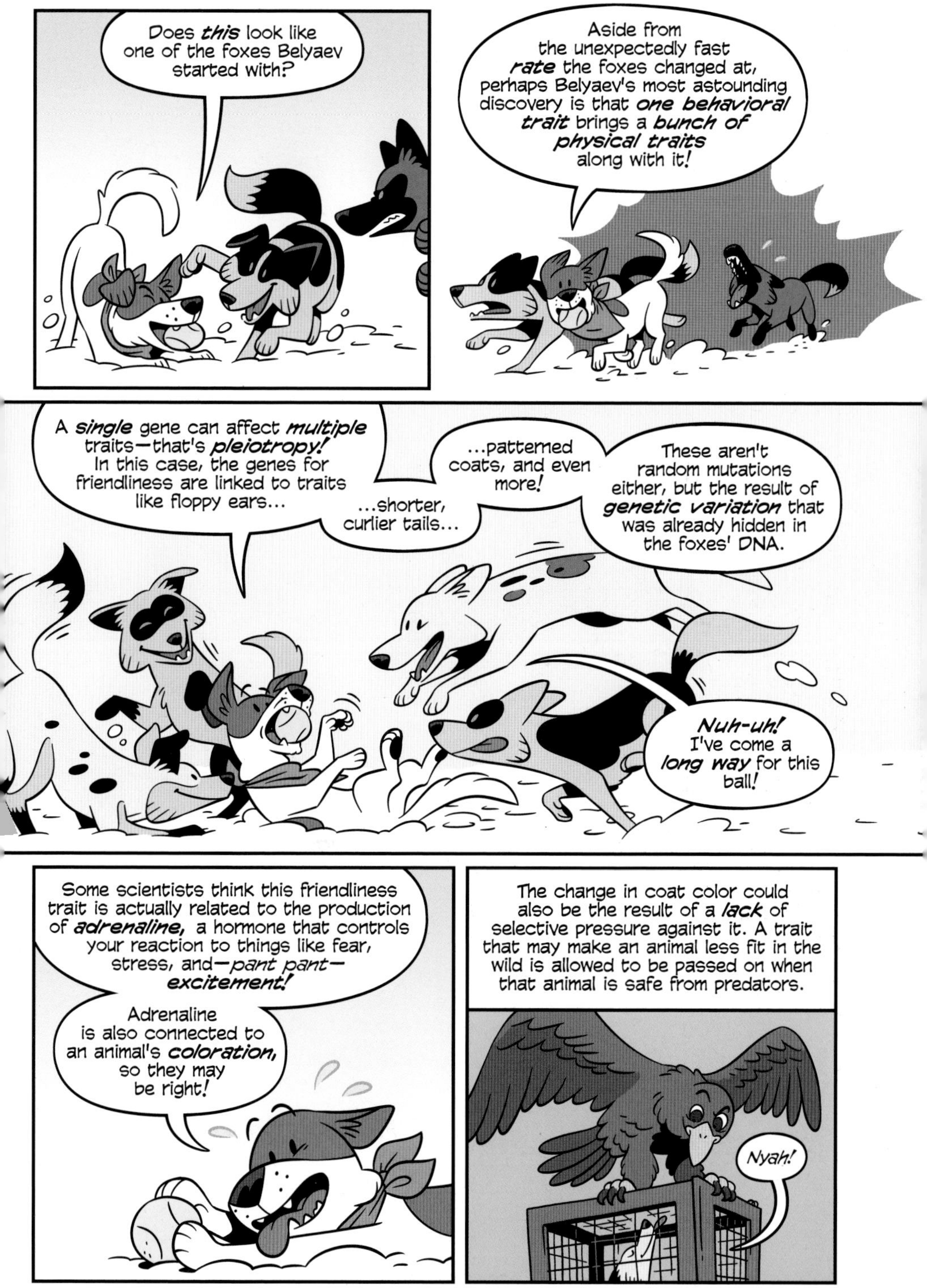
Does this look like one of the foxes Belyaev started with?
Aside from the unexpectedly fast rate the foxes changed at, perhaps Belyaev's most astounding discovery is that one behavioral trait brings a bunch of physical traits along with it!
A single gene can affect multiple traits—that's pleiotropy! In this case, the genes for friendliness are linked to traits like floppy ears...
...shorter, curlier tails...
...patterned coats, and even more!
These aren't random mutations either, but the result of genetic variation that was already hidden in the foxes' DNA.
Nuh-uh! I've come a long way for this ball!
Some scientists think this friendliness trait is actually related to the production of adrenaline, a hormone that controls your reaction to things like fear, stress, and—pant pant—excitement!
Adrenaline is also connected to an animal's coloration, so they may be right!
The change in coat color could also be the result of a lack of selective pressure against it. A trait that may make an animal less fit in the wild is allowed to be passed on when that animal is safe from predators.
Nyah!

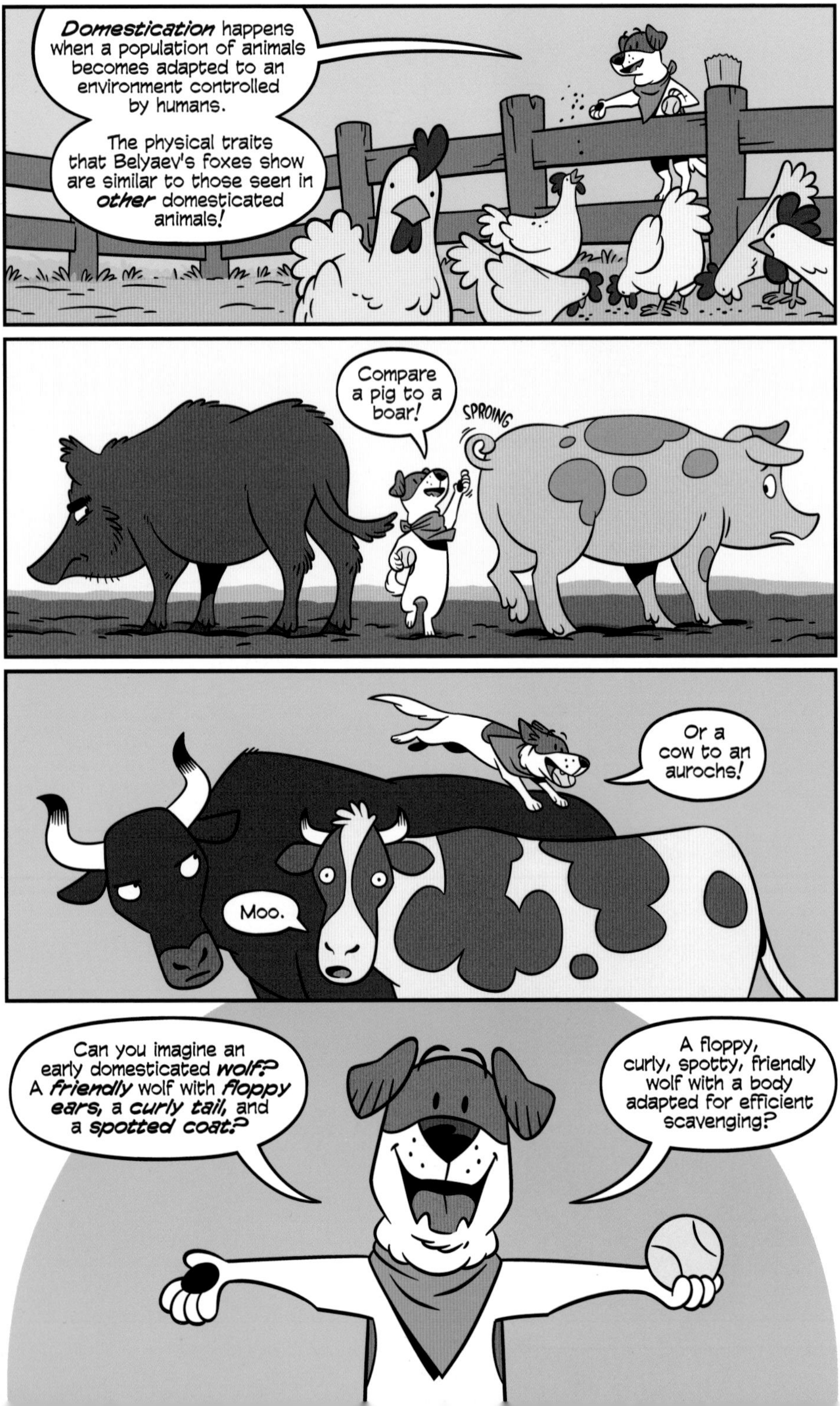
Domestication happens when a population of animals becomes adapted to an environment controlled by humans.
The physical traits that Belyaev's foxes show are similar to those seen in other domesticated animals!
Compare a pig to a boar!
SPROING
Or a cow to an aurochs!
Moo.
Can you imagine an early domesticated wolf? A friendly wolf with floppy ears, a curly tail, and a spotted coat?
A floppy, curly, spotty, friendly wolf with a body adapted for efficient scavenging?

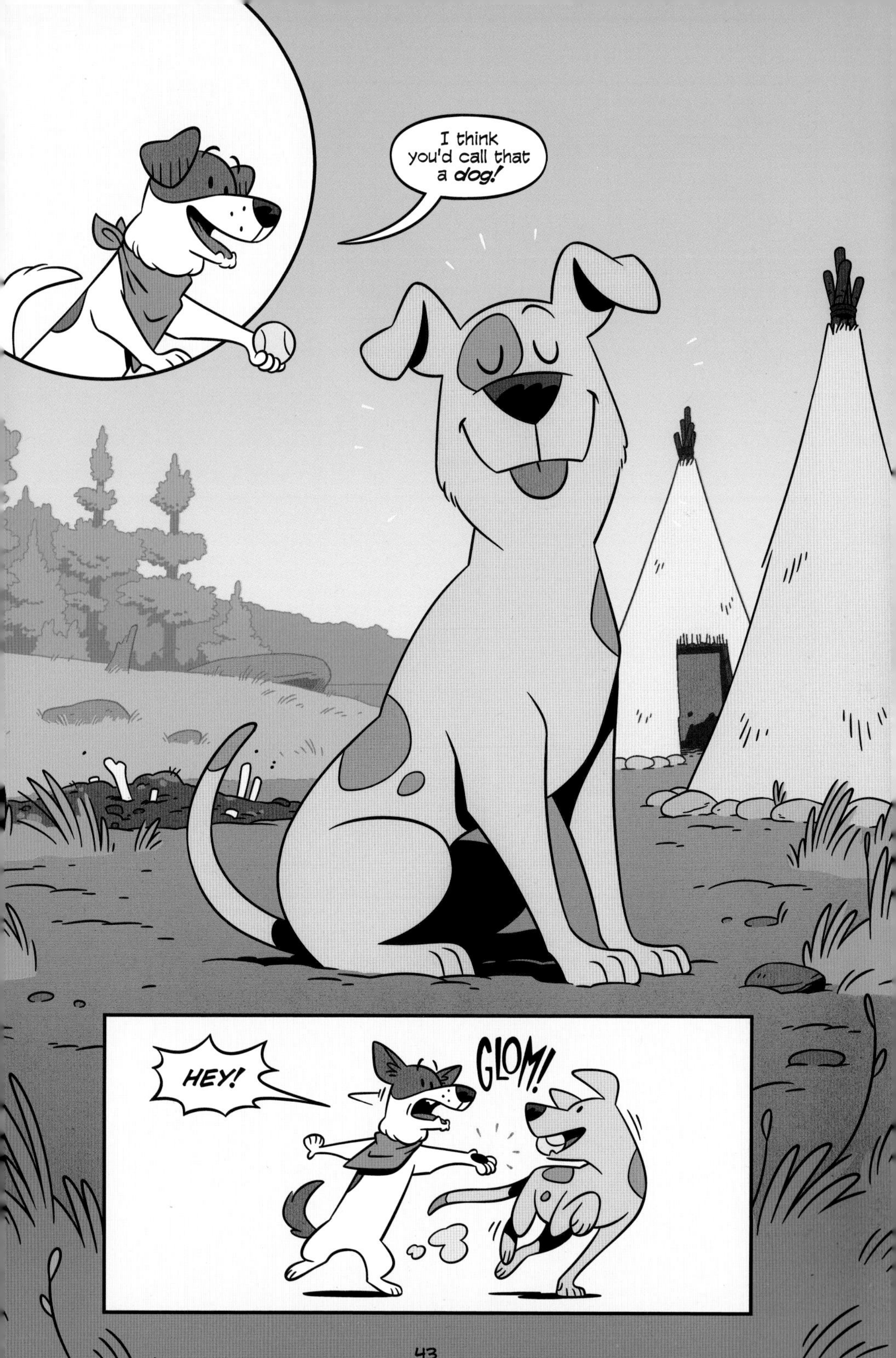
I think you'd call that a *dog!*
HEY!
GLOM!

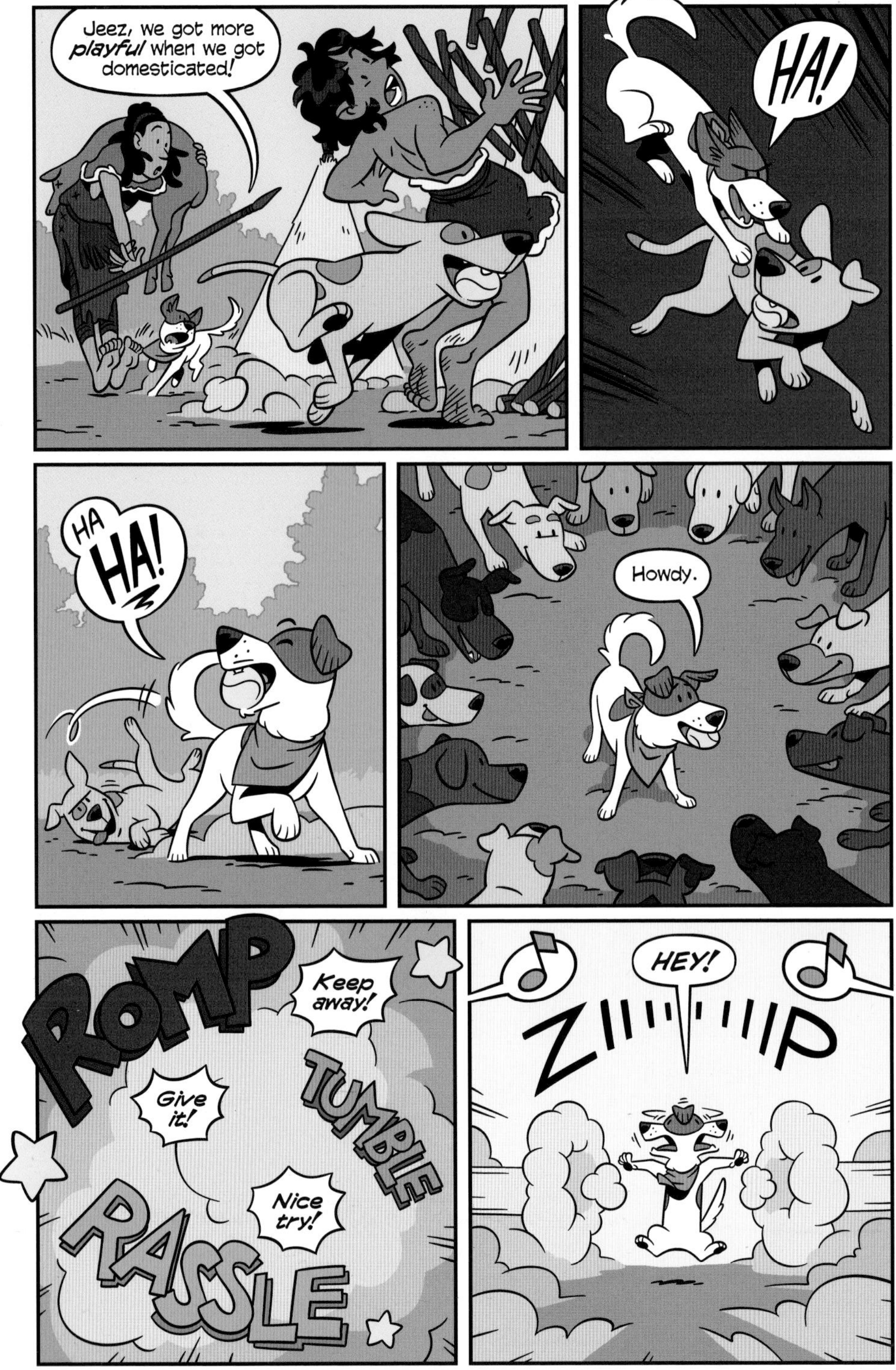
Jeez, we got more *playful* when we got domesticated!
HA!
HA HA!
Howdy.
ROMP
Keep away!
Give it!
TUMBLE
Nice try!
RASSLE
HEY!
ZIIIIIIP

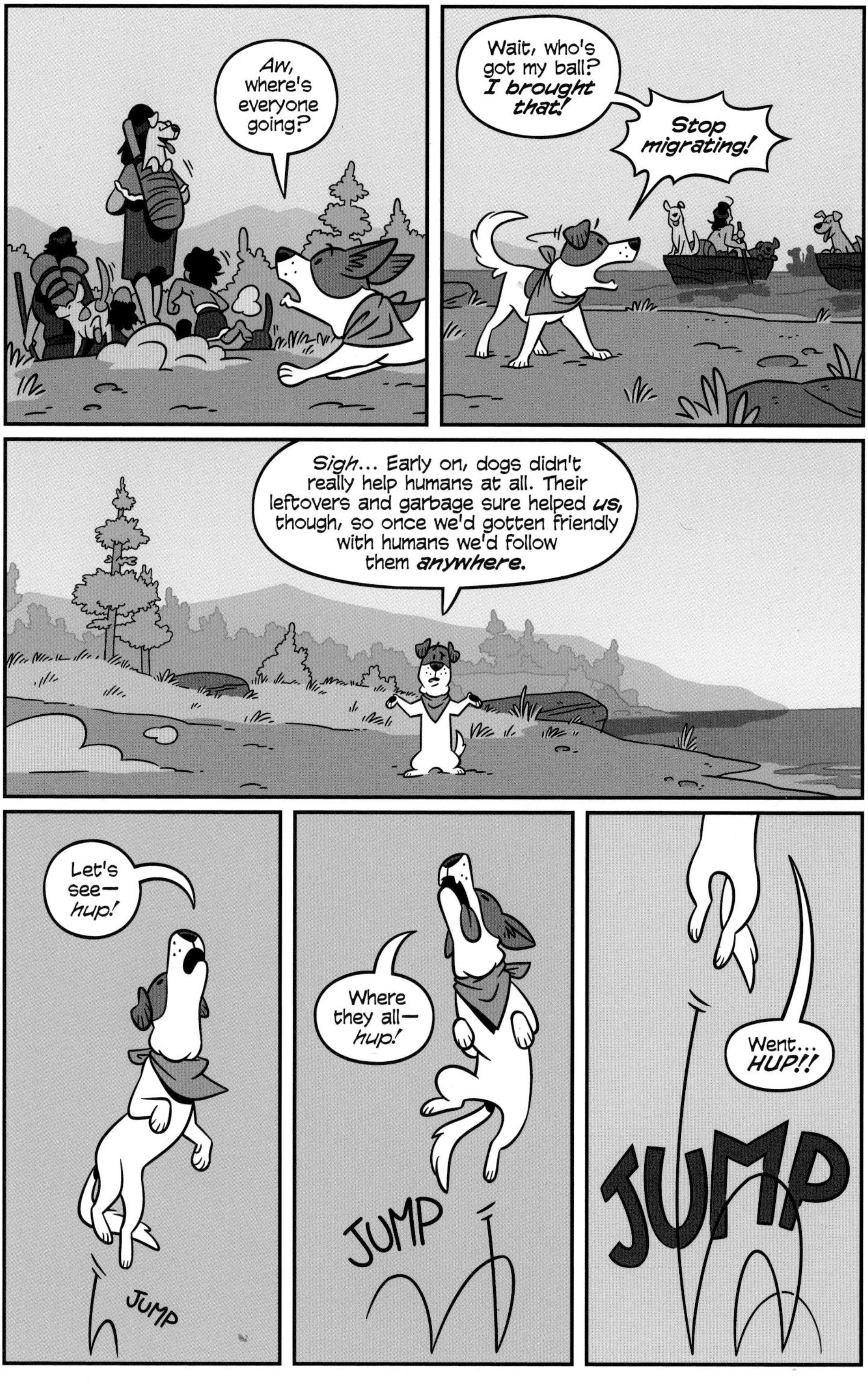

Aw, where's everyone going?
Wait, who's got my ball? ***I brought that!***
Stop migrating!
Sigh... Early on, dogs didn't really help humans at all. Their leftovers and garbage sure helped ***us,*** though, so once we'd gotten friendly with humans we'd follow them ***anywhere.***
Let's see— *hup!*
JUMP
Where they all— *hup!*
JUMP
Went... ***HUP!!***
JUMP

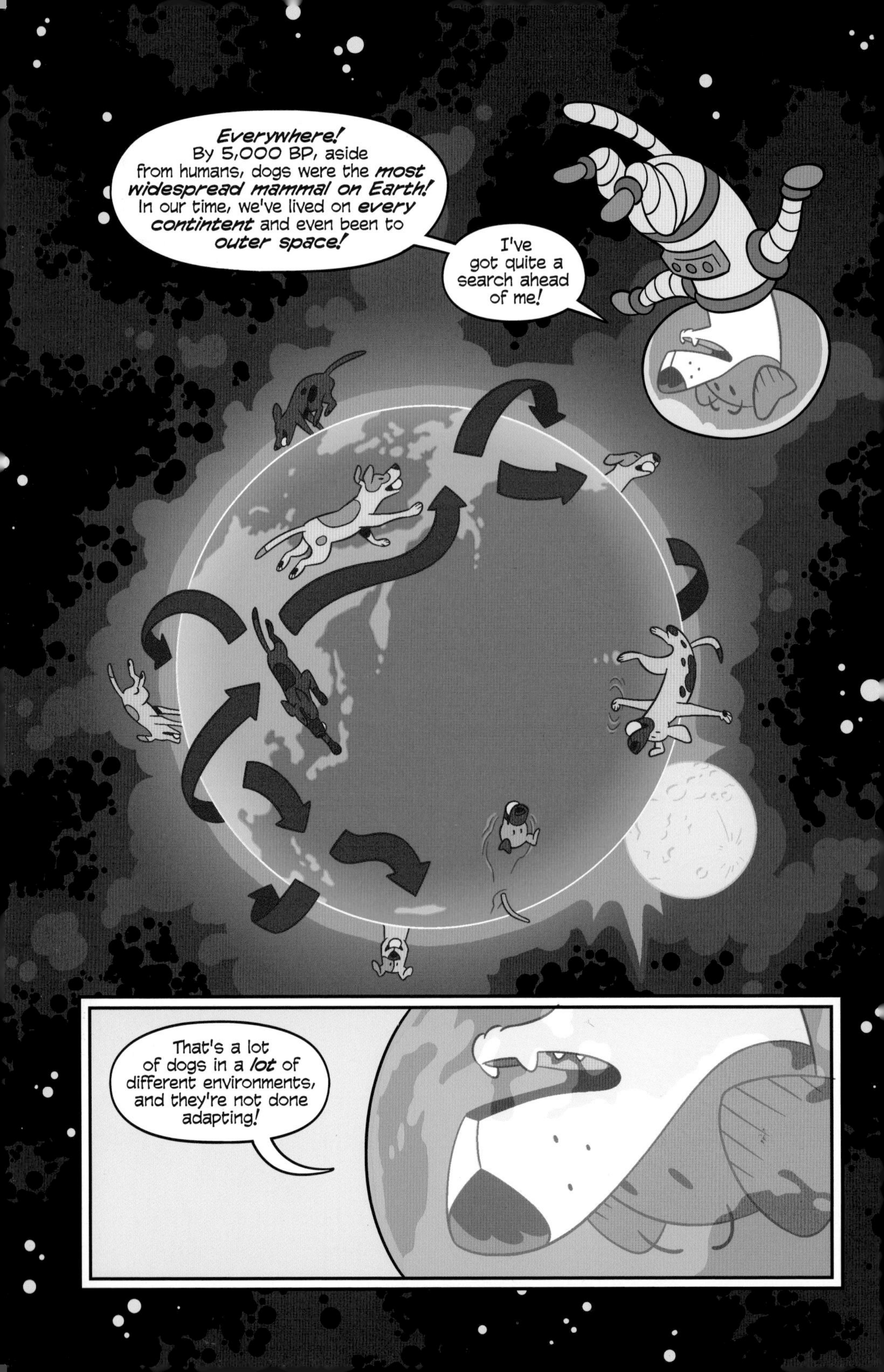

Everywhere! By 5,000 BP, aside from humans, dogs were the ***most widespread mammal on Earth!*** In our time, we've lived on ***every contintent*** and even been to ***outer space!***
I've got quite a search ahead of me!
That's a lot of dogs in a *lot* of different environments, and they're not done adapting!

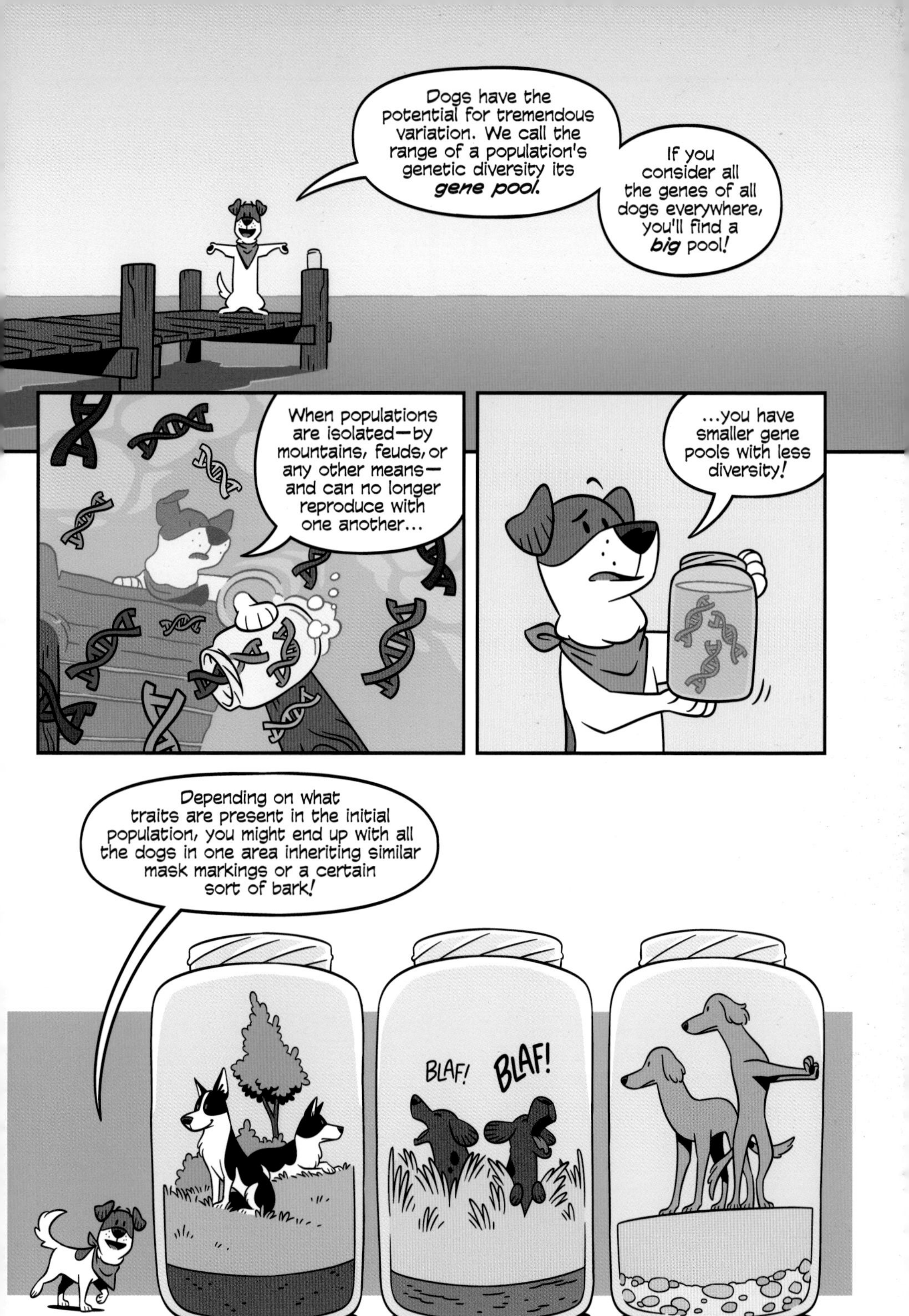
Dogs have the potential for tremendous variation. We call the range of a population's genetic diversity its ***gene pool.***
If you consider all the genes of all dogs everywhere, you'll find a ***big*** pool!
When populations are isolated—by mountains, feuds, or any other means—and can no longer reproduce with one another...
...you have smaller gene pools with less diversity!
Depending on what traits are present in the initial population, you might end up with all the dogs in one area inheriting similar mask markings or a certain sort of bark!
BLAF!
BLAF!

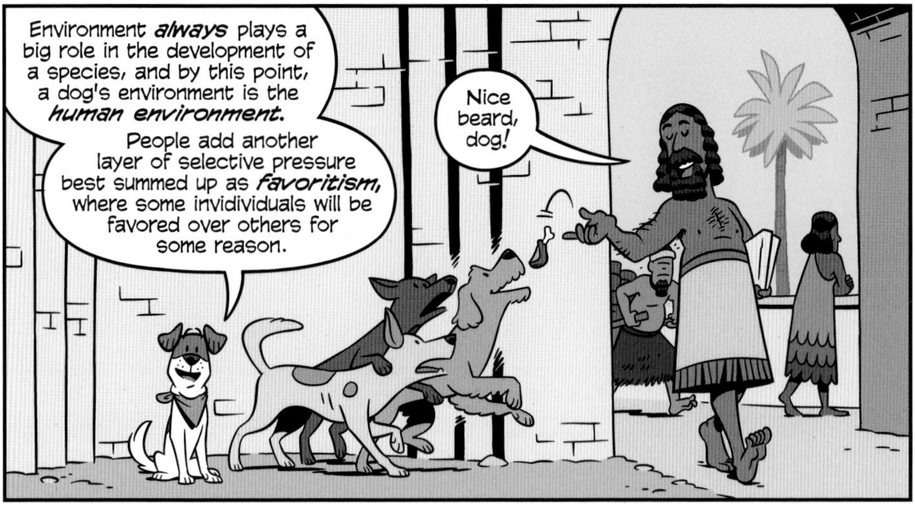
Environment *always* plays a big role in the development of a species, and by this point, a dog's environment is the *human environment.*
People add another layer of selective pressure best summed up as *favoritism,* where some invidividuals will be favored over others for some reason.
Nice beard, dog!

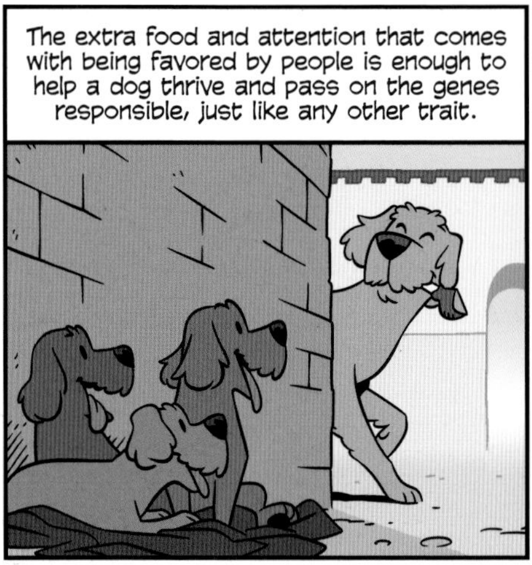
The extra food and attention that comes with being favored by people is enough to help a dog thrive and pass on the genes responsible, just like any other trait.

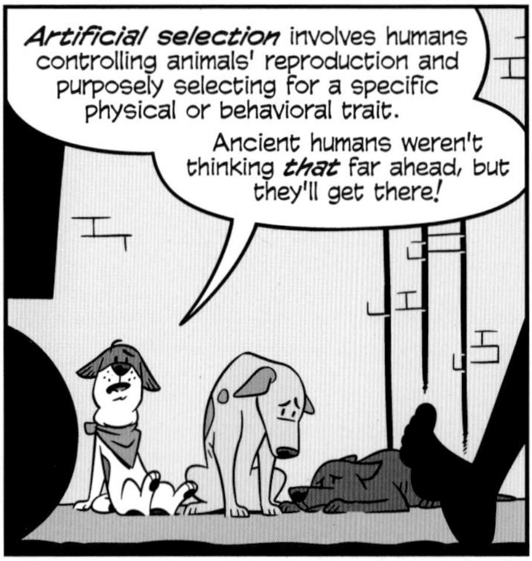
Artificial selection involves humans controlling animals' reproduction and purposely selecting for a specific physical or behavioral trait.
Ancient humans weren't thinking *that* far ahead, but they'll get there!

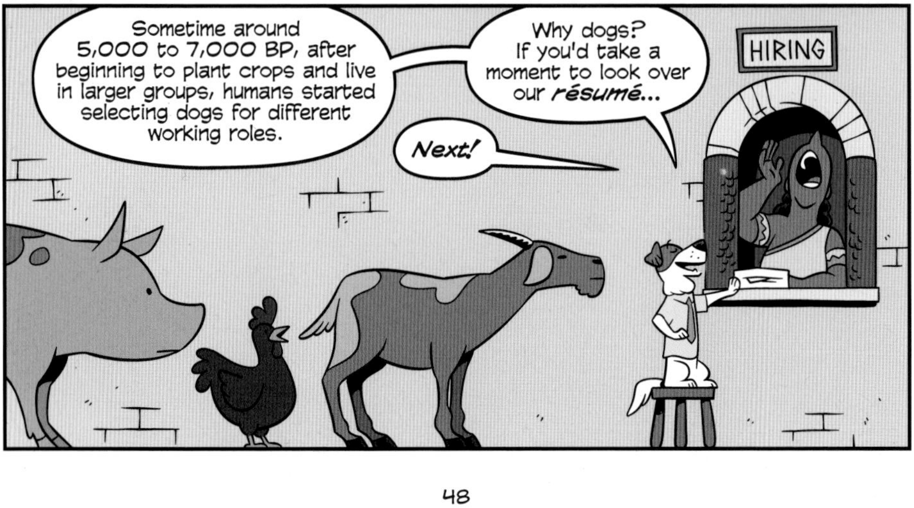
Sometime around 5,000 to 7,000 BP, after beginning to plant crops and live in larger groups, humans started selecting dogs for different working roles.
Why dogs? If you'd take a moment to look over our *résumé*...
HIRING
Next!

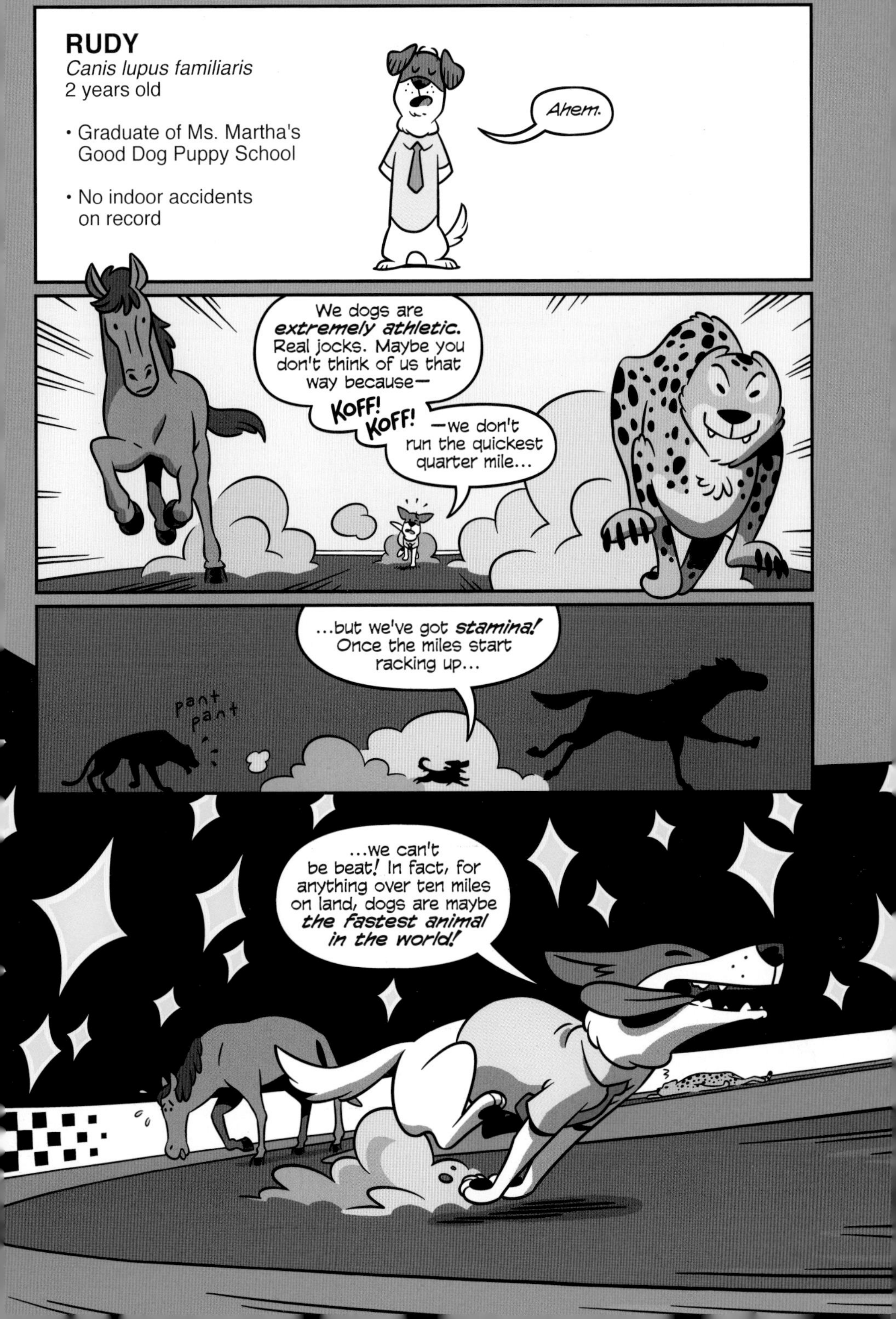
RUDY
Canis lupus familiaris
2 years old
• Graduate of Ms. Martha's Good Dog Puppy School
• No indoor accidents on record
Ahem.
We dogs are extremely athletic. Real jocks. Maybe you don't think of us that way because—
KOFF! KOFF!
—we don't run the quickest quarter mile...
...but we've got stamina! Once the miles start racking up...
pant pant
...we can't be beat! In fact, for anything over ten miles on land, dogs are maybe the fastest animal in the world!

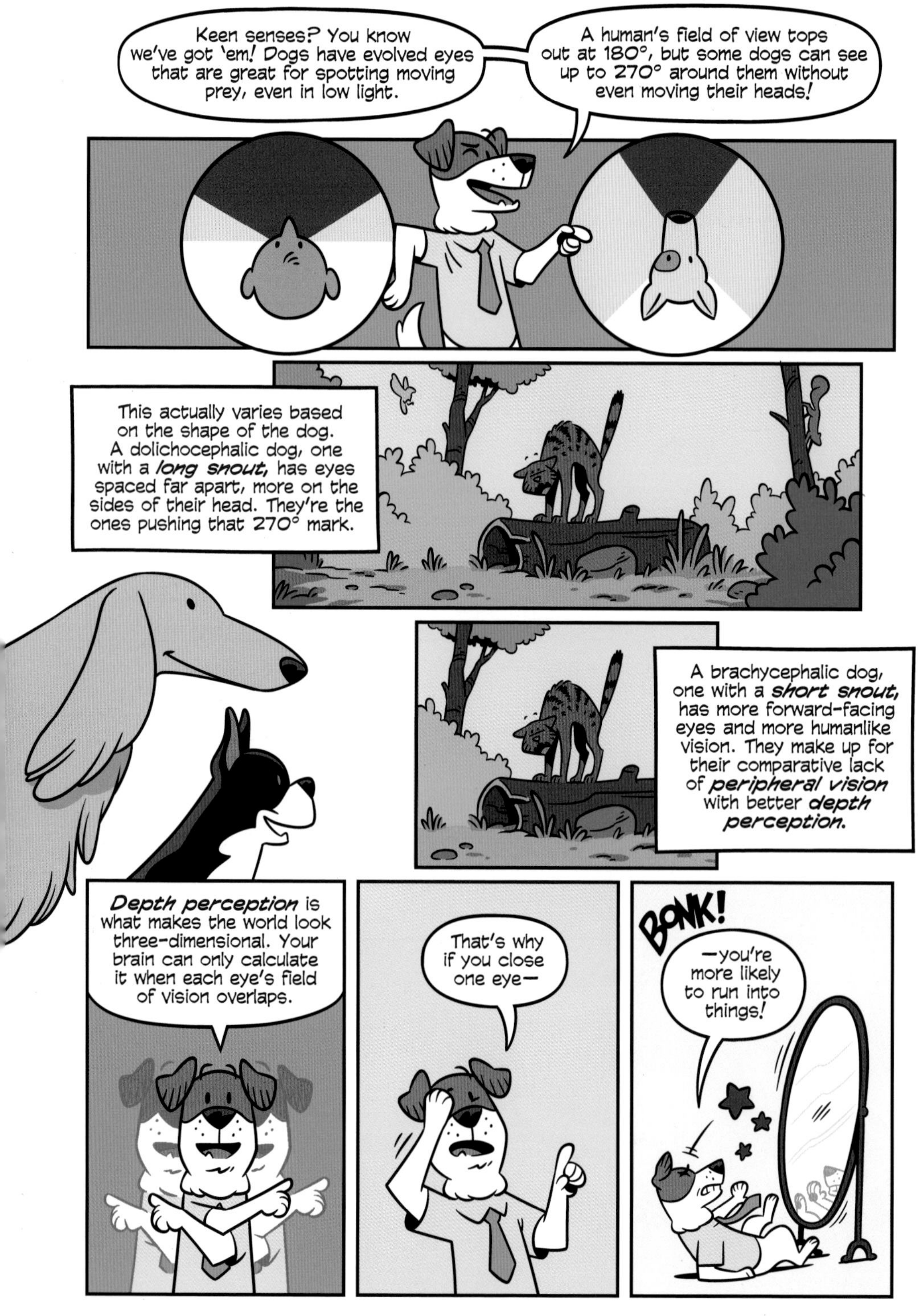
Keen senses? You know we've got 'em! Dogs have evolved eyes that are great for spotting moving prey, even in low light.
A human's field of view tops out at 180°, but some dogs can see up to 270° around them without even moving their heads!
This actually varies based on the shape of the dog. A dolichocephalic dog, one with a *long snout,* has eyes spaced far apart, more on the sides of their head. They're the ones pushing that 270° mark.
A brachycephalic dog, one with a *short snout,* has more forward-facing eyes and more humanlike vision. They make up for their comparative lack of *peripheral vision* with better *depth perception.*
Depth perception is what makes the world look three-dimensional. Your brain can only calculate it when each eye's field of vision overlaps.
That's why if you close one eye—
BONK!
—you're more likely to run into things!

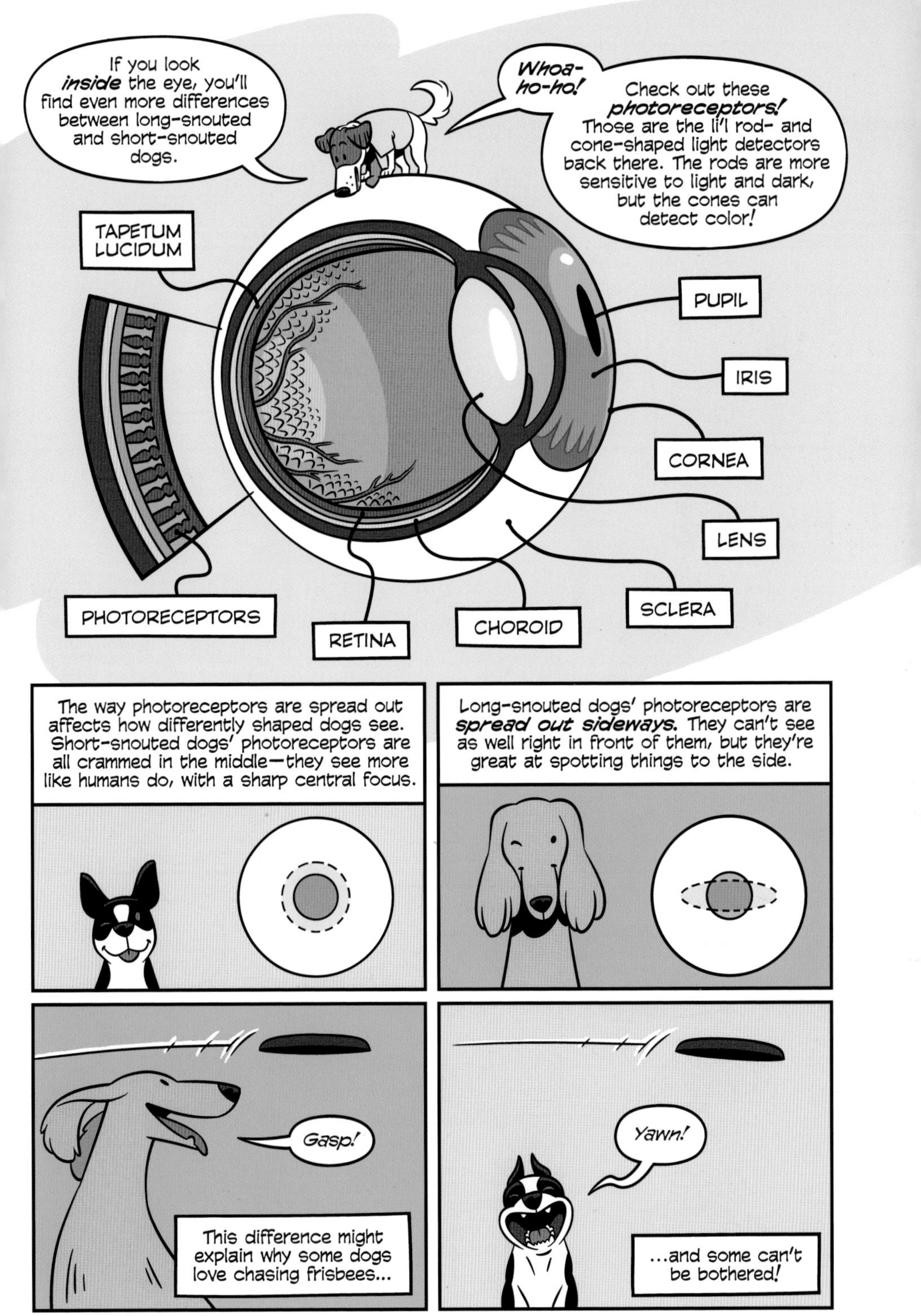
If you look *inside* the eye, you'll find even more differences between long-snouted and short-snouted dogs.
Whoa-ho-ho!
Check out these *photoreceptors!* Those are the li'l rod- and cone-shaped light detectors back there. The rods are more sensitive to light and dark, but the cones can detect color!
TAPETUM LUCIDUM
PUPIL
IRIS
CORNEA
LENS
SCLERA
PHOTORECEPTORS
RETINA
CHOROID
The way photoreceptors are spread out affects how differently shaped dogs see. Short-snouted dogs' photoreceptors are all crammed in the middle—they see more like humans do, with a sharp central focus.
Long-snouted dogs' photoreceptors are *spread out sideways.* They can't see as well right in front of them, but they're great at spotting things to the side.
Gasp!
This difference might explain why some dogs love chasing frisbees...
Yawn!
...and some can't be bothered!

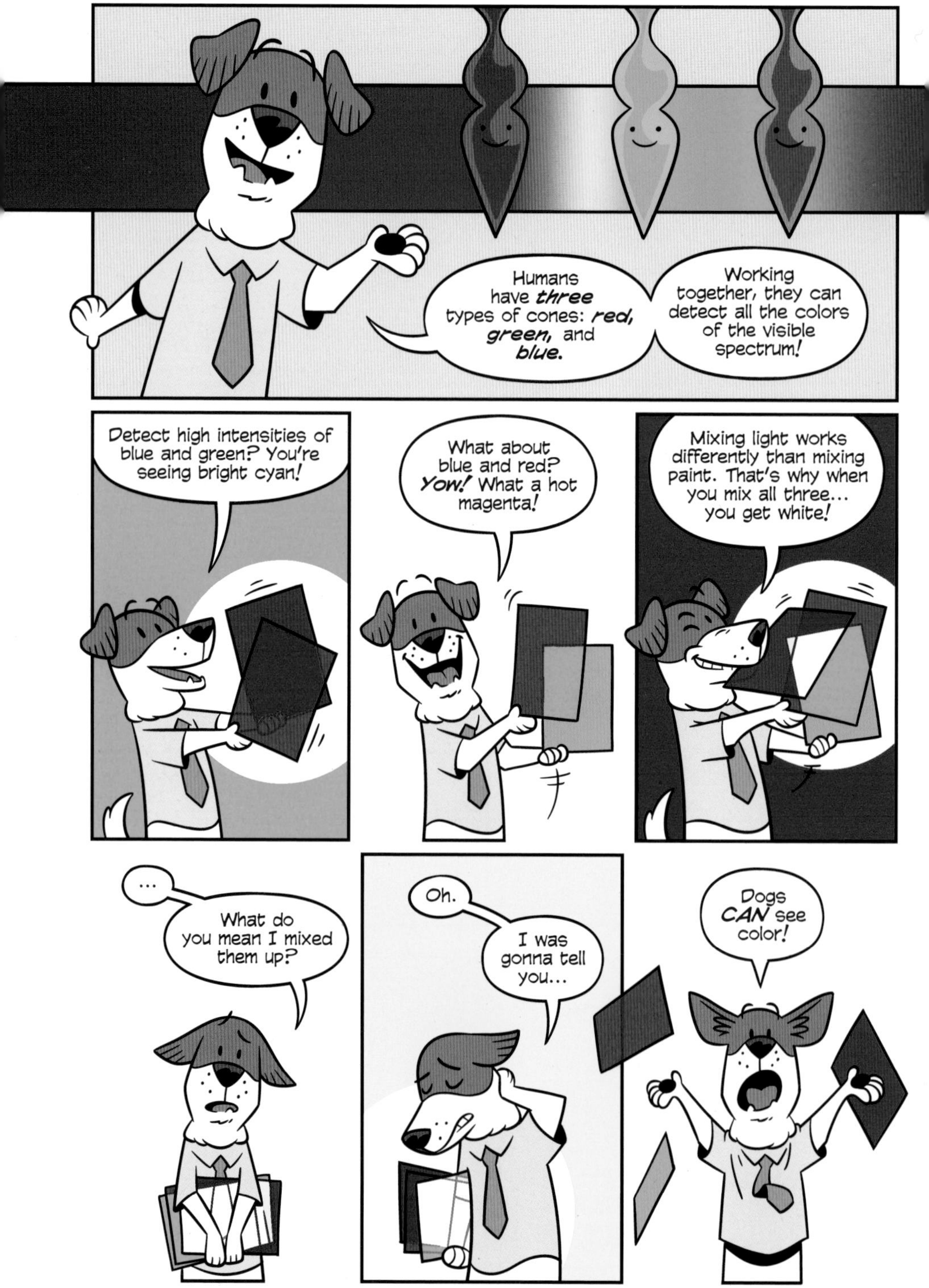
Humans have *three* types of cones: *red, green,* and *blue.*
Working together, they can detect all the colors of the visible spectrum!
Detect high intensities of blue and green? You're seeing bright cyan!
What about blue and red? *YOW!* What a hot magenta!
Mixing light works differently than mixing paint. That's why when you mix all three... you get white!
...
What do you mean I mixed them up?
Oh.
I was gonna tell you...
Dogs *CAN* see color!

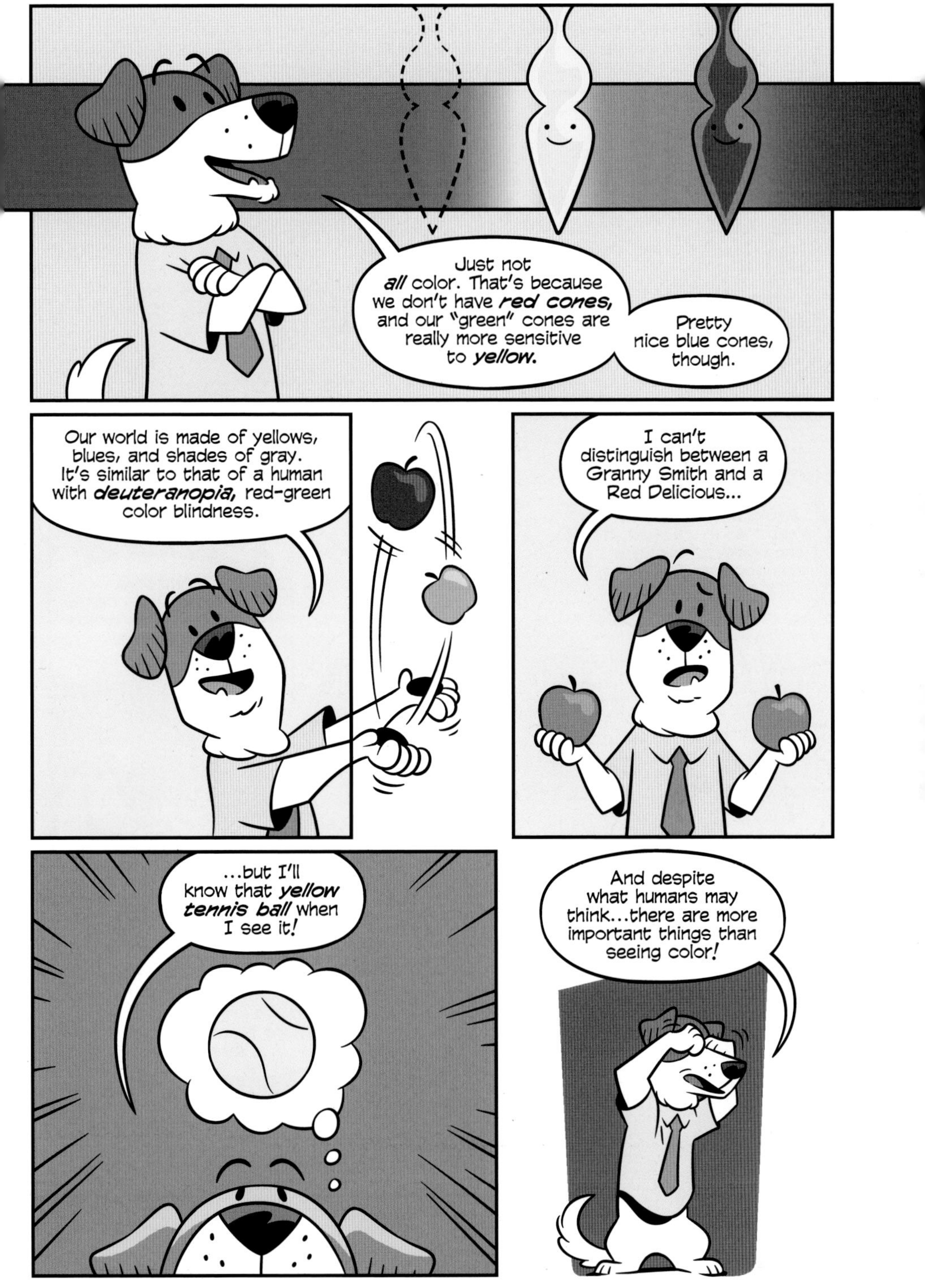
Just not *all* color. That's because we don't have ***red cones,*** and our "green" cones are really more sensitive to ***yellow.***
Pretty nice blue cones, though.
Our world is made of yellows, blues, and shades of gray. It's similar to that of a human with ***deuteranopia,*** red-green color blindness.
I can't distinguish between a Granny Smith and a Red Delicious...
...but I'll know that ***yellow tennis ball*** when I see it!
And despite what humans may think...there are more important things than seeing color!

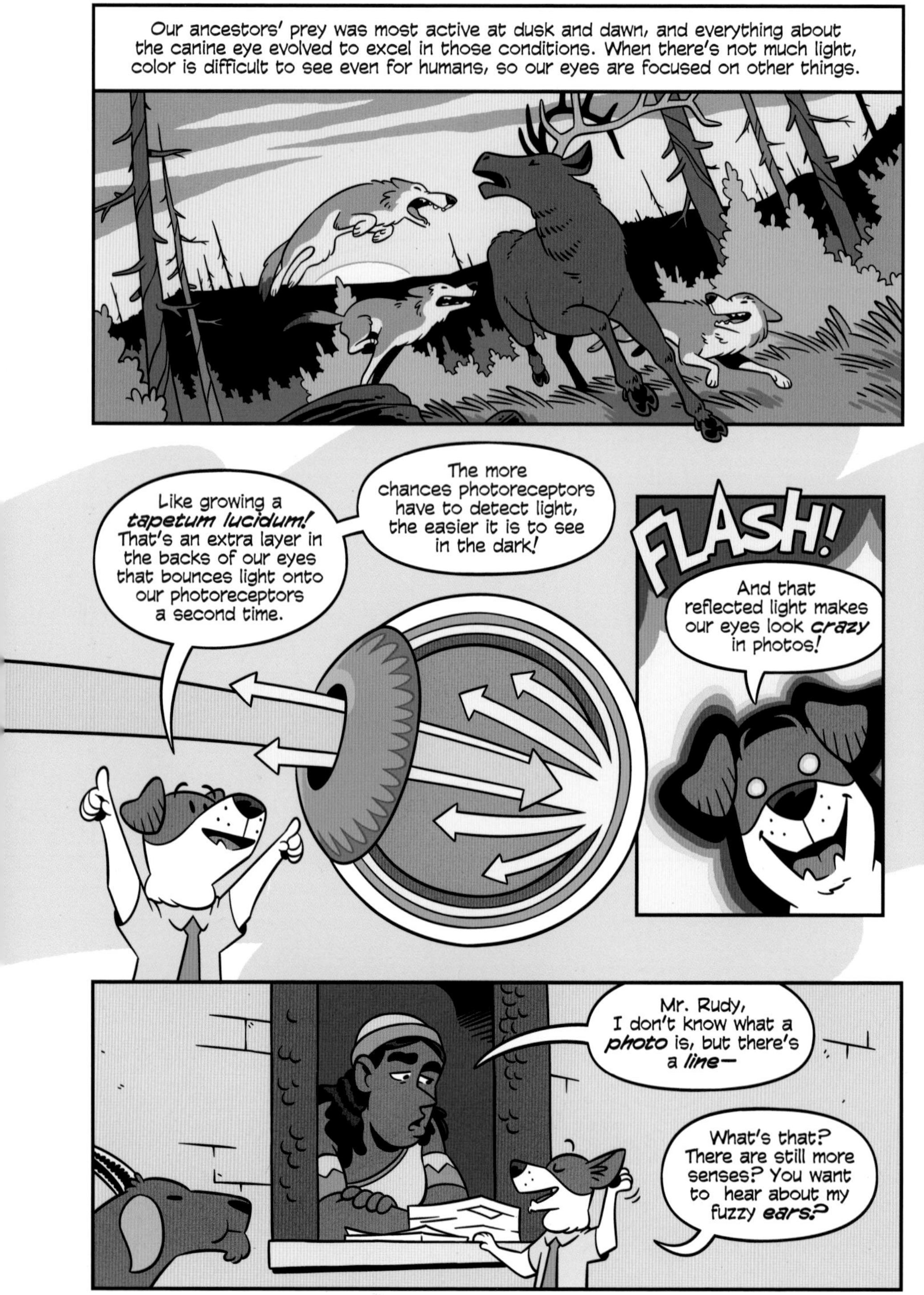
Our ancestors' prey was most active at dusk and dawn, and everything about the canine eye evolved to excel in those conditions. When there's not much light, color is difficult to see even for humans, so our eyes are focused on other things.
Like growing a *tapetum lucidum!* That's an extra layer in the backs of our eyes that bounces light onto our photoreceptors a second time.
The more chances photoreceptors have to detect light, the easier it is to see in the dark!
FLASH!
And that reflected light makes our eyes look *crazy* in photos!
Mr. Rudy, I don't know what a *photo* is, but there's a *line*—
What's that? There are still more senses? You want to hear about my fuzzy *ears?*

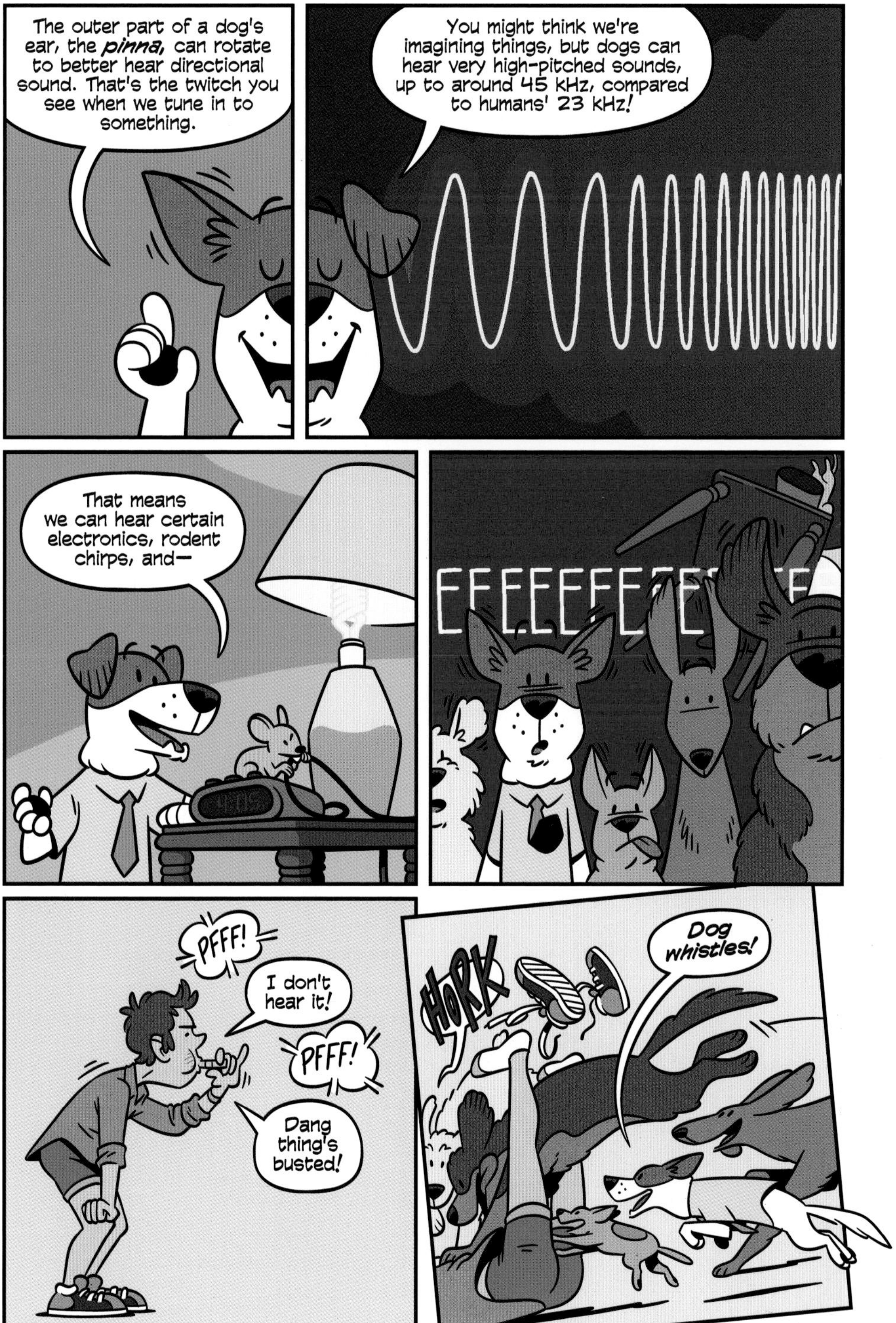
The outer part of a dog's ear, the *pinna,* can rotate to better hear directional sound. That's the twitch you see when we tune in to something.
You might think we're imagining things, but dogs can hear very high-pitched sounds, up to around 45 kHz, compared to humans' 23 kHz!
That means we can hear certain electronics, rodent chirps, and—
4:05
EEEEEEEEEEE
PFFF!
I don't hear it!
PFFF!
Dang thing's busted!
HORK
Dog whistles!

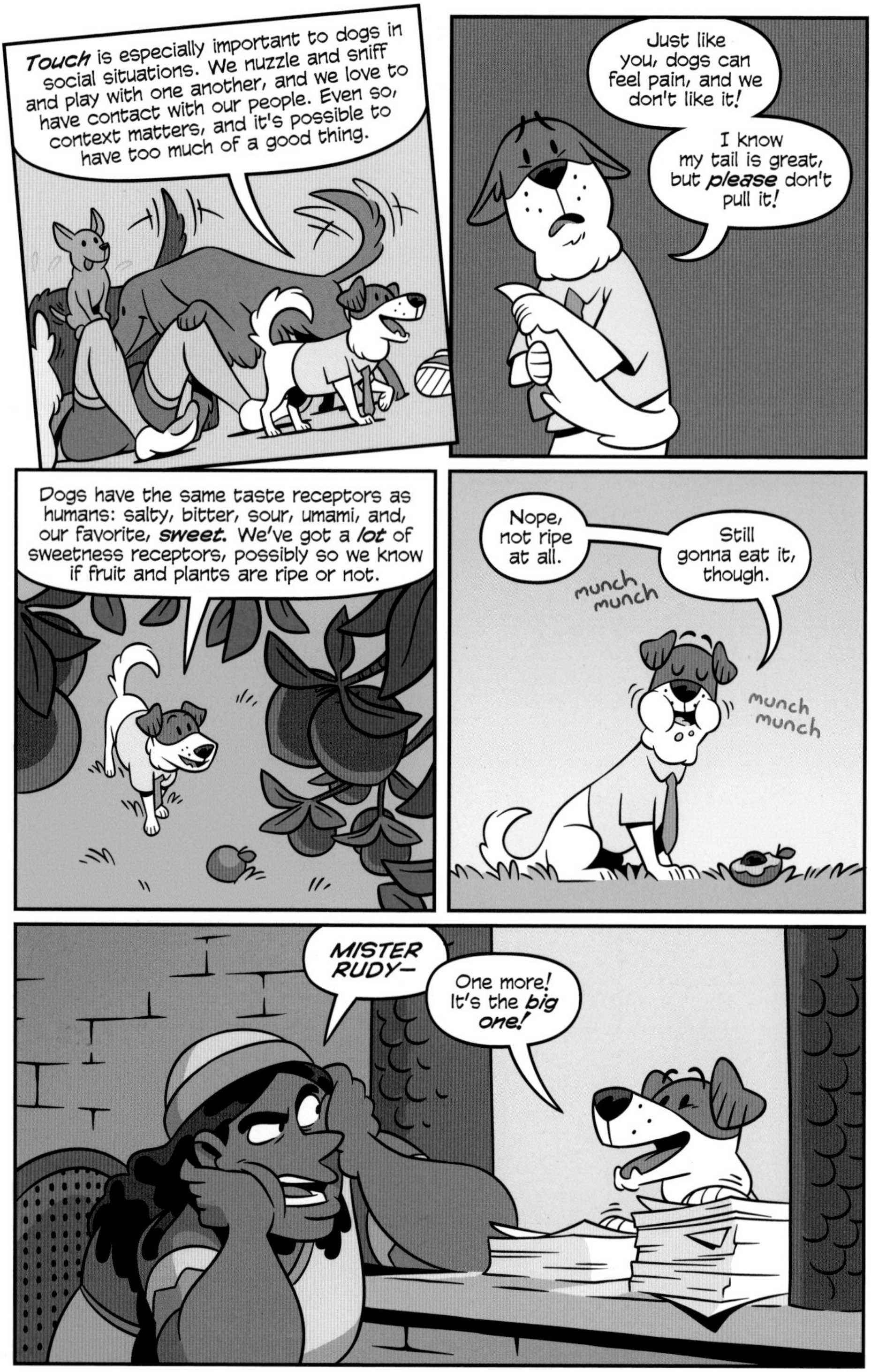
Touch is especially important to dogs in social situations. We nuzzle and sniff and play with one another, and we love to have contact with our people. Even so, context matters, and it's possible to have too much of a good thing.
Just like you, dogs can feel pain, and we don't like it!
I know my tail is great, but *please* don't pull it!
Dogs have the same taste receptors as humans: salty, bitter, sour, umami, and, our favorite, ***sweet.*** We've got a *lot* of sweetness receptors, possibly so we know if fruit and plants are ripe or not.
Nope, not ripe at all.
munch munch
Still gonna eat it, though.
munch munch
MISTER RUDY—
One more! It's the ***big one!***

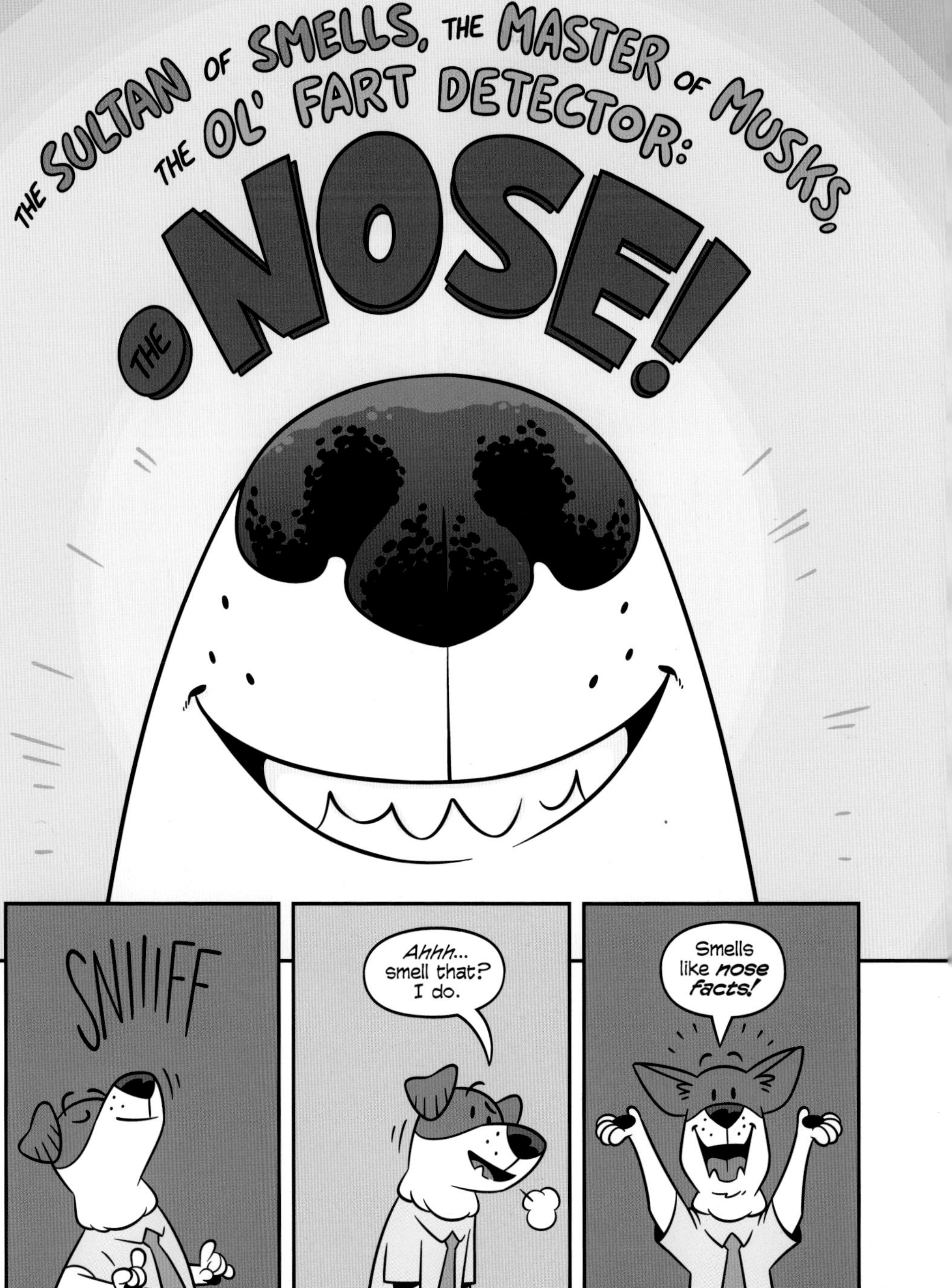

THE SULTAN OF SMELLS, THE MASTER OF MUSKS, THE OL' FART DETECTOR:
THE NOSE!
SNIIIFF
Ahhh... smell that? I do.
Smells like ***nose facts!***

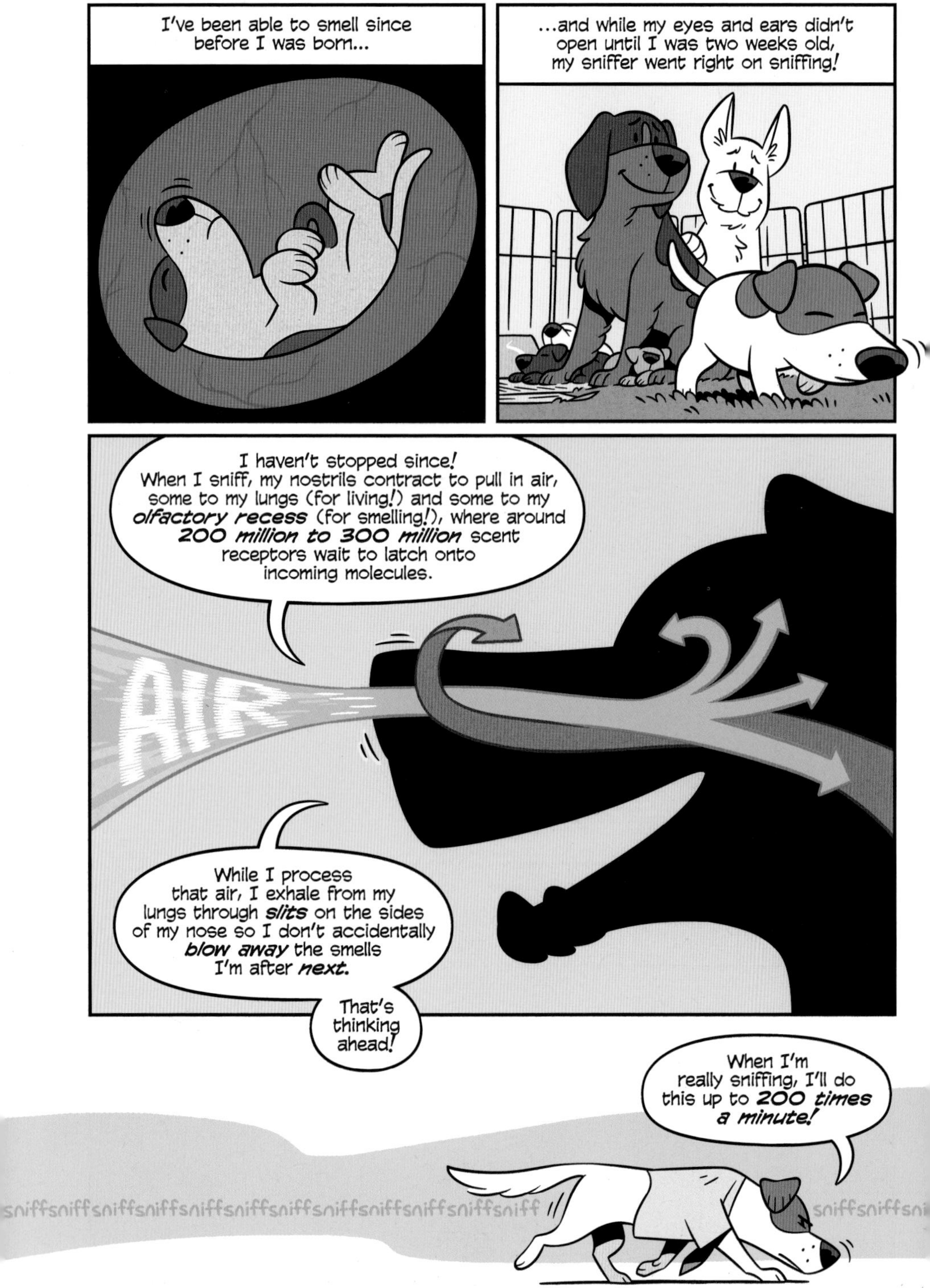

I've been able to smell since before I was born...
...and while my eyes and ears didn't open until I was two weeks old, my sniffer went right on sniffing!
I haven't stopped since! When I sniff, my nostrils contract to pull in air, some to my lungs (for living!) and some to my olfactory recess (for smelling!), where around 200 million to 300 million scent receptors wait to latch onto incoming molecules.
AIR
While I process that air, I exhale from my lungs through slits on the sides of my nose so I don't accidentally blow away the smells I'm after next.
That's thinking ahead!
When I'm really sniffing, I'll do this up to 200 times a minute!
sniffsniffsniffsniffsniffsniffsniffsniffsniffsniffsniff

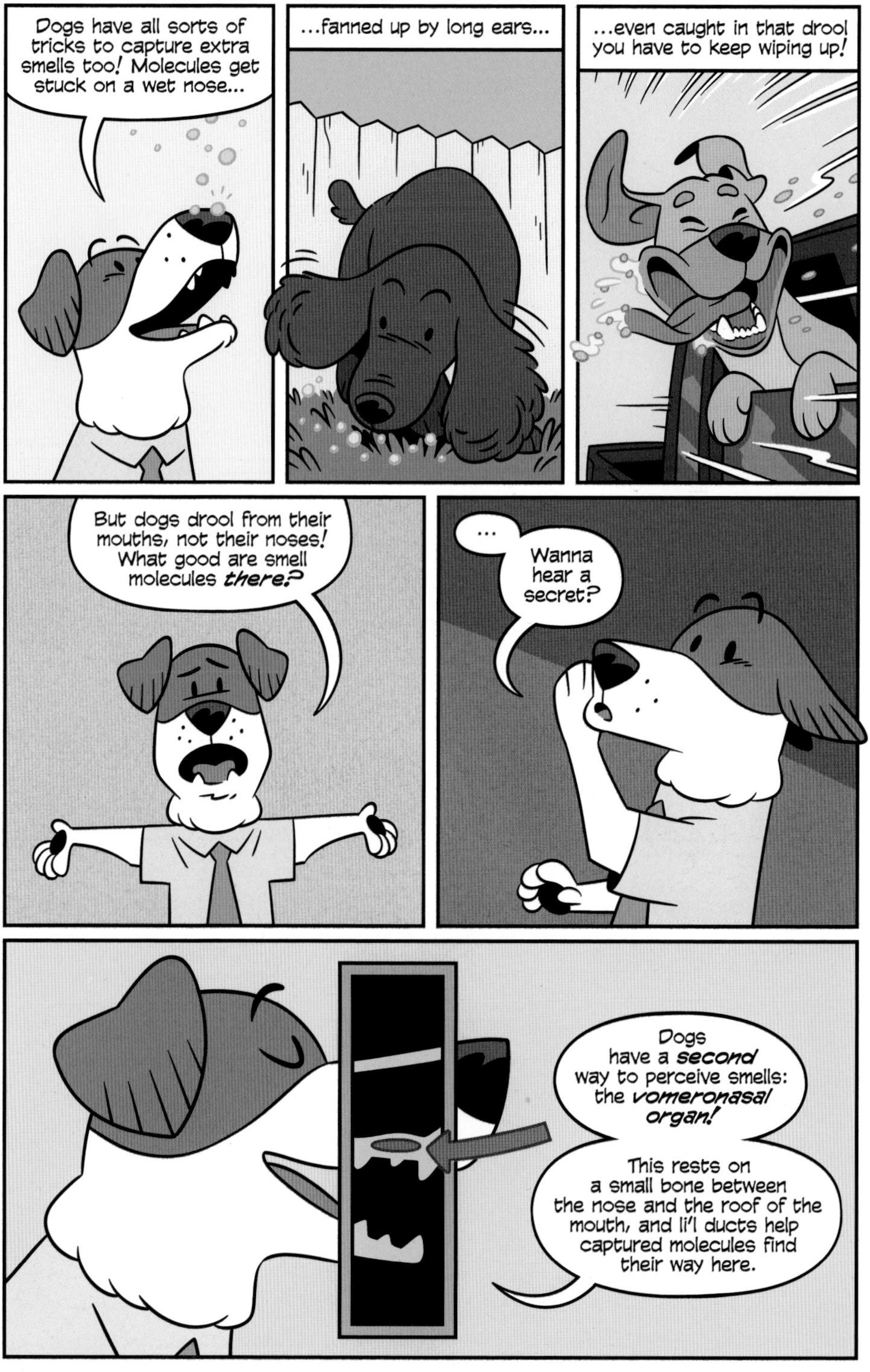

Dogs have all sorts of tricks to capture extra smells too! Molecules get stuck on a wet nose...
...fanned up by long ears...
...even caught in that drool you have to keep wiping up!
But dogs drool from their mouths, not their noses! What good are smell molecules *there?*
...
Wanna hear a secret?
Dogs have a ***second*** way to perceive smells: the ***vomeronasal organ!***
This rests on a small bone between the nose and the roof of the mouth, and li'l ducts help captured molecules find their way here.

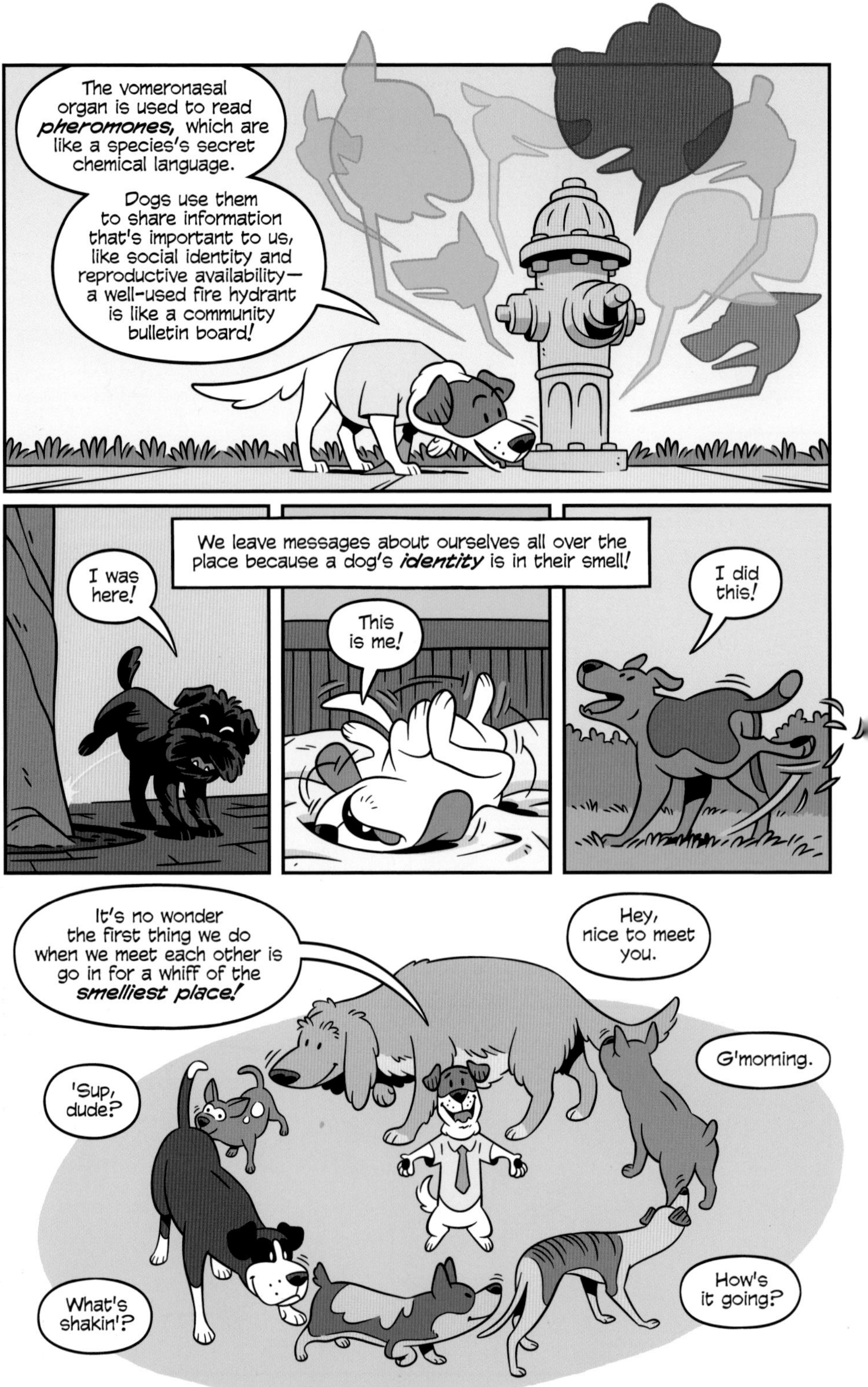
The vomeronasal organ is used to read ***pheromones,*** which are like a species's secret chemical language.
Dogs use them to share information that's important to us, like social identity and reproductive availability— a well-used fire hydrant is like a community bulletin board!
We leave messages about ourselves all over the place because a dog's ***identity*** is in their smell!
I was here!
This is me!
I did this!
It's no wonder the first thing we do when we meet each other is go in for a whiff of the ***smelliest place!***
Hey, nice to meet you.
G'morning.
'Sup, dude?
What's shakin'?
How's it going?

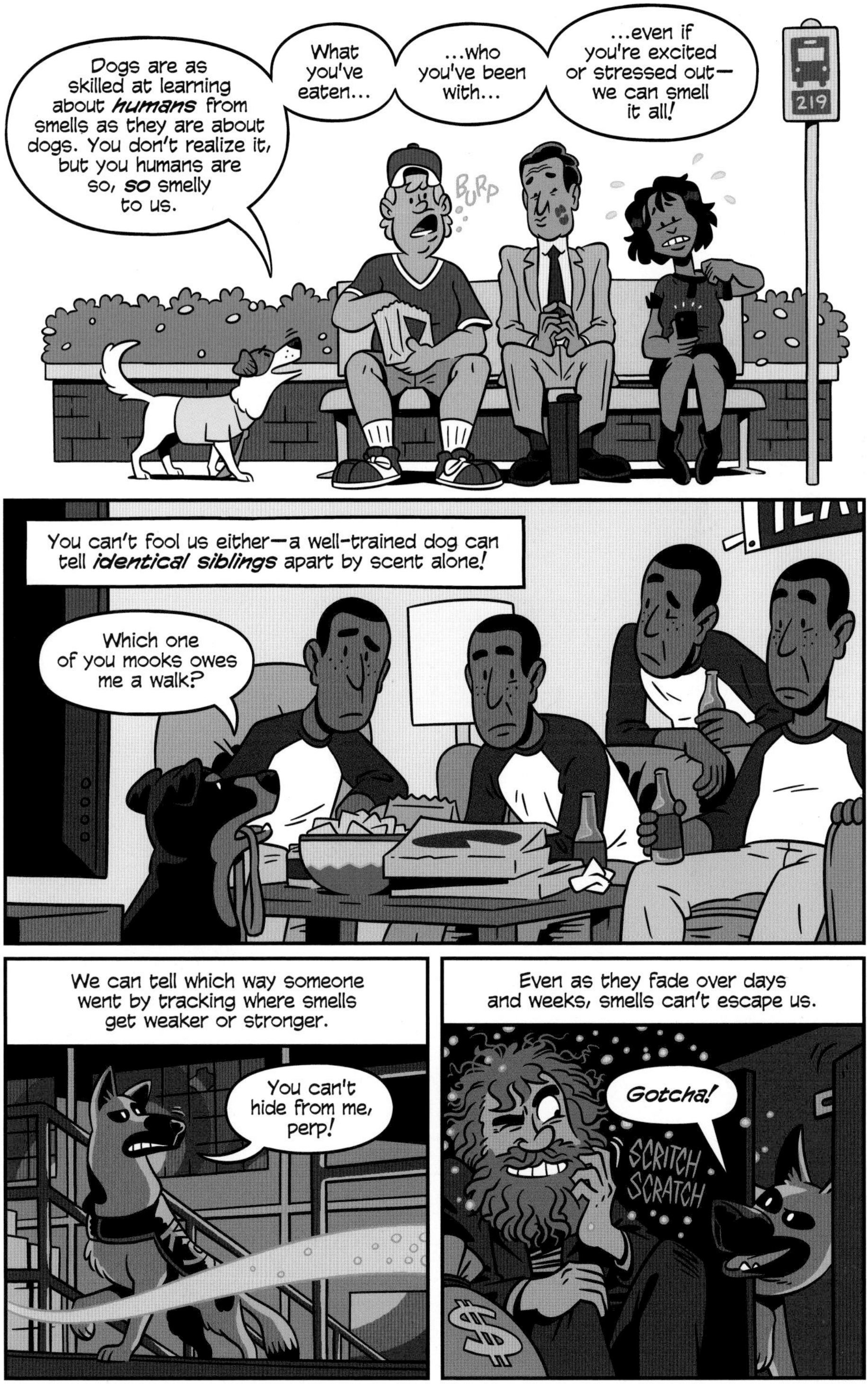

Dogs are as skilled at learning about *humans* from smells as they are about dogs. You don't realize it, but you humans are so, *so* smelly to us.
What you've eaten...
...who you've been with...
...even if you're excited or stressed out—we can smell it all!
219
BURP
You can't fool us either—a well-trained dog can tell *identical siblings* apart by scent alone!
Which one of you mooks owes me a walk?
We can tell which way someone went by tracking where smells get weaker or stronger.
You can't hide from me, perp!
Even as they fade over days and weeks, smells can't escape us.
Gotcha!
SCRITCH SCRATCH

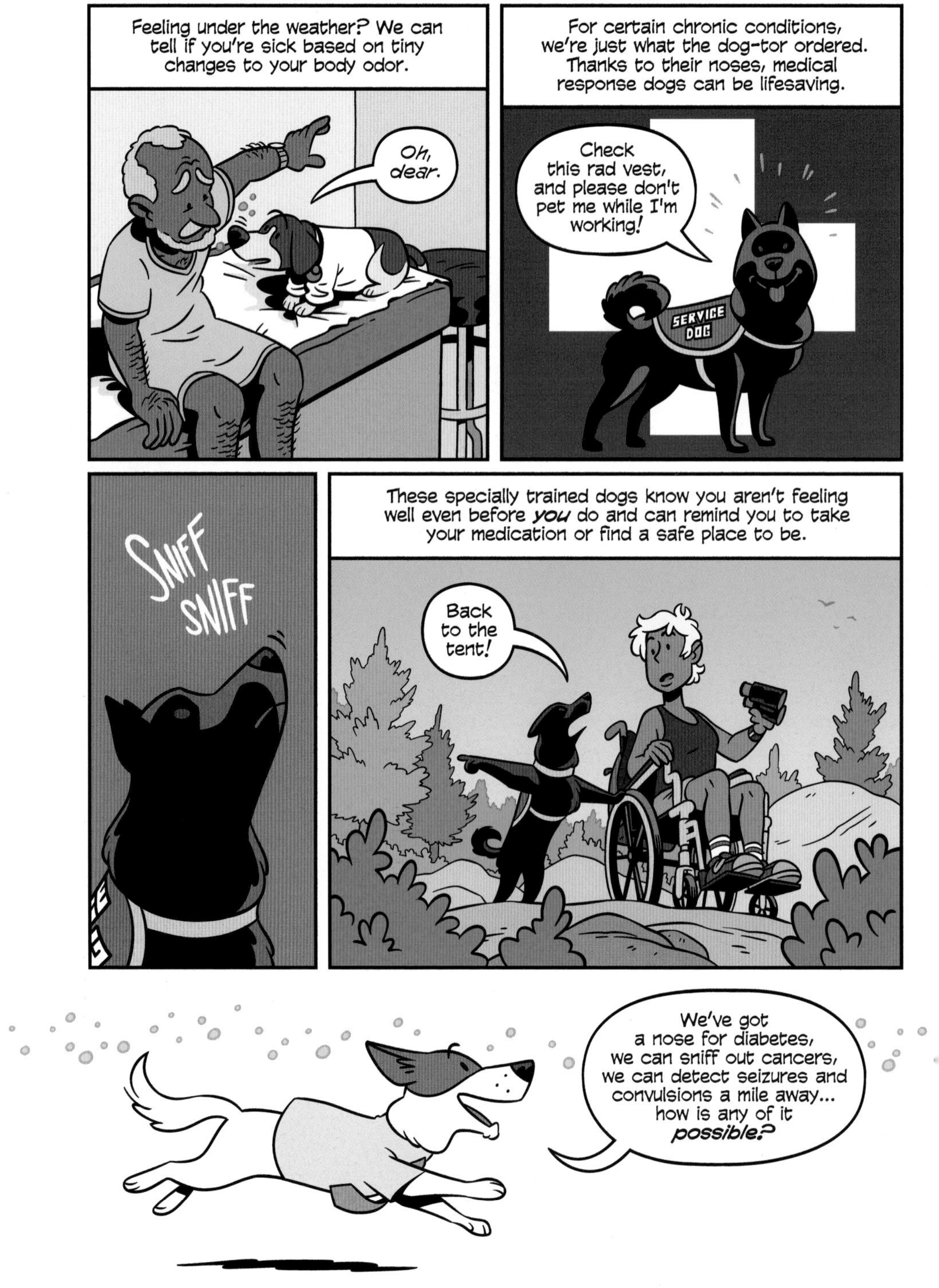
Feeling under the weather? We can tell if you're sick based on tiny changes to your body odor.
Oh, dear.
For certain chronic conditions, we're just what the dog-tor ordered. Thanks to their noses, medical response dogs can be lifesaving.
Check this rad vest, and please don't pet me while I'm working!
SERVICE DOG
SNIFF SNIFF
These specially trained dogs know you aren't feeling well even before *you* do and can remind you to take your medication or find a safe place to be.
Back to the tent!
We've got a nose for diabetes, we can sniff out cancers, we can detect seizures and convulsions a mile away... how is any of it *possible?*

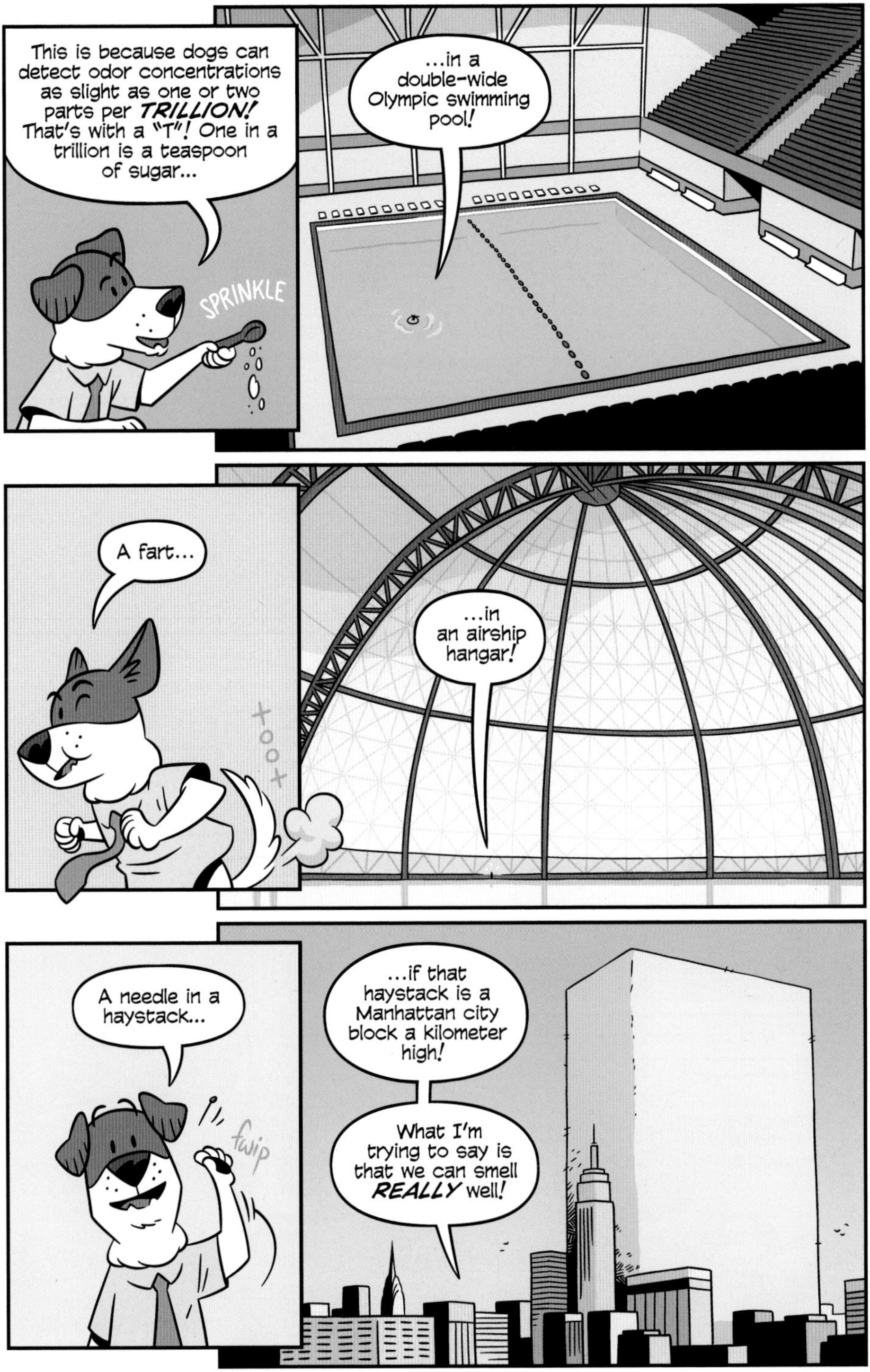
This is because dogs can detect odor concentrations as slight as one or two parts per *TRILLION!* That's with a "T"! One in a trillion is a teaspoon of sugar...
SPRINKLE
...in a double-wide Olympic swimming pool!
A fart...
toot
...in an airship hangar!
A needle in a haystack...
fwip
...if that haystack is a Manhattan city block a kilometer high!
What I'm trying to say is that we can smell *REALLY* well!

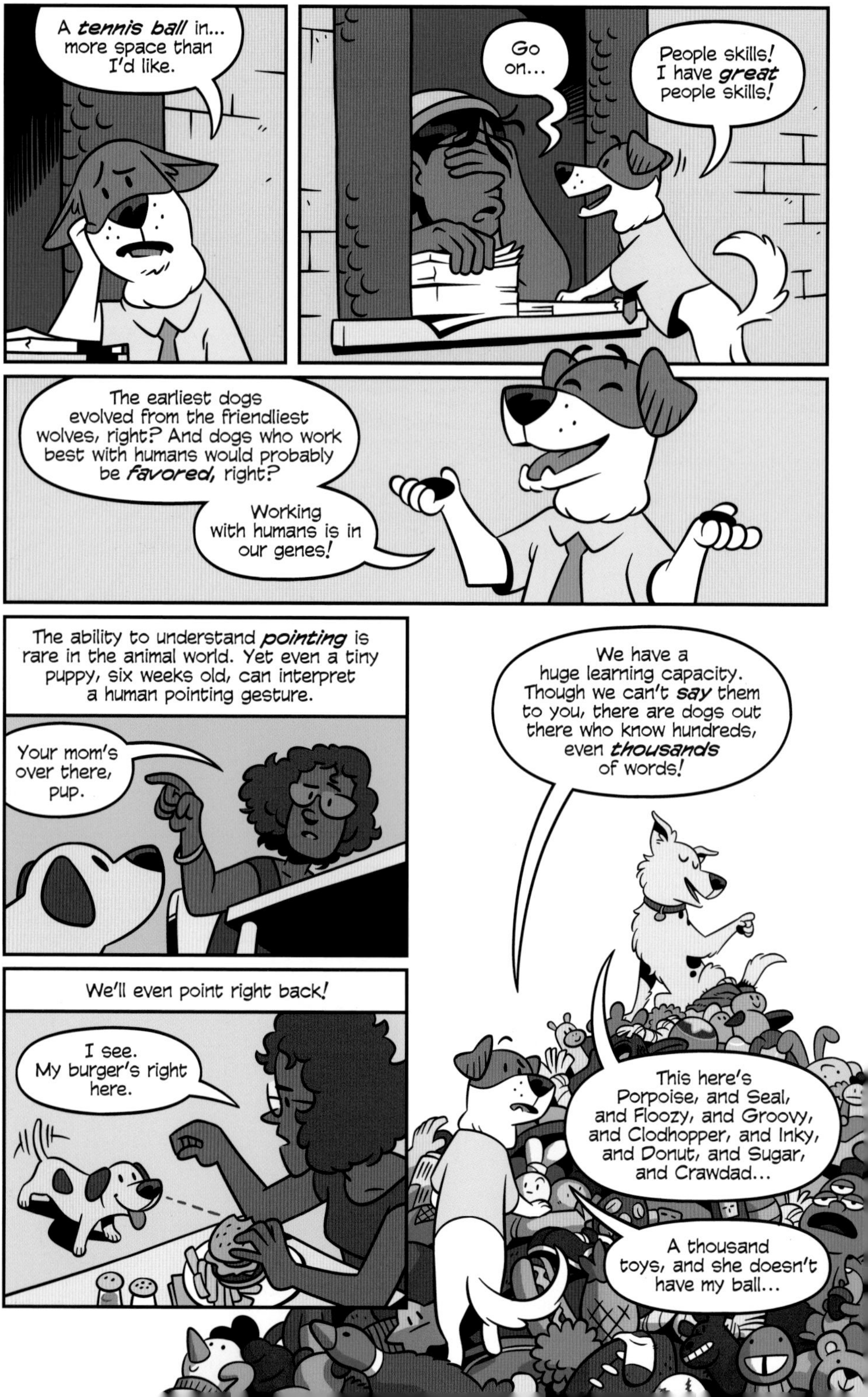
A *tennis ball* in... more space than I'd like.
Go on...
People skills! I have *great* people skills!
The earliest dogs evolved from the friendliest wolves, right? And dogs who work best with humans would probably be *favored*, right?
Working with humans is in our genes!
The ability to understand *pointing* is rare in the animal world. Yet even a tiny puppy, six weeks old, can interpret a human pointing gesture.
Your mom's over there, pup.
We'll even point right back!
I see. My burger's right here.
We have a huge learning capacity. Though we can't *say* them to you, there are dogs out there who know hundreds, even *thousands* of words!
This here's Porpoise, and Seal, and Floozy, and Groovy, and Clodhopper, and Inky, and Donut, and Sugar, and Crawdad...
A thousand toys, and she doesn't have my ball...

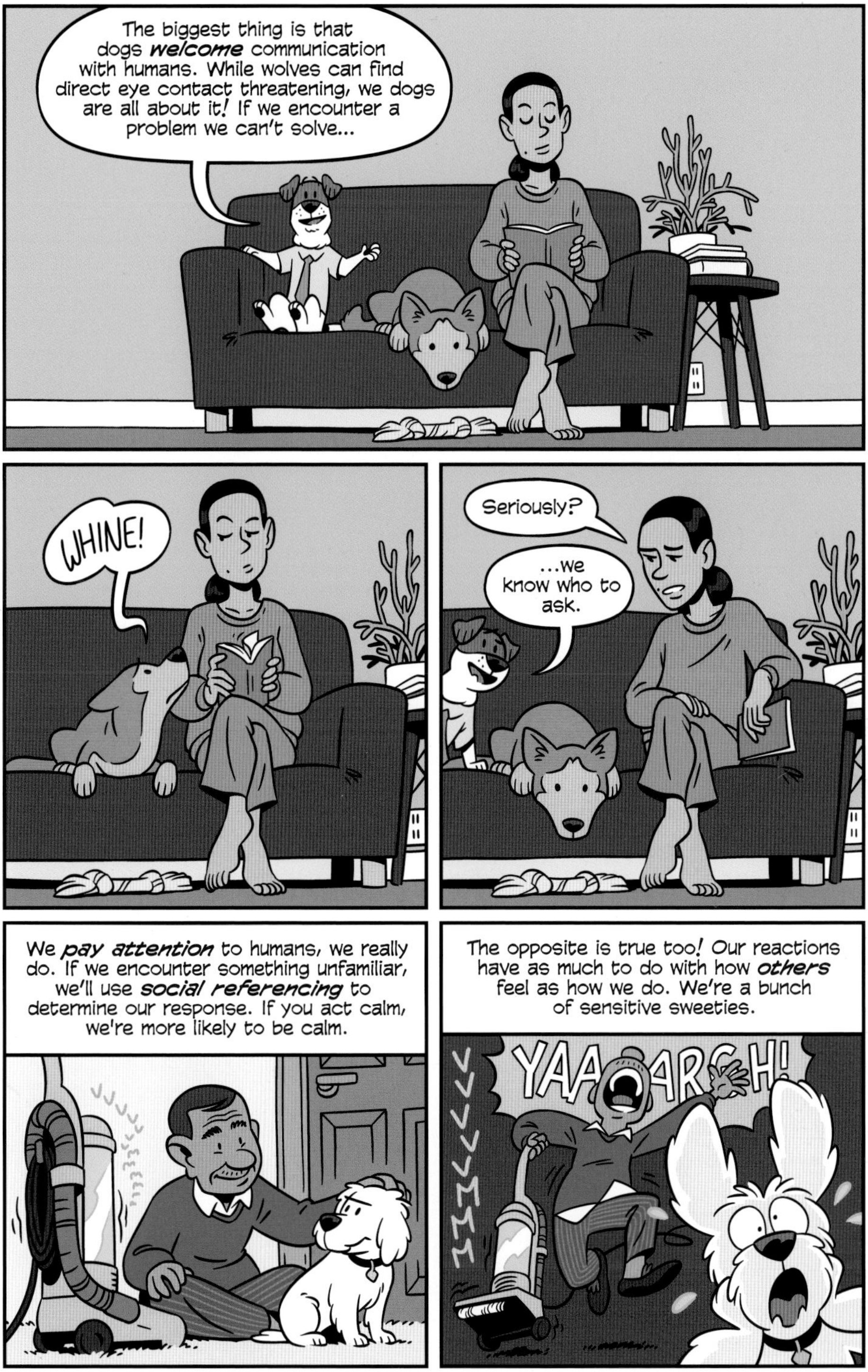

The biggest thing is that dogs *welcome* communication with humans. While wolves can find direct eye contact threatening, we dogs are all about it! If we encounter a problem we can't solve...
WHINE!
Seriously?
...we know who to ask.
We *pay attention* to humans, we really do. If we encounter something unfamiliar, we'll use *social referencing* to determine our response. If you act calm, we're more likely to be calm.
The opposite is true too! Our reactions have as much to do with how *others* feel as how we do. We're a bunch of sensitive sweeties.
YAAARGH!

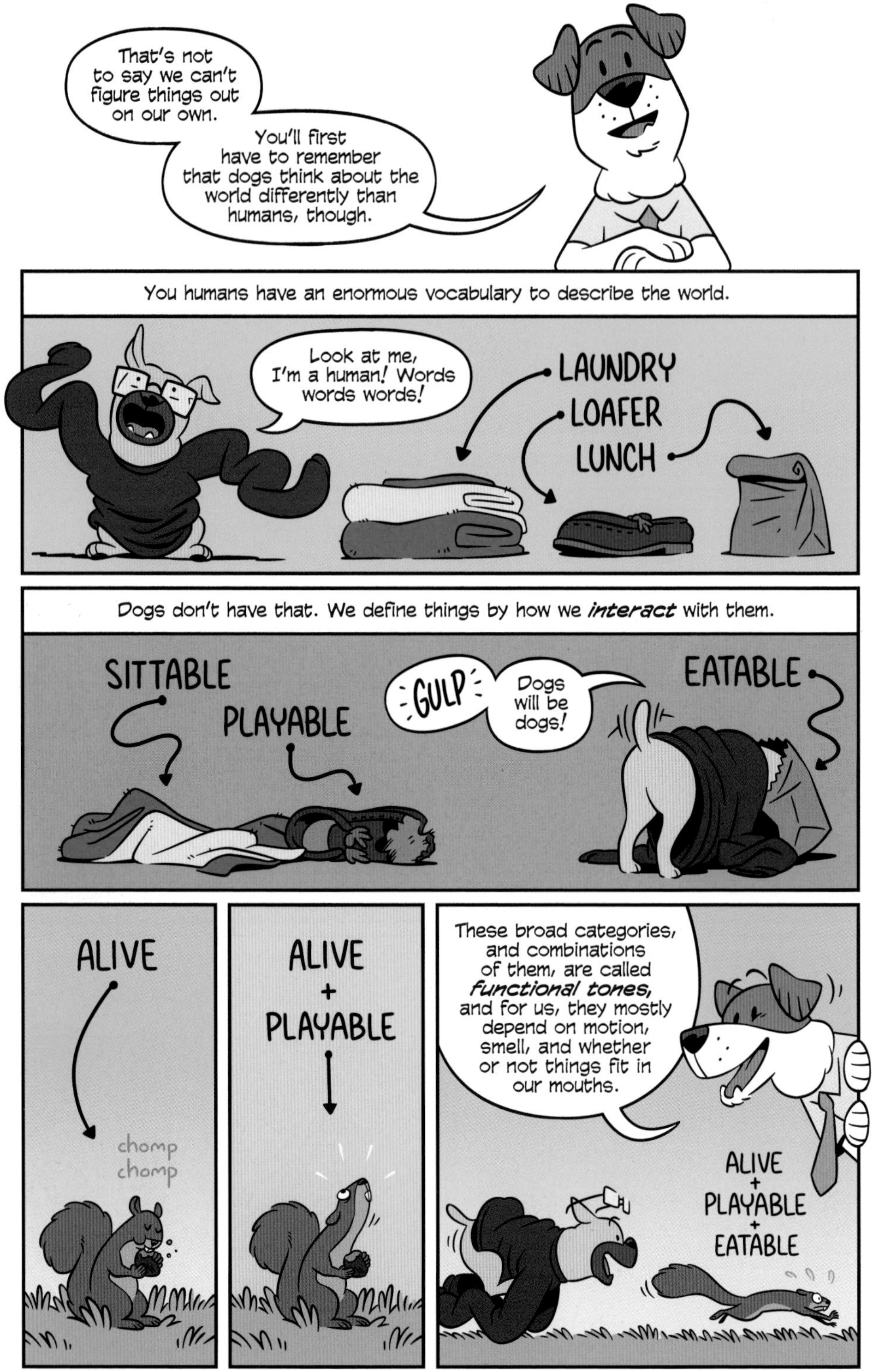
That's not to say we can't figure things out on our own.
You'll first have to remember that dogs think about the world differently than humans, though.
You humans have an enormous vocabulary to describe the world.
Look at me, I'm a human! Words words words!
LAUNDRY
LOAFER
LUNCH
Dogs don't have that. We define things by how we *interact* with them.
SITTABLE
PLAYABLE
GULP
Dogs will be dogs!
EATABLE
ALIVE
chomp chomp
ALIVE + PLAYABLE
These broad categories, and combinations of them, are called ***functional tones,*** and for us, they mostly depend on motion, smell, and whether or not things fit in our mouths.
ALIVE + PLAYABLE + EATABLE

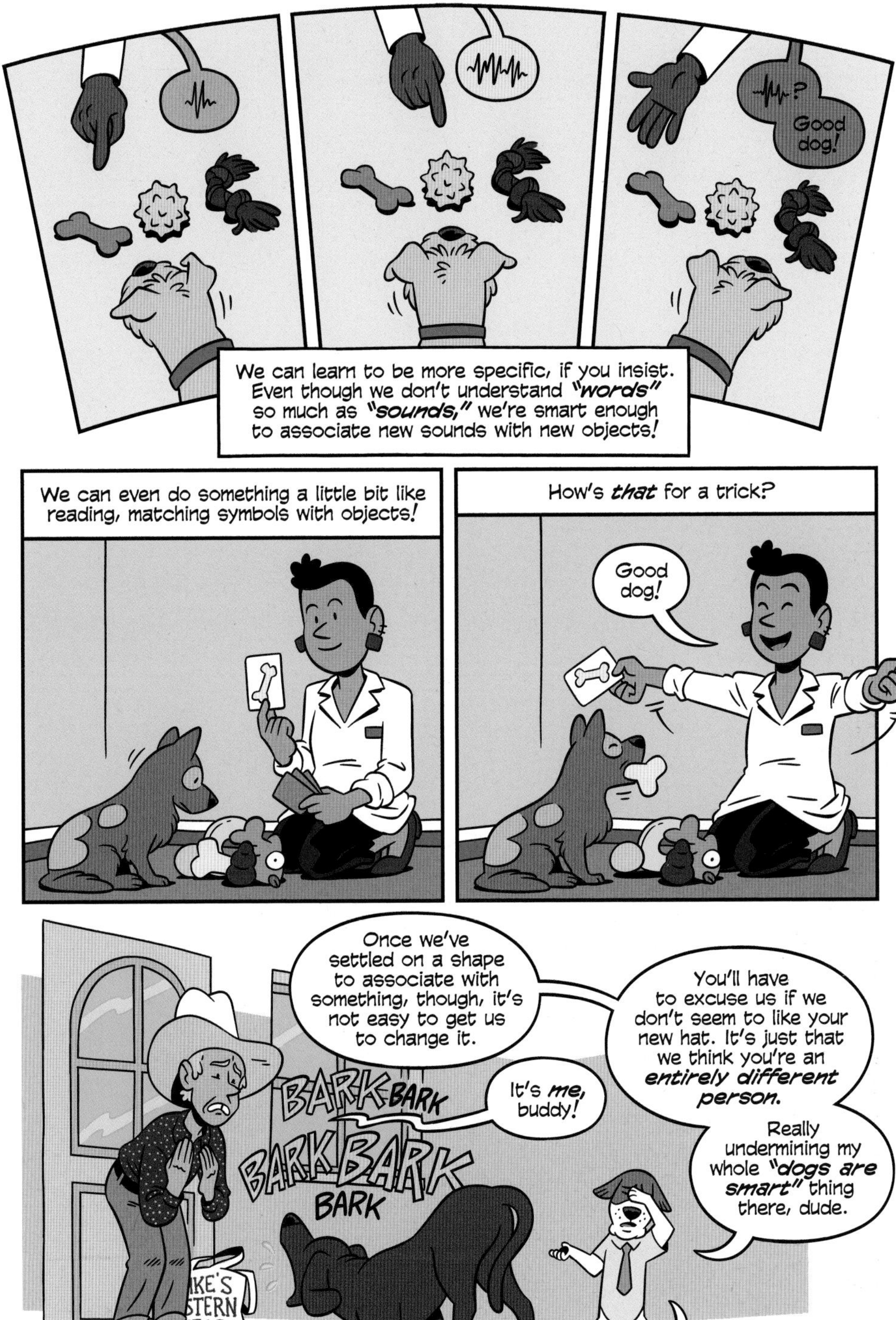

Good dog!
We can learn to be more specific, if you insist. Even though we don't understand "words" so much as "sounds," we're smart enough to associate new sounds with new objects!
We can even do something a little bit like reading, matching symbols with objects!
How's that for a trick?
Good dog!
Once we've settled on a shape to associate with something, though, it's not easy to get us to change it.
You'll have to excuse us if we don't seem to like your new hat. It's just that we think you're an entirely different person.
BARK BARK
BARK BARK
BARK
It's me, buddy!
Really undermining my whole "dogs are smart" thing there, dude.

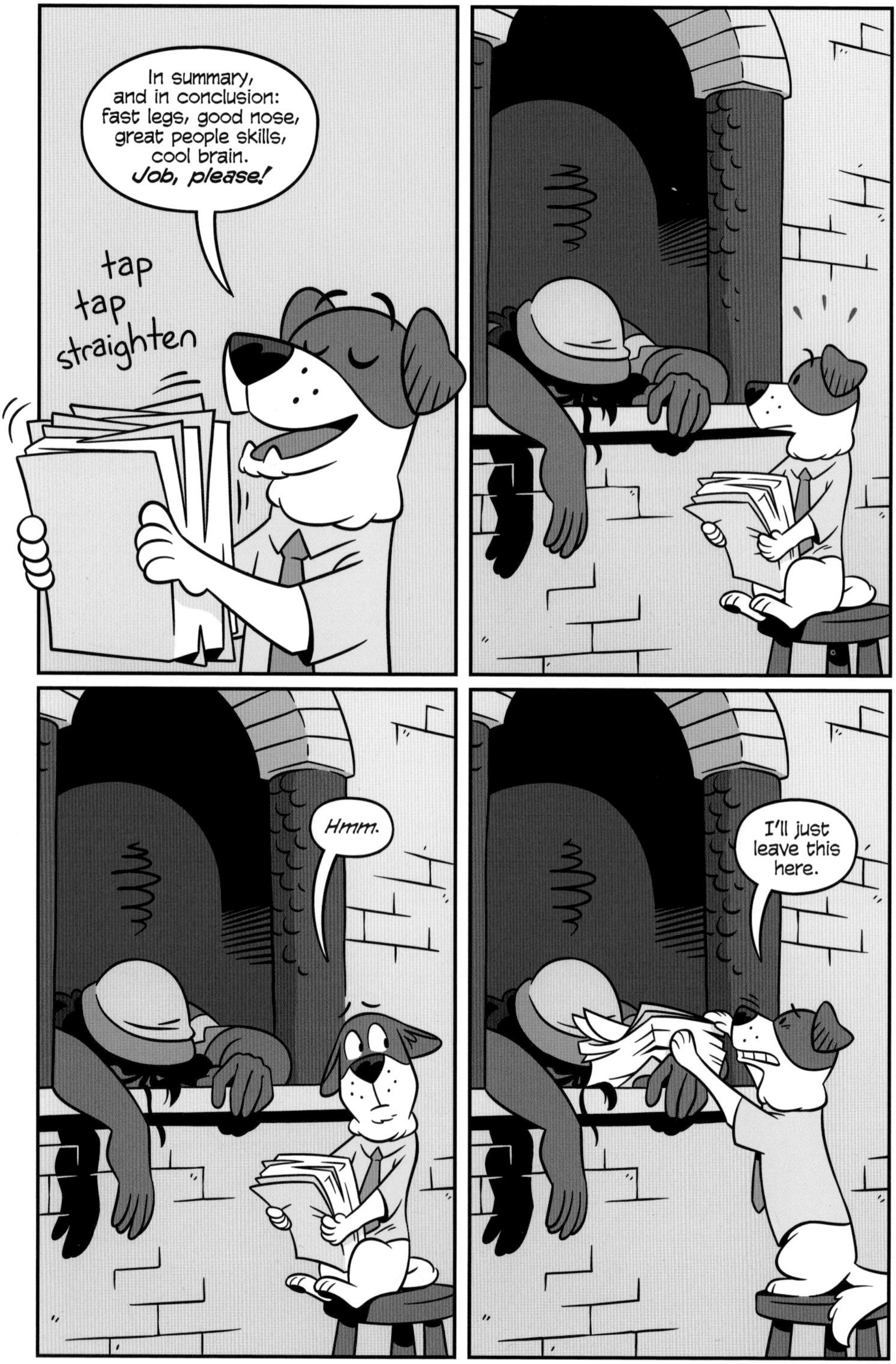
In summary,
and in conclusion:
fast legs, good nose,
great people skills,
cool brain.
Job, please!
tap
tap
straighten
Hmm.
I'll just
leave this
here.

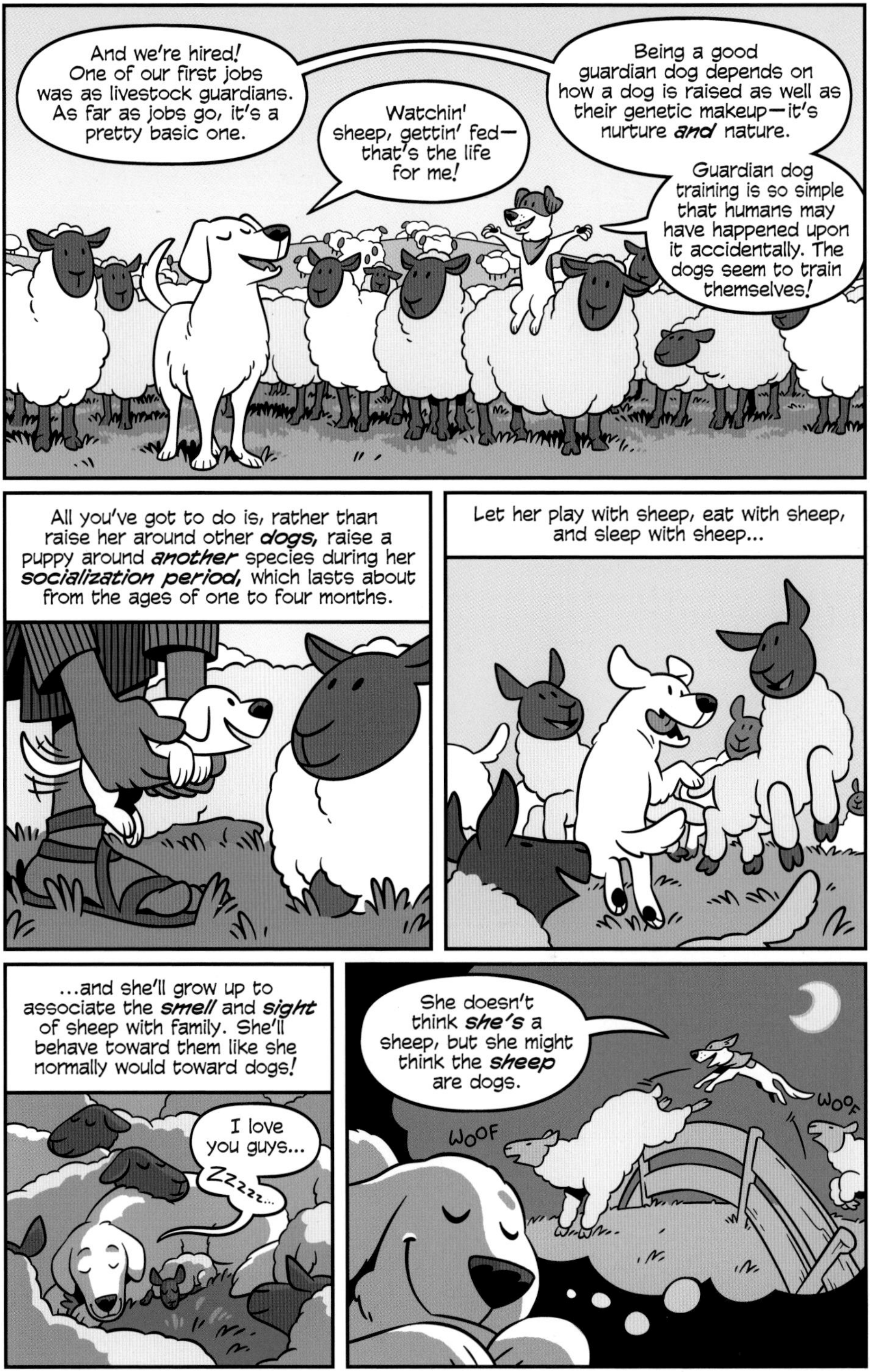
And we're hired! One of our first jobs was as livestock guardians. As far as jobs go, it's a pretty basic one.
Watchin' sheep, gettin' fed—that's the life for me!
Being a good guardian dog depends on how a dog is raised as well as their genetic makeup—it's nurture *and* nature.
Guardian dog training is so simple that humans may have happened upon it accidentally. The dogs seem to train themselves!
All you've got to do is, rather than raise her around other *dogs,* raise a puppy around *another* species during her *socialization period,* which lasts about from the ages of one to four months.
Let her play with sheep, eat with sheep, and sleep with sheep...
...and she'll grow up to associate the *smell* and *sight* of sheep with family. She'll behave toward them like she normally would toward dogs!
I love you guys...
Zzzzz...
She doesn't think *she's* a sheep, but she might think the *sheep* are dogs.
WOOF
WOOF

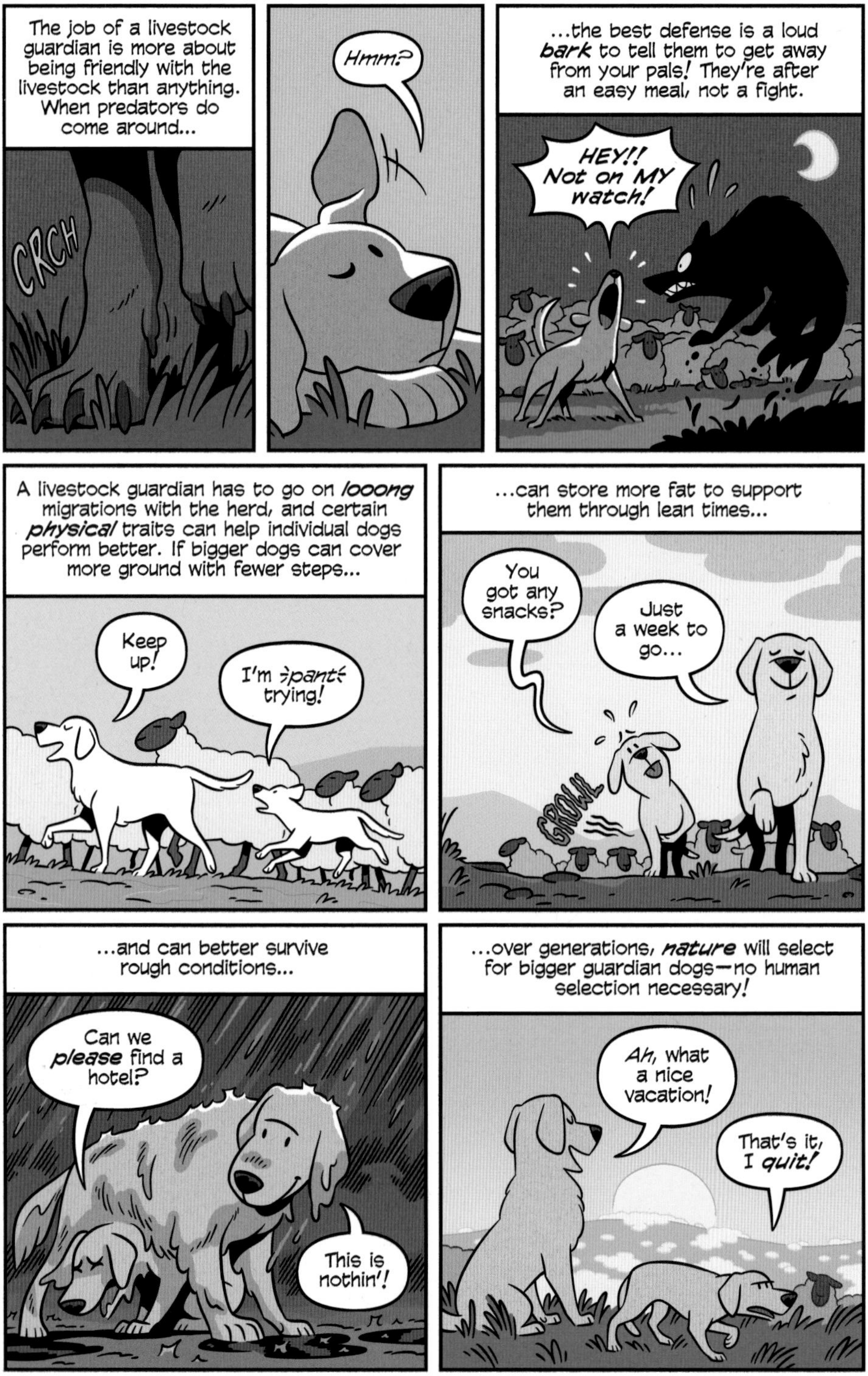
The job of a livestock guardian is more about being friendly with the livestock than anything. When predators do come around...
CRCH
Hmm?
...the best defense is a loud *bark* to tell them to get away from your pals! They're after an easy meal, not a fight.
HEY!! Not on MY watch!
A livestock guardian has to go on *looong* migrations with the herd, and certain *physical* traits can help individual dogs perform better. If bigger dogs can cover more ground with fewer steps...
Keep up!
I'm *pant* trying!
...can store more fat to support them through lean times...
You got any snacks?
Just a week to go...
GROWL
...and can better survive rough conditions...
Can we *please* find a hotel?
This is nothin'!
...over generations, *nature* will select for bigger guardian dogs—no human selection necessary!
Ah, what a nice vacation!
That's it, I *quit!*

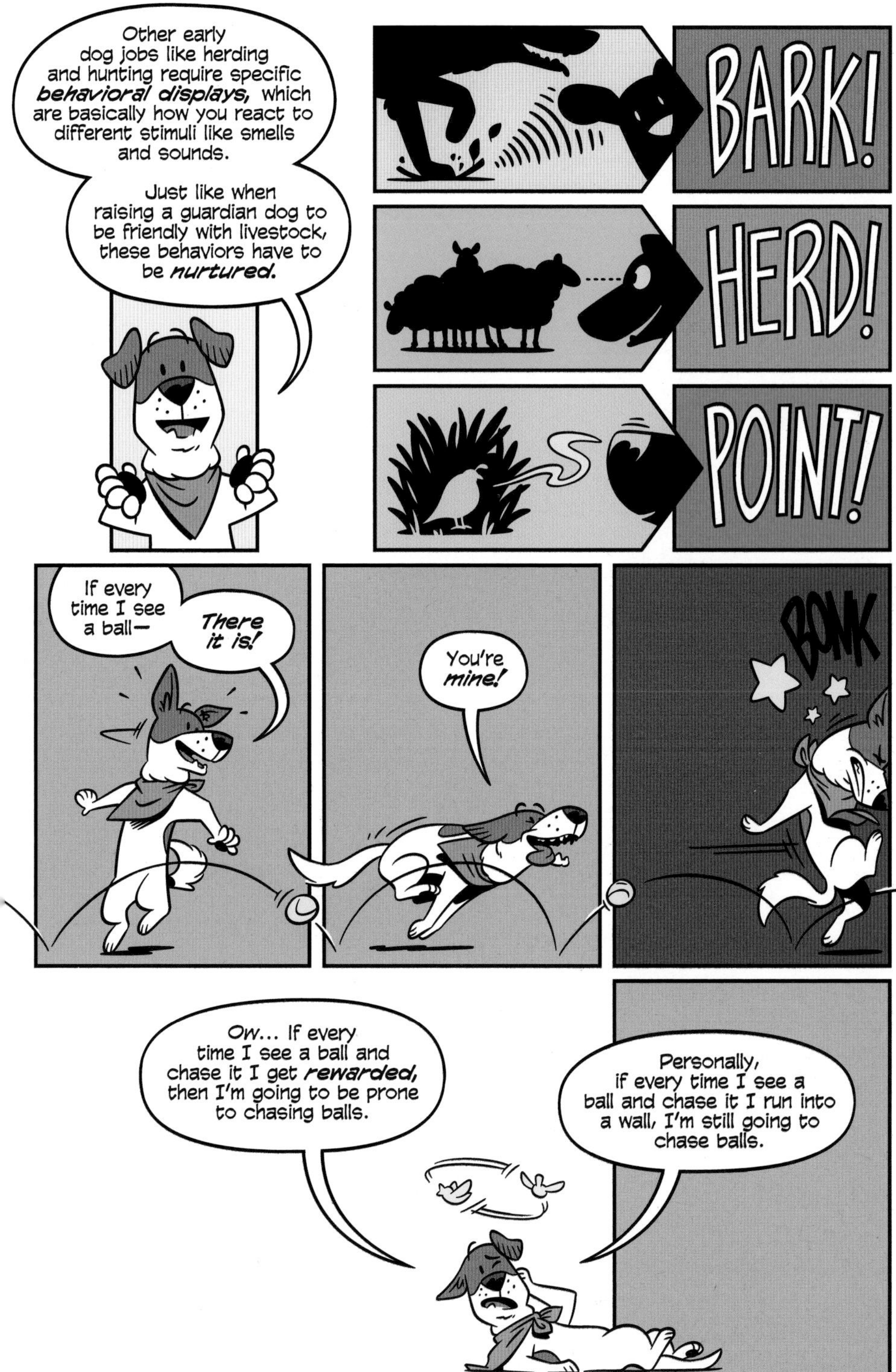

Other early dog jobs like herding and hunting require specific *behavioral displays,* which are basically how you react to different stimuli like smells and sounds.
Just like when raising a guardian dog to be friendly with livestock, these behaviors have to be *nurtured.*
BARK!
HERD!
POINT!
If every time I see a ball—
There it is!
You're *mine!*
BONK
Ow... If every time I see a ball and chase it I get *rewarded,* then I'm going to be prone to chasing balls.
Personally, if every time I see a ball and chase it I run into a wall, I'm still going to chase balls.

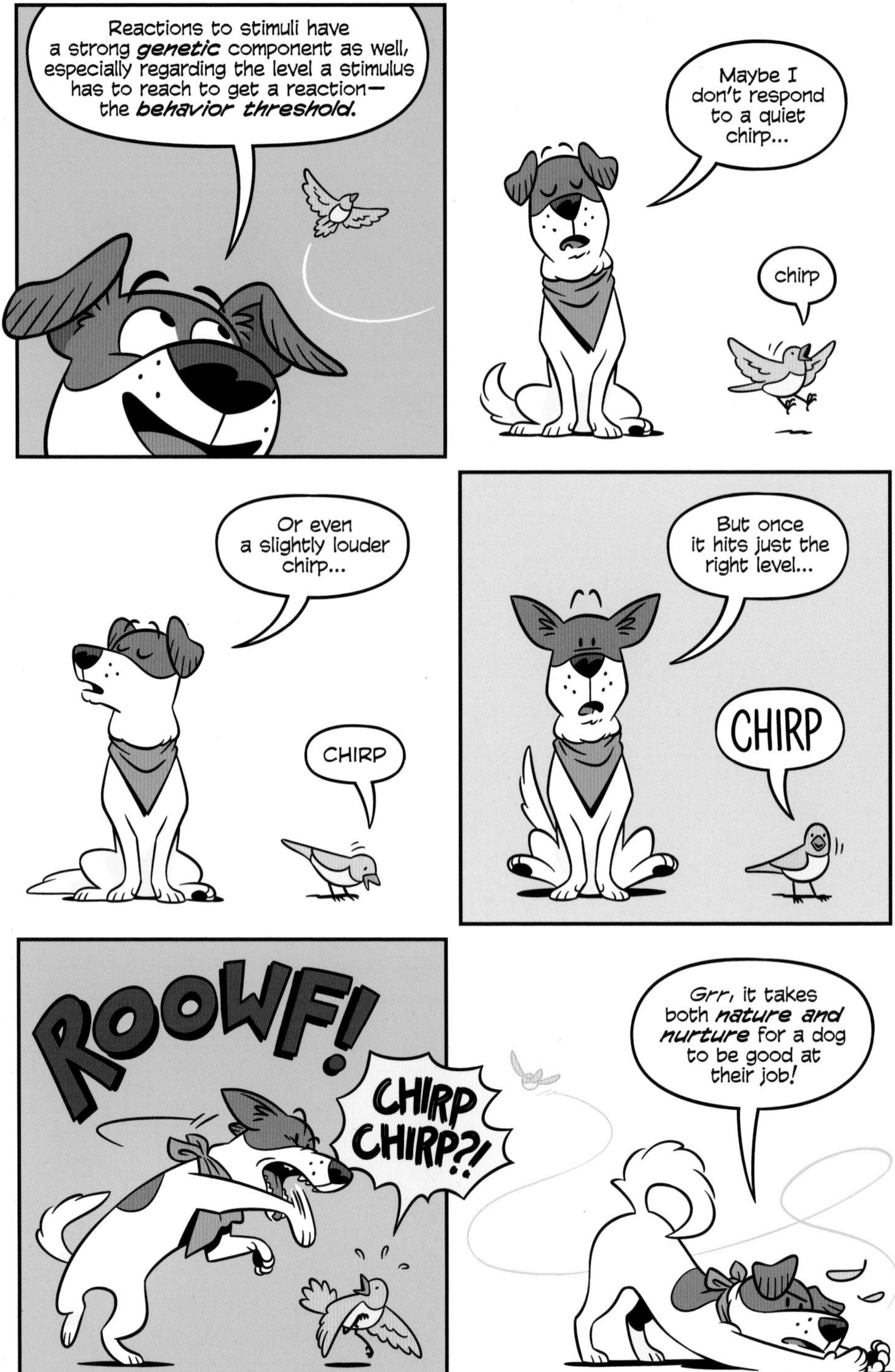

Reactions to stimuli have a strong ***genetic*** component as well, especially regarding the level a stimulus has to reach to get a reaction— the ***behavior threshold.***
Maybe I don't respond to a quiet chirp...
chirp
Or even a slightly louder chirp...
CHIRP
But once it hits just the right level...
CHIRP
ROOWF!
CHIRP CHIRP?!
Grr, it takes both ***nature and nurture*** for a dog to be good at their job!

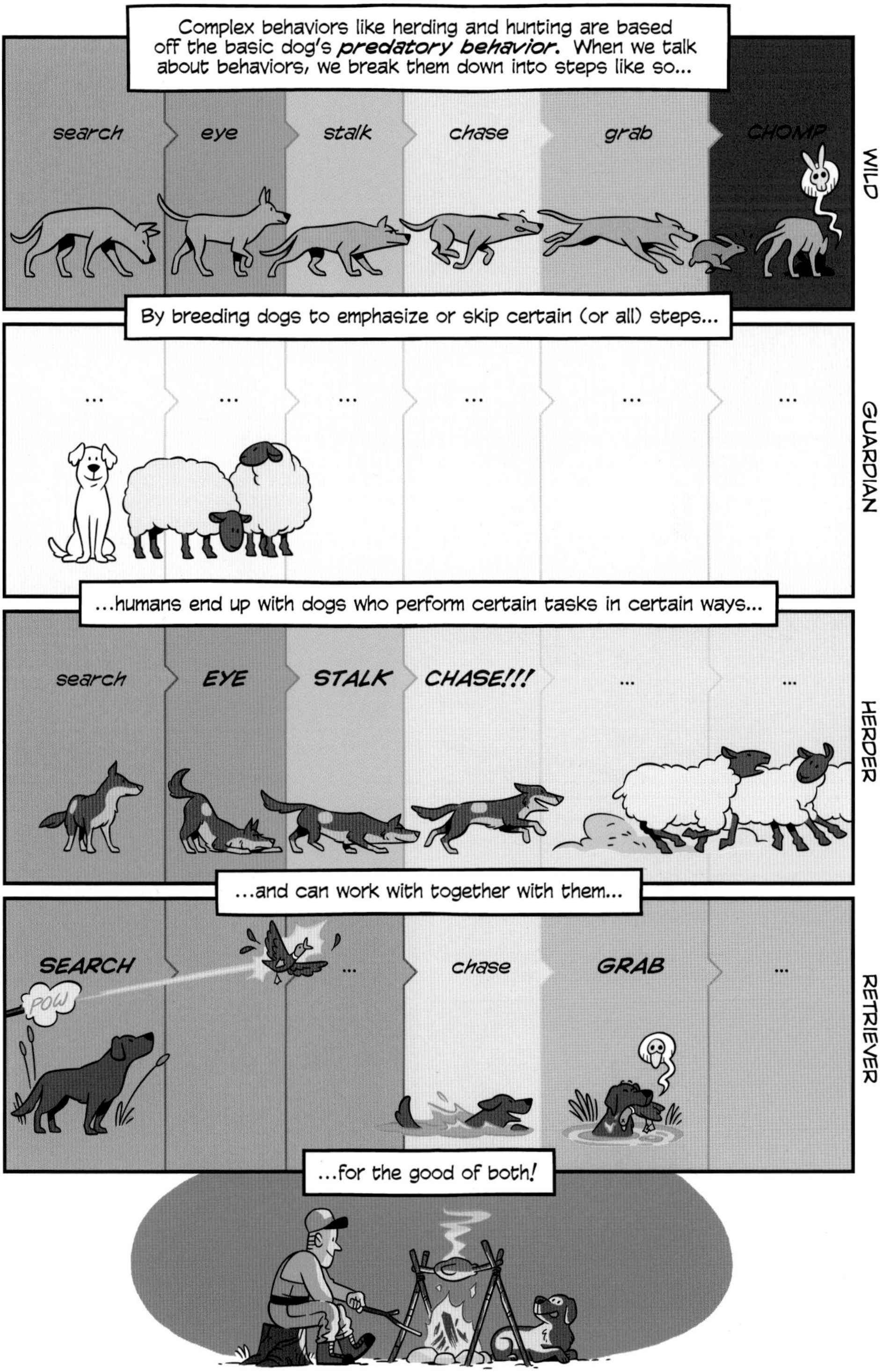

Complex behaviors like herding and hunting are based off the basic dog's ***predatory behavior.*** When we talk about behaviors, we break them down into steps like so...
search
eye
stalk
chase
grab
CHOMP
WILD
By breeding dogs to emphasize or skip certain (or all) steps...
...
...
...
...
...
...
GUARDIAN
...humans end up with dogs who perform certain tasks in certain ways...
search
EYE
STALK
CHASE!!!
...
...
HERDER
...and can work with together with them...
SEARCH
POW
...
chase
GRAB
...
RETRIEVER
...for the good of both!

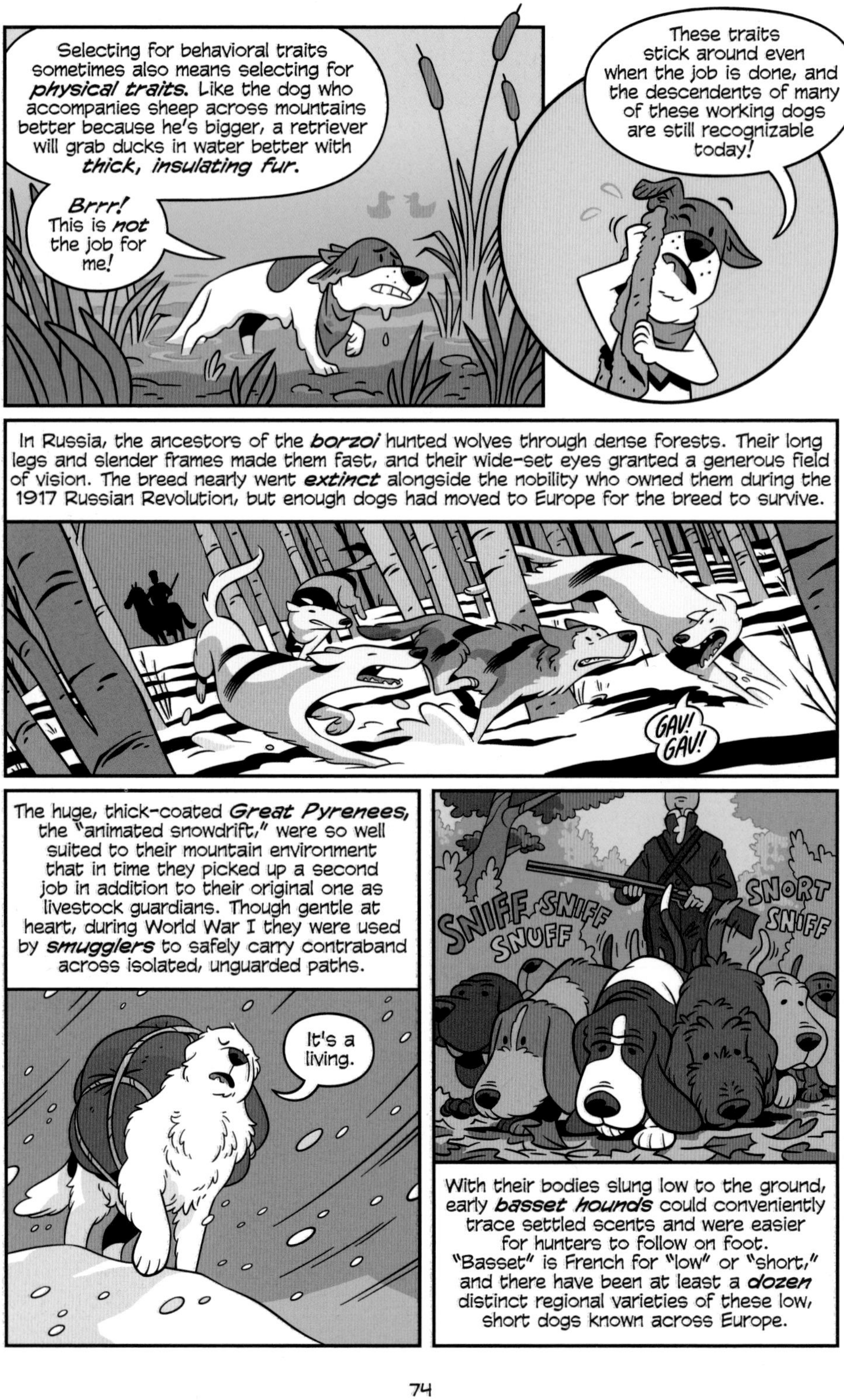
Selecting for behavioral traits sometimes also means selecting for physical traits. Like the dog who accompanies sheep across mountains better because he's bigger, a retriever will grab ducks in water better with thick, insulating fur.
Brrr! This is not the job for me!
These traits stick around even when the job is done, and the descendents of many of these working dogs are still recognizable today!
In Russia, the ancestors of the borzoi hunted wolves through dense forests. Their long legs and slender frames made them fast, and their wide-set eyes granted a generous field of vision. The breed nearly went extinct alongside the nobility who owned them during the 1917 Russian Revolution, but enough dogs had moved to Europe for the breed to survive.
GAV! GAV!
The huge, thick-coated Great Pyrenees, the "animated snowdrift," were so well suited to their mountain environment that in time they picked up a second job in addition to their original one as livestock guardians. Though gentle at heart, during World War I they were used by smugglers to safely carry contraband across isolated, unguarded paths.
It's a living.
SNIFF SNIFF SNUFF
SNORT SNIFF
With their bodies slung low to the ground, early basset hounds could conveniently trace settled scents and were easier for hunters to follow on foot. "Basset" is French for "low" or "short," and there have been at least a dozen distinct regional varieties of these low, short dogs known across Europe.

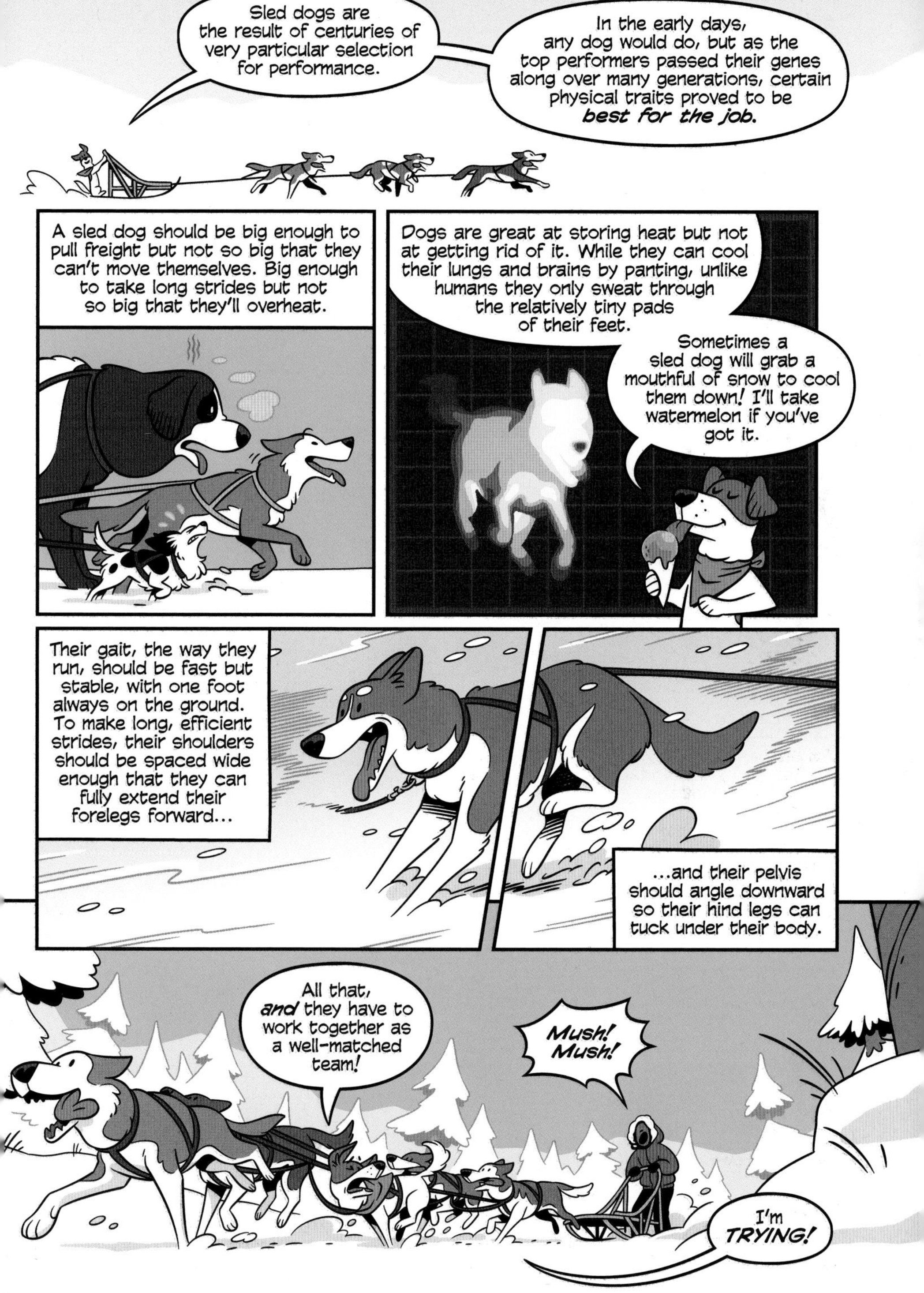
Sled dogs are the result of centuries of very particular selection for performance.
In the early days, any dog would do, but as the top performers passed their genes along over many generations, certain physical traits proved to be ***best for the job.***
A sled dog should be big enough to pull freight but not so big that they can't move themselves. Big enough to take long strides but not so big that they'll overheat.
Dogs are great at storing heat but not at getting rid of it. While they can cool their lungs and brains by panting, unlike humans they only sweat through the relatively tiny pads of their feet.
Sometimes a sled dog will grab a mouthful of snow to cool them down! I'll take watermelon if you've got it.
Their gait, the way they run, should be fast but stable, with one foot always on the ground. To make long, efficient strides, their shoulders should be spaced wide enough that they can fully extend their forelegs forward...
...and their pelvis should angle downward so their hind legs can tuck under their body.
All that, ***and*** they have to work together as a well-matched team!
Mush! Mush!
I'm ***TRYING!***

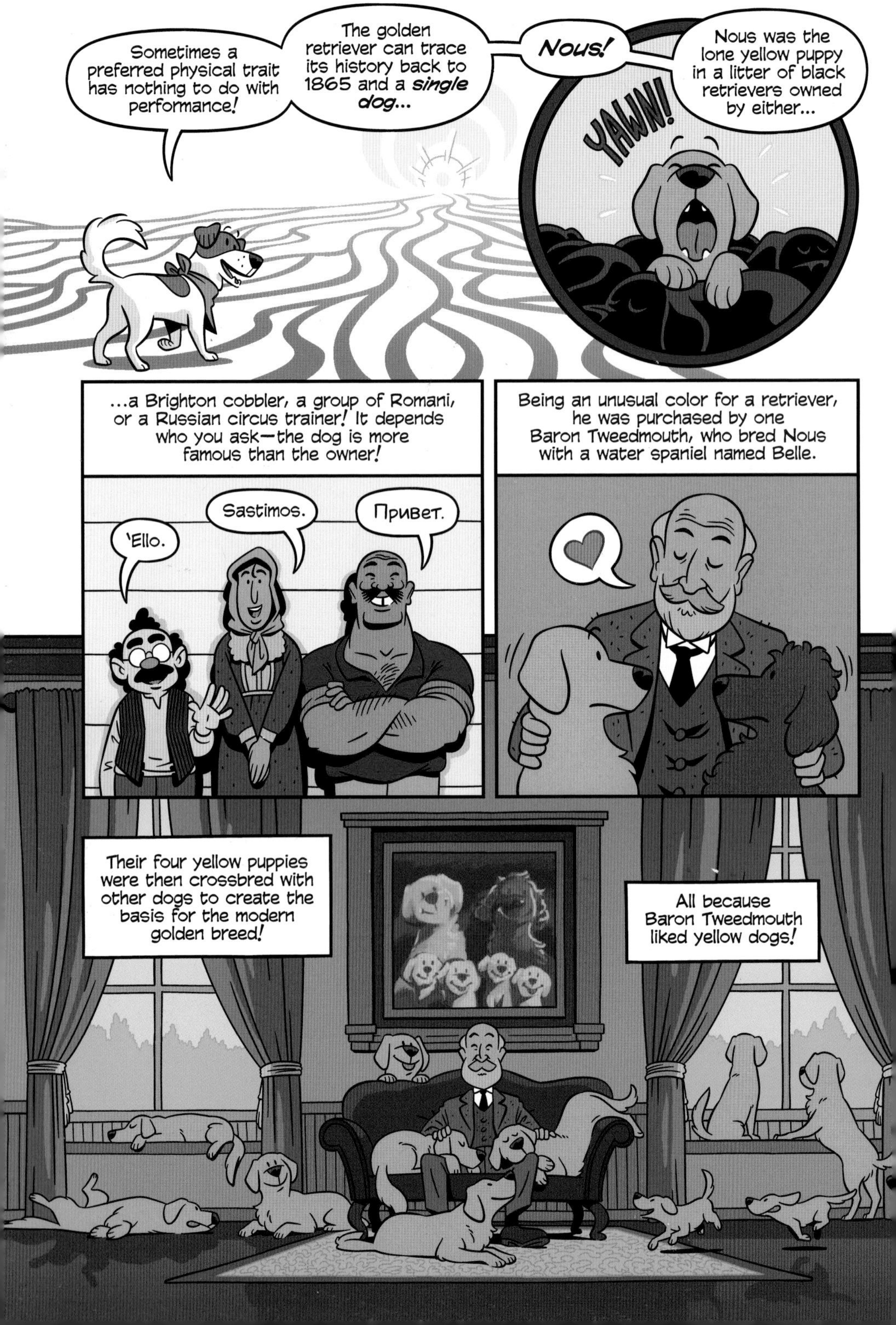

Sometimes a preferred physical trait has nothing to do with performance!
The golden retriever can trace its history back to 1865 and a *single dog...*
Nous!
Nous was the lone yellow puppy in a litter of black retrievers owned by either...
YAWN!
...a Brighton cobbler, a group of Romani, or a Russian circus trainer! It depends who you ask—the dog is more famous than the owner!
'Ello.
Sastimos.
Привет.
Being an unusual color for a retriever, he was purchased by one Baron Tweedmouth, who bred Nous with a water spaniel named Belle.
Their four yellow puppies were then crossbred with other dogs to create the basis for the modern golden breed!
All because Baron Tweedmouth liked yellow dogs!

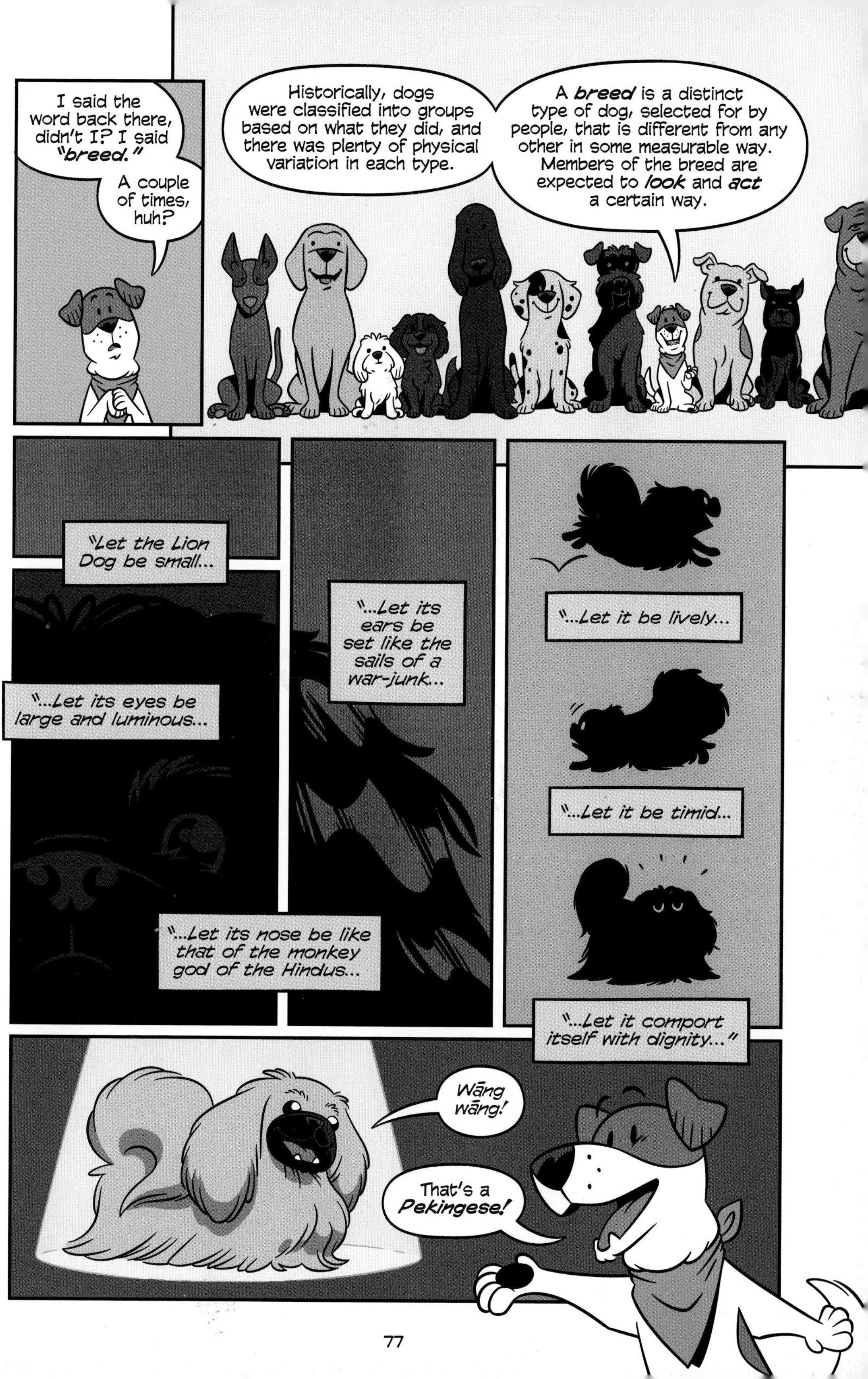

I said the word back there, didn't I? I said **"breed."**
A couple of times, huh?
Historically, dogs were classified into groups based on what they did, and there was plenty of physical variation in each type.
A **breed** is a distinct type of dog, selected for by people, that is different from any other in some measurable way. Members of the breed are expected to ***look*** and ***act*** a certain way.
"Let the Lion Dog be small...
"...Let its eyes be large and luminous...
"...Let its nose be like that of the monkey god of the Hindus...
"...Let its ears be set like the sails of a war-junk...
"...Let it be lively...
"...Let it be timid...
"...Let it comport itself with dignity..."
Wāng wāng!
That's a ***Pekingese!***

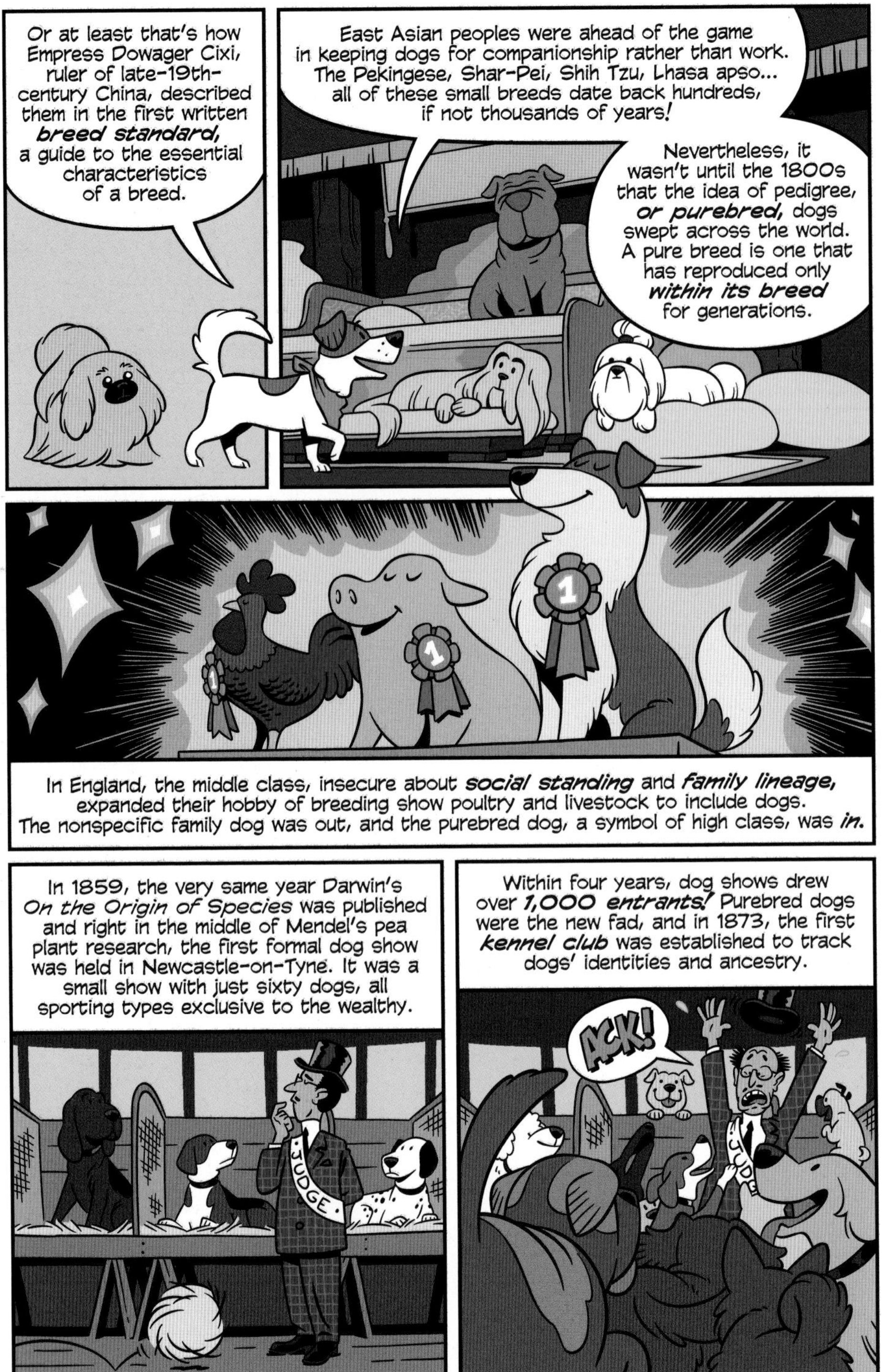
Or at least that's how Empress Dowager Cixi, ruler of late-19th-century China, described them in the first written *breed standard,* a guide to the essential characteristics of a breed.
East Asian peoples were ahead of the game in keeping dogs for companionship rather than work. The Pekingese, Shar-Pei, Shih Tzu, Lhasa apso... all of these small breeds date back hundreds, if not thousands of years!
Nevertheless, it wasn't until the 1800s that the idea of pedigree, *or purebred,* dogs swept across the world. A pure breed is one that has reproduced only *within its breed* for generations.
1
1
1
In England, the middle class, insecure about *social standing* and *family lineage,* expanded their hobby of breeding show poultry and livestock to include dogs. The nonspecific family dog was out, and the purebred dog, a symbol of high class, was *in.*
In 1859, the very same year Darwin's *On the Origin of Species* was published and right in the middle of Mendel's pea plant research, the first formal dog show was held in Newcastle-on-Tyne. It was a small show with just sixty dogs, all sporting types exclusive to the wealthy.
JUDGE
Within four years, dog shows drew over *1,000 entrants!* Purebred dogs were the new fad, and in 1873, the first *kennel club* was established to track dogs' identities and ancestry.
ACK!
JUDGE

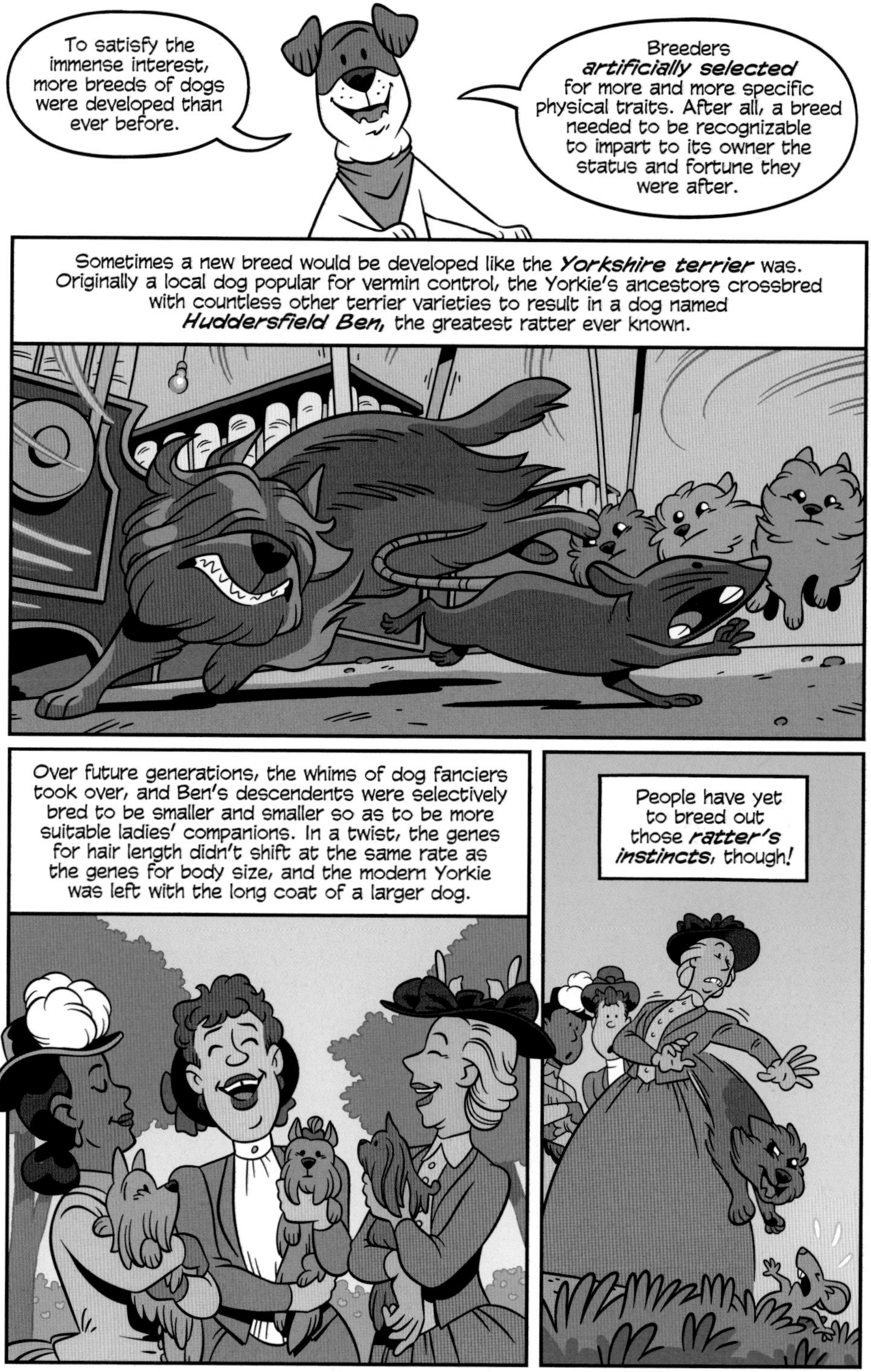
To satisfy the immense interest, more breeds of dogs were developed than ever before.
Breeders *artificially selected* for more and more specific physical traits. After all, a breed needed to be recognizable to impart to its owner the status and fortune they were after.
Sometimes a new breed would be developed like the *Yorkshire terrier* was. Originally a local dog popular for vermin control, the Yorkie's ancestors crossbred with countless other terrier varieties to result in a dog named *Huddersfield Ben,* the greatest ratter ever known.
Over future generations, the whims of dog fanciers took over, and Ben's descendents were selectively bred to be smaller and smaller so as to be more suitable ladies' companions. In a twist, the genes for hair length didn't shift at the same rate as the genes for body size, and the modern Yorkie was left with the long coat of a larger dog.
People have yet to breed out those *ratter's instincts,* though!

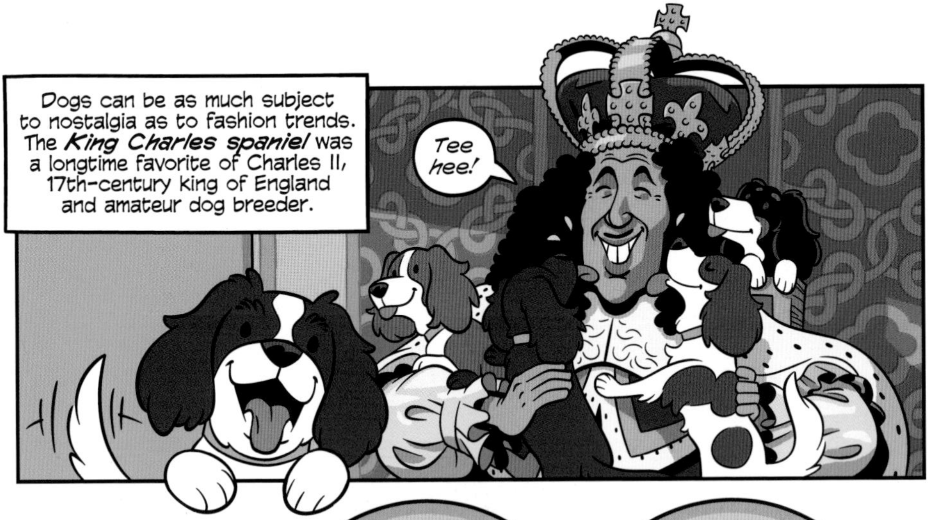
Dogs can be as much subject to nostalgia as to fashion trends. The ***King Charles spaniel*** was a longtime favorite of Charles II, 17th-century king of England and amateur dog breeder.
Tee hee!

In the Victorian period of the late 1800s, contemporary fashion demanded smaller dogs with ***flatter*** faces. Those traits were selectively bred for, and the people got what they wanted.

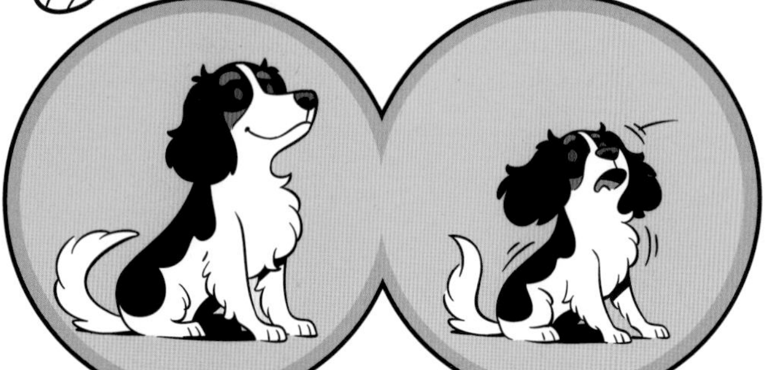

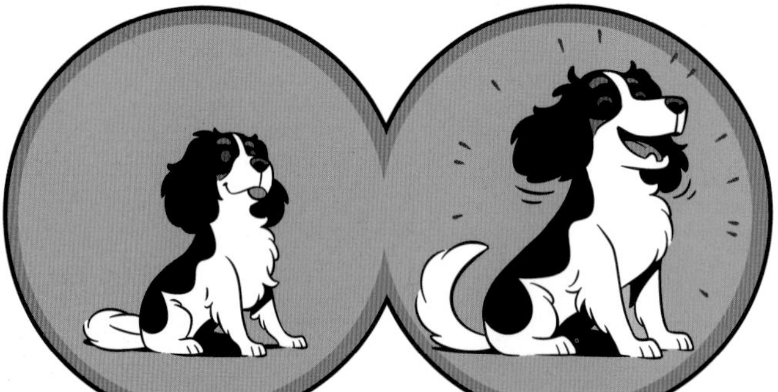

Fans of the original dogs weren't crazy about the changes bred into their favorite pets, and in the 1920s, nostalgic breeders developed the ***Cavalier King Charles spaniel*** in an attempt to re-create the dogs of Charles II's time.

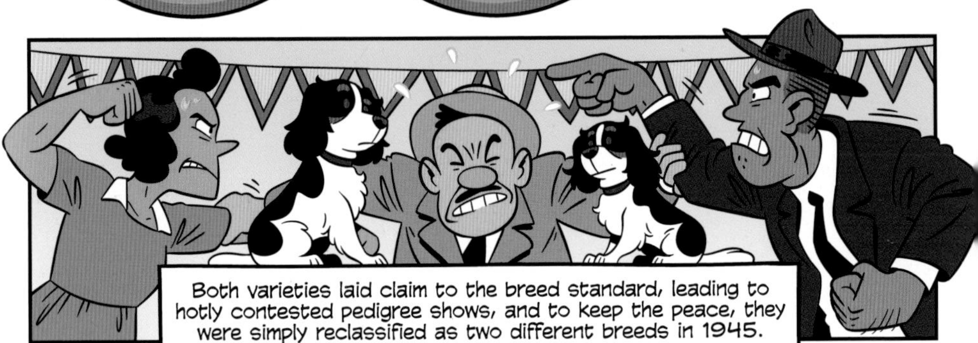
Both varieties laid claim to the breed standard, leading to hotly contested pedigree shows, and to keep the peace, they were simply reclassified as two different breeds in 1945.

Why else might humans select for traits? The English bulldog got an upturned nose so they could breathe while their powerful jaws were locked to their targets during the cruel sport of bull baiting...

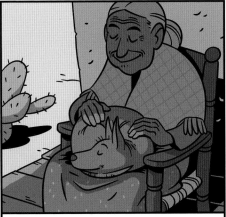

...hairless dogs like the Xoloitzcuintli became hot-bodied pain relievers...

...the short-legged dachshund could pursue prey into their burrows...

...and while the pharaoh hound *looks* like dogs depicted in ancient Egyptian art, don't be fooled—they're a relatively recent crossbreed callback!

The backgrounds of some dogs, like the *pug*, remain utter mysteries. Did they originate in China, Russia, Holland?

Are they dwarf mastiffs? Smooth-coated, long-legged Pekingese?

What about the name? "Pug" could be the word for monkey, fist, goblin... What's your deal?!

I just gotta be me, y'all.

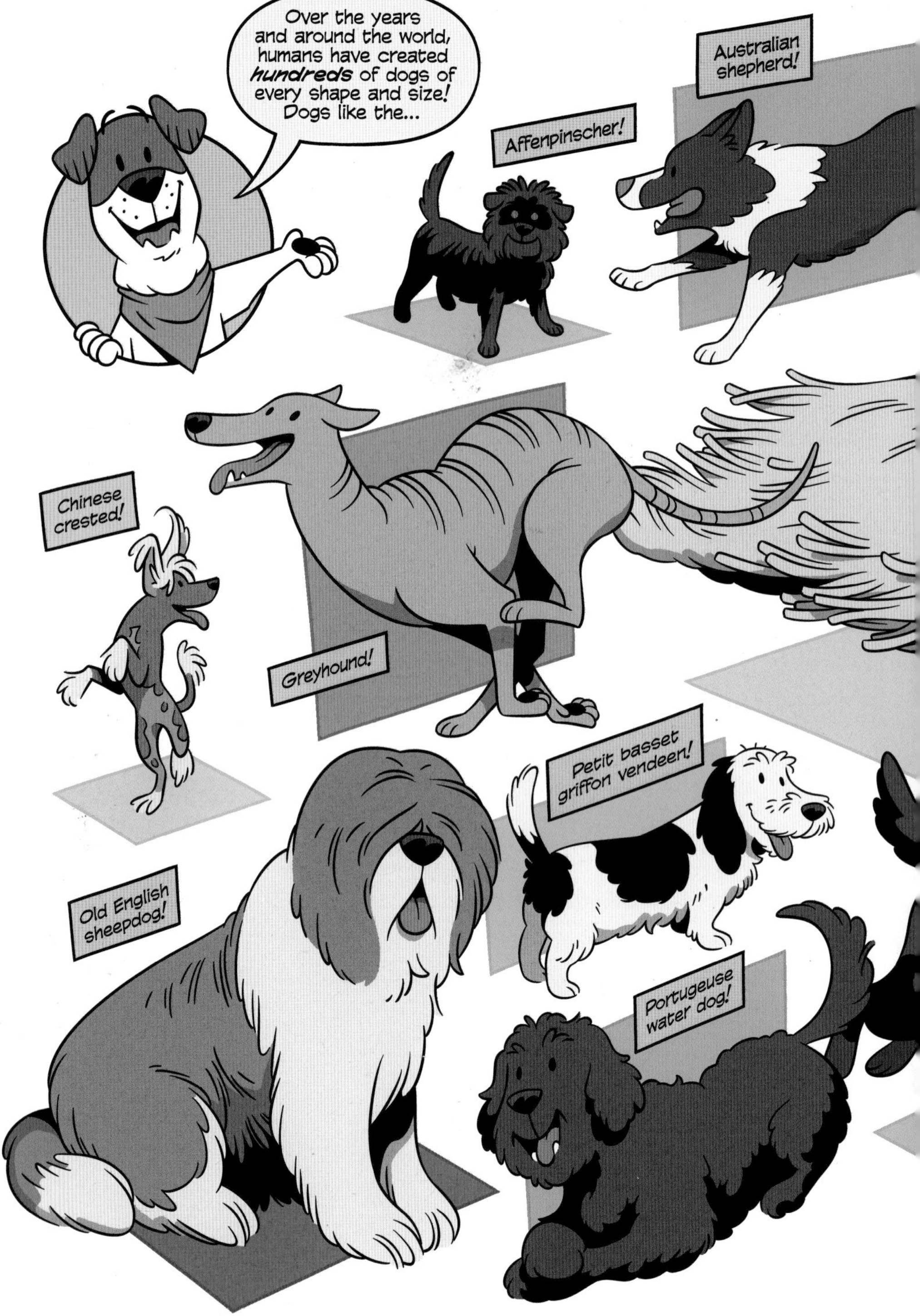
Over the years and around the world, humans have created *hundreds* of dogs of every shape and size! Dogs like the...
Affenpinscher!
Australian shepherd!
Chinese crested!
Greyhound!
Petit basset griffon vendeen!
Old English sheepdog!
Portuguese water dog!

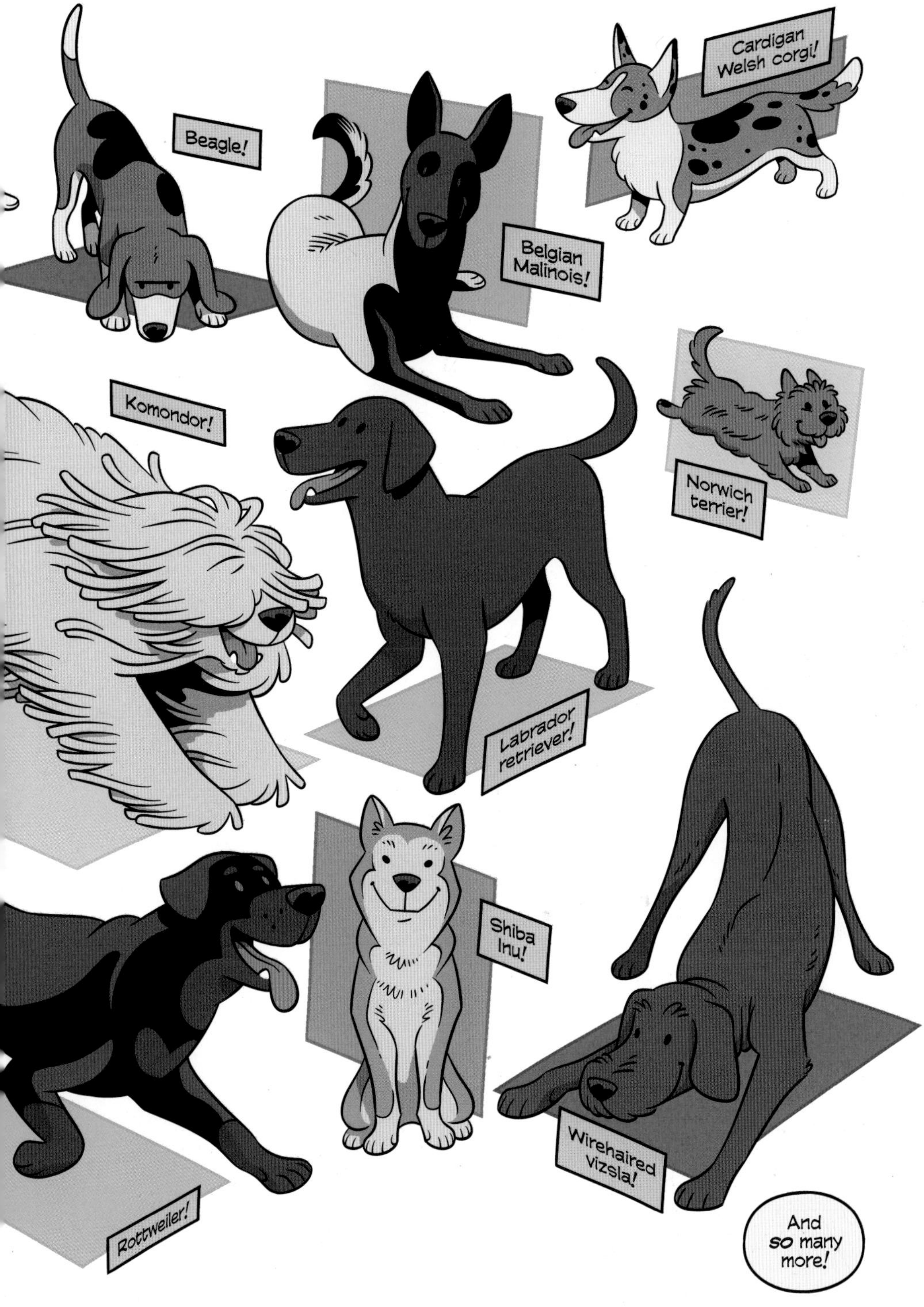

Beagle!
Belgian Malinois!
Cardigan Welsh corgi!
Komondor!
Labrador retriever!
Norwich terrier!
Rottweiler!
Shiba Inu!
Wirehaired vizsla!
And so many more!

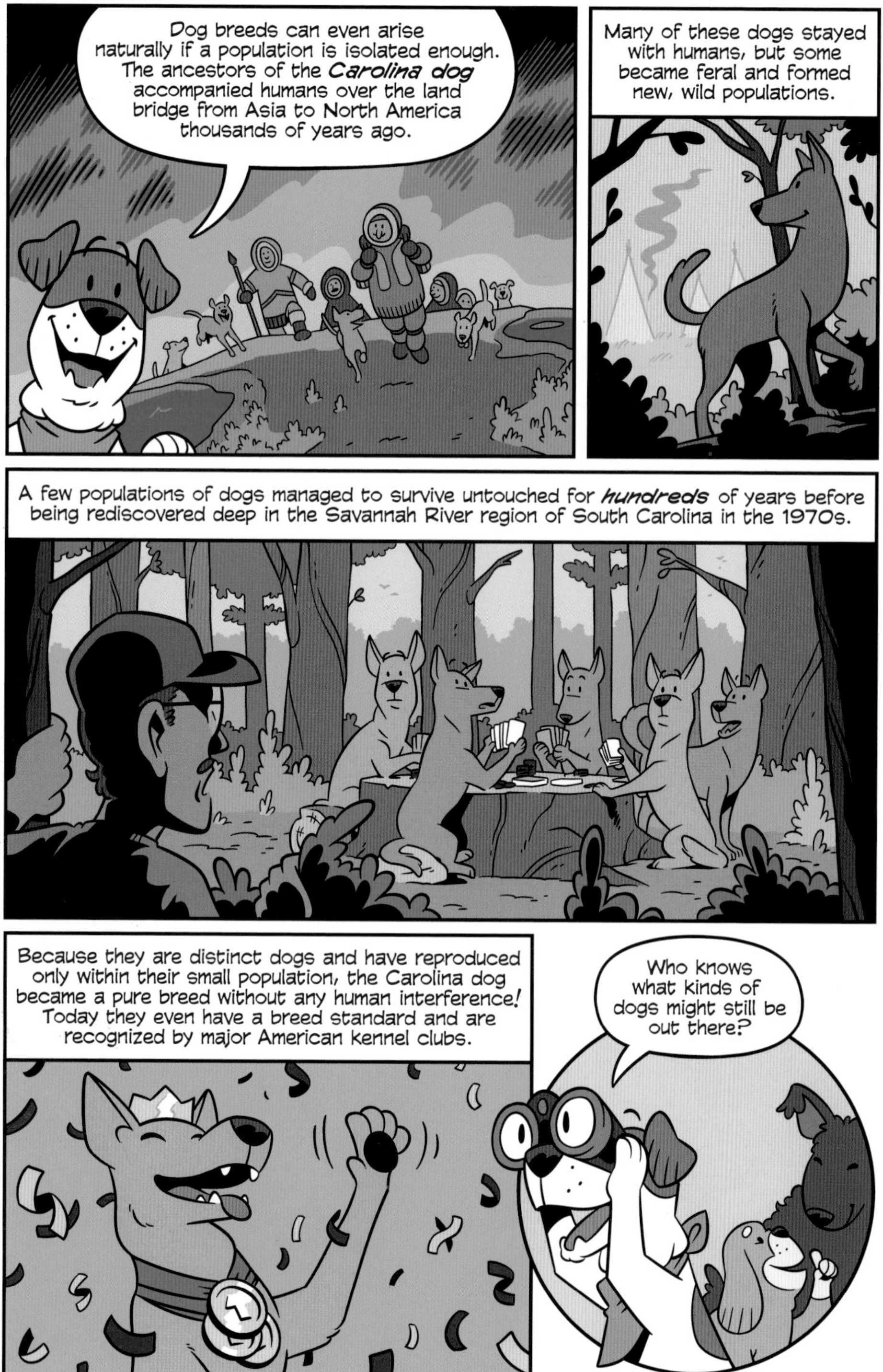
Dog breeds can even arise naturally if a population is isolated enough. The ancestors of the *Carolina dog* accompanied humans over the land bridge from Asia to North America thousands of years ago.
Many of these dogs stayed with humans, but some became feral and formed new, wild populations.
A few populations of dogs managed to survive untouched for *hundreds* of years before being rediscovered deep in the Savannah River region of South Carolina in the 1970s.
Because they are distinct dogs and have reproduced only within their small population, the Carolina dog became a pure breed without any human interference! Today they even have a breed standard and are recognized by major American kennel clubs.
Who knows what kinds of dogs might still be out there?

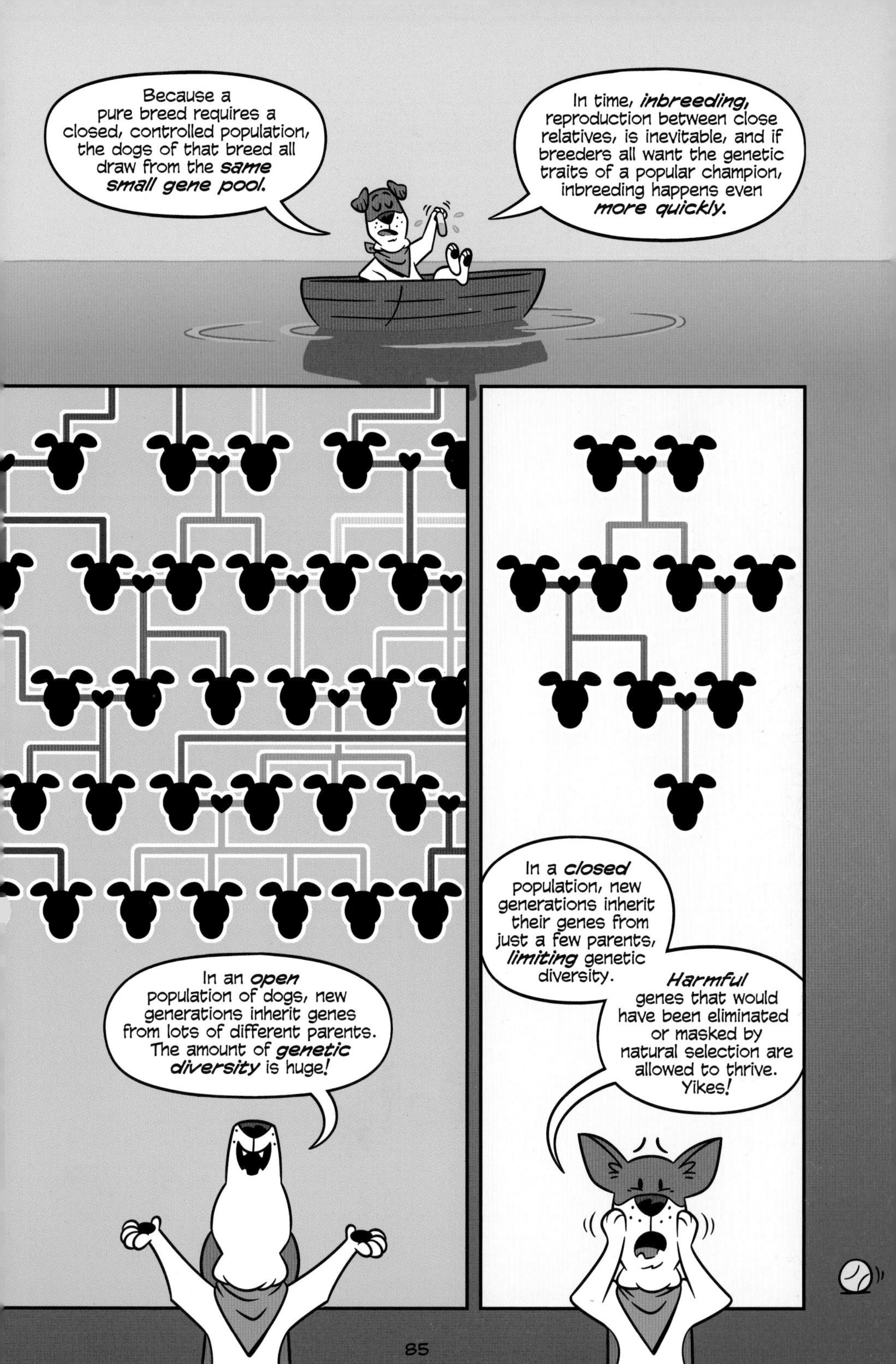
Because a pure breed requires a closed, controlled population, the dogs of that breed all draw from the *same small gene pool.*
In time, *inbreeding,* reproduction between close relatives, is inevitable, and if breeders all want the genetic traits of a popular champion, inbreeding happens even *more quickly.*
In an *open* population of dogs, new generations inherit genes from lots of different parents. The amount of *genetic diversity* is huge!
In a *closed* population, new generations inherit their genes from just a few parents, *limiting* genetic diversity.
Harmful genes that would have been eliminated or masked by natural selection are allowed to thrive. Yikes!

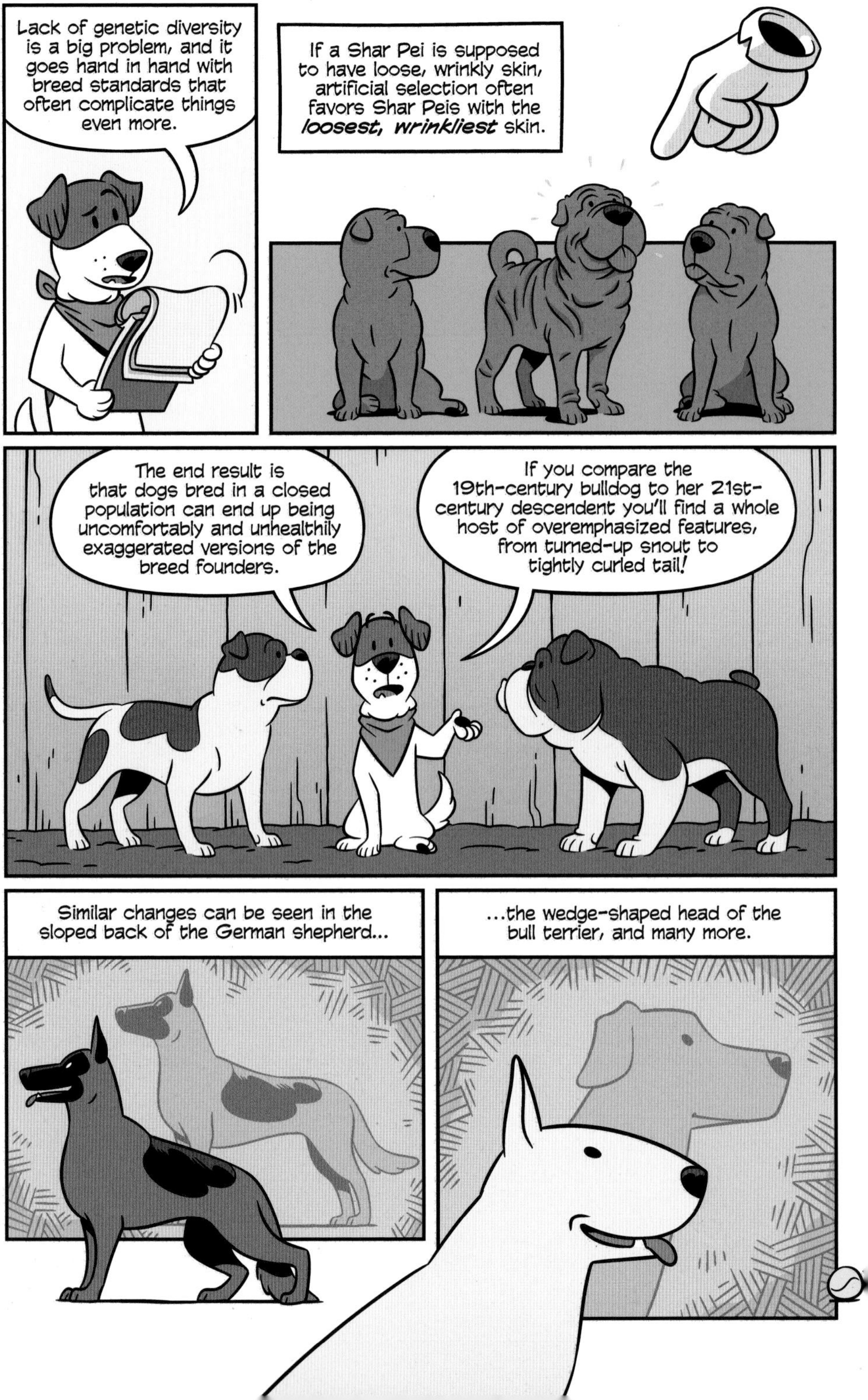
Lack of genetic diversity is a big problem, and it goes hand in hand with breed standards that often complicate things even more.
If a Shar Pei is supposed to have loose, wrinkly skin, artificial selection often favors Shar Peis with the *loosest, wrinkliest* skin.
The end result is that dogs bred in a closed population can end up being uncomfortably and unhealthily exaggerated versions of the breed founders.
If you compare the 19th-century bulldog to her 21st-century descendent you'll find a whole host of overemphasized features, from turned-up snout to tightly curled tail!
Similar changes can be seen in the sloped back of the German shepherd...
...the wedge-shaped head of the bull terrier, and many more.

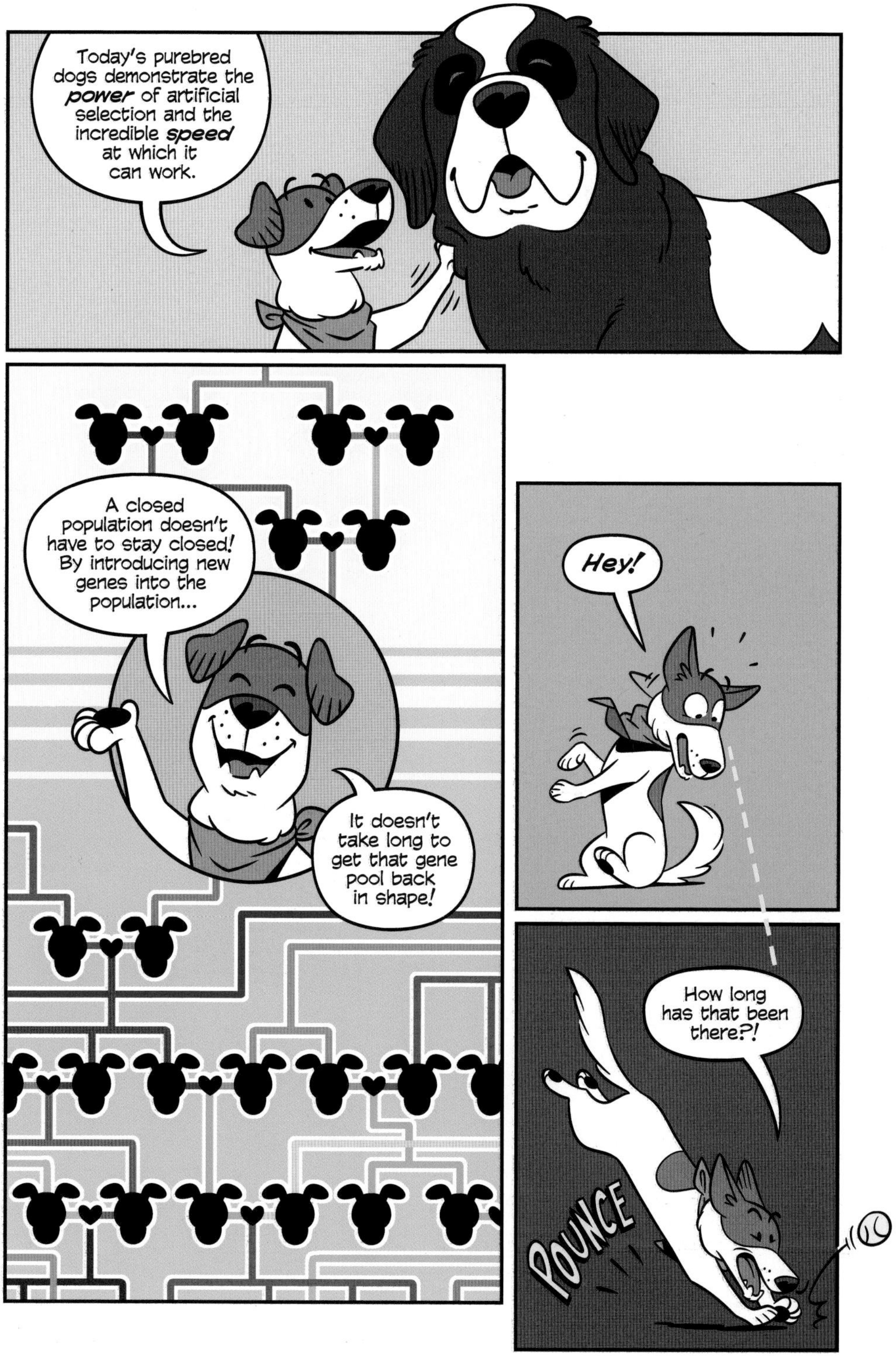
Today's purebred dogs demonstrate the *power* of artificial selection and the incredible *speed* at which it can work.
A closed population doesn't have to stay closed! By introducing new genes into the population...
It doesn't take long to get that gene pool back in shape!
Hey!
How long has that been there?!
POUNCE

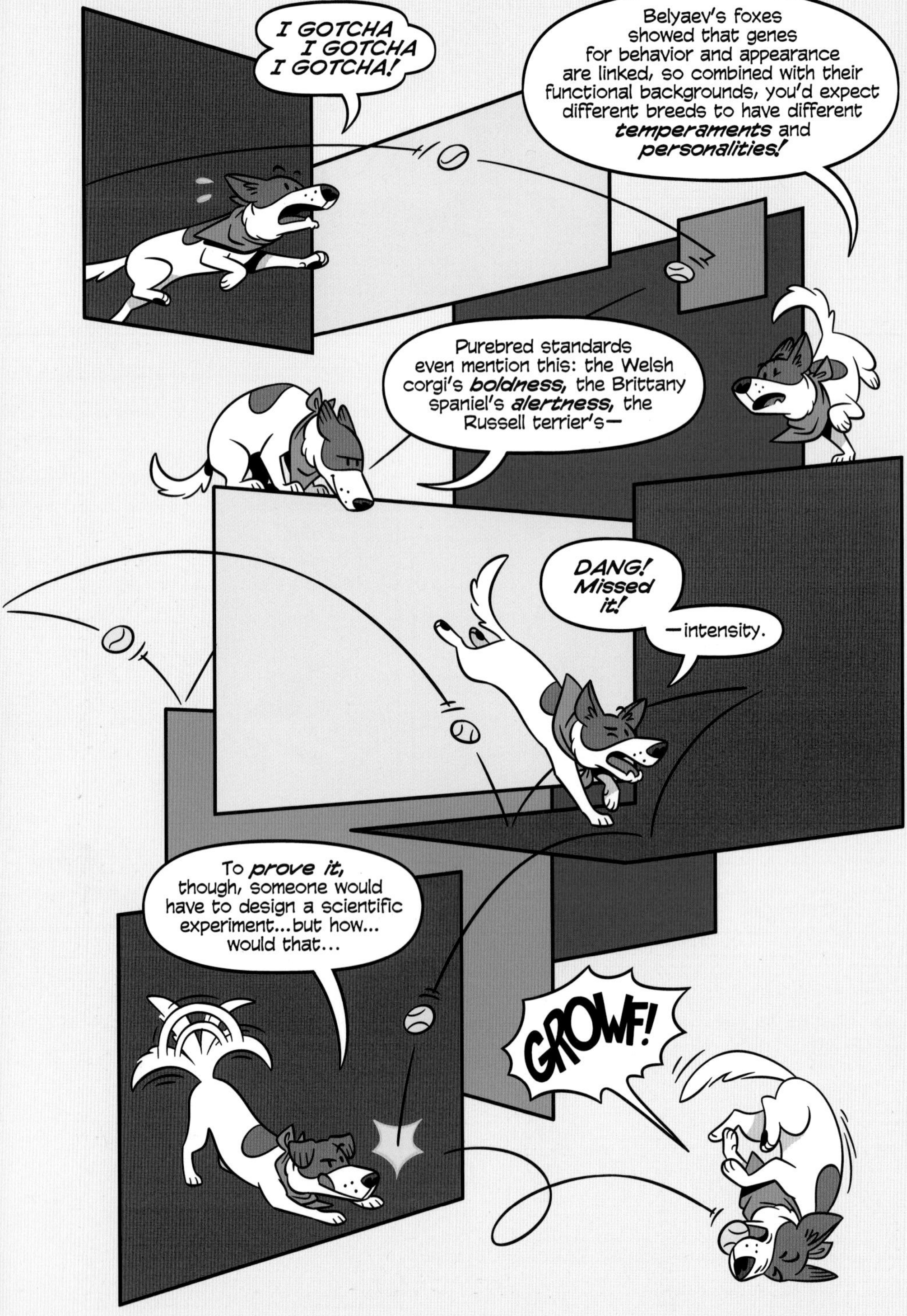

I GOTCHA I GOTCHA I GOTCHA!
Belyaev's foxes showed that genes for behavior and appearance are linked, so combined with their functional backgrounds, you'd expect different breeds to have different *temperaments* and *personalities!*
Purebred standards even mention this: the Welsh corgi's *boldness*, the Brittany spaniel's *alertness*, the Russell terrier's—
DANG! Missed it!
—intensity.
To *prove it*, though, someone would have to design a scientific experiment...but how... would that...
GROWF!

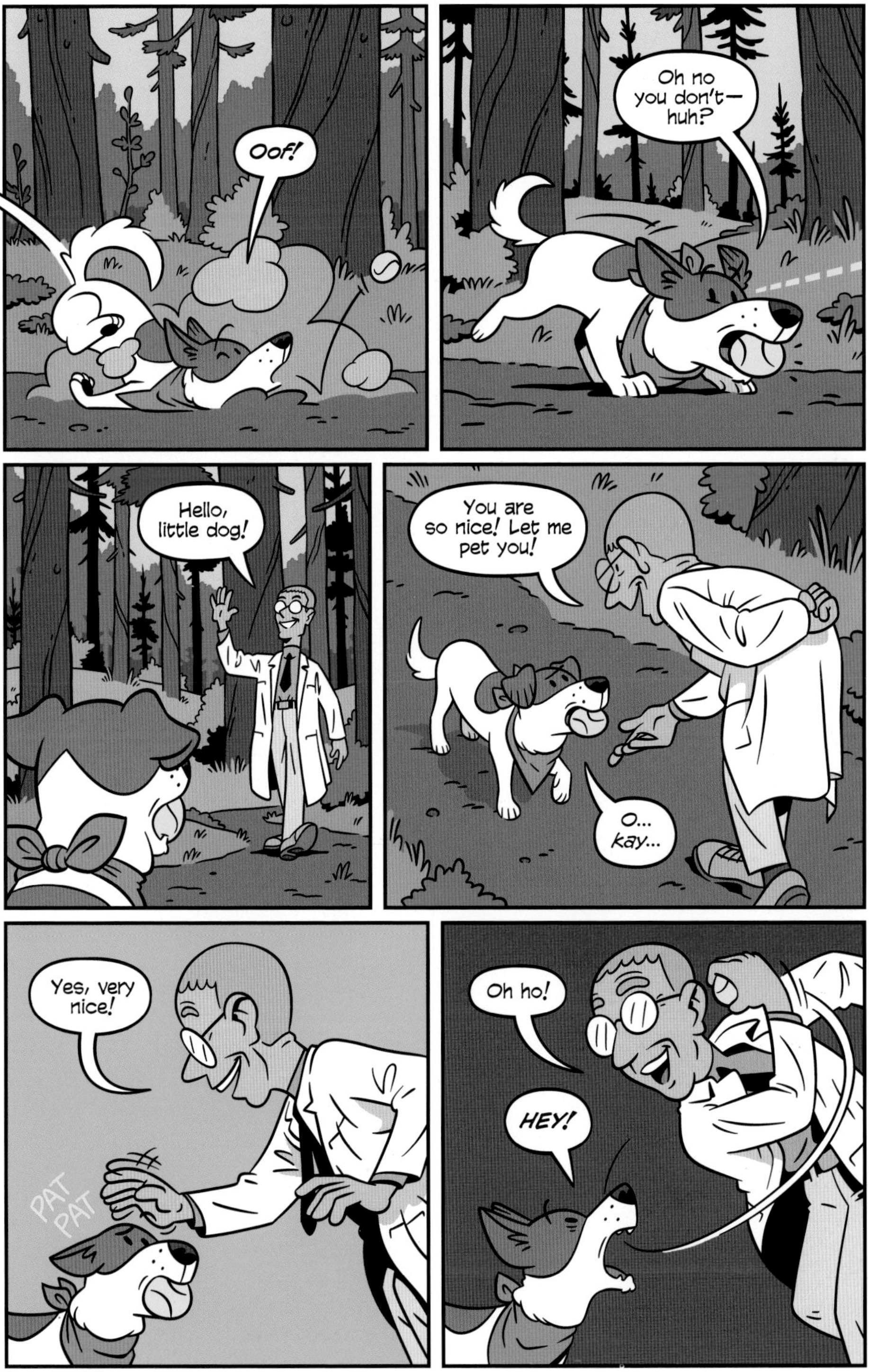

Oof!
Oh no you don't— huh?
Hello, little dog!
You are so nice! Let me pet you!
O... kay...
Yes, very nice!
PAT PAT
Oh ho!
HEY!

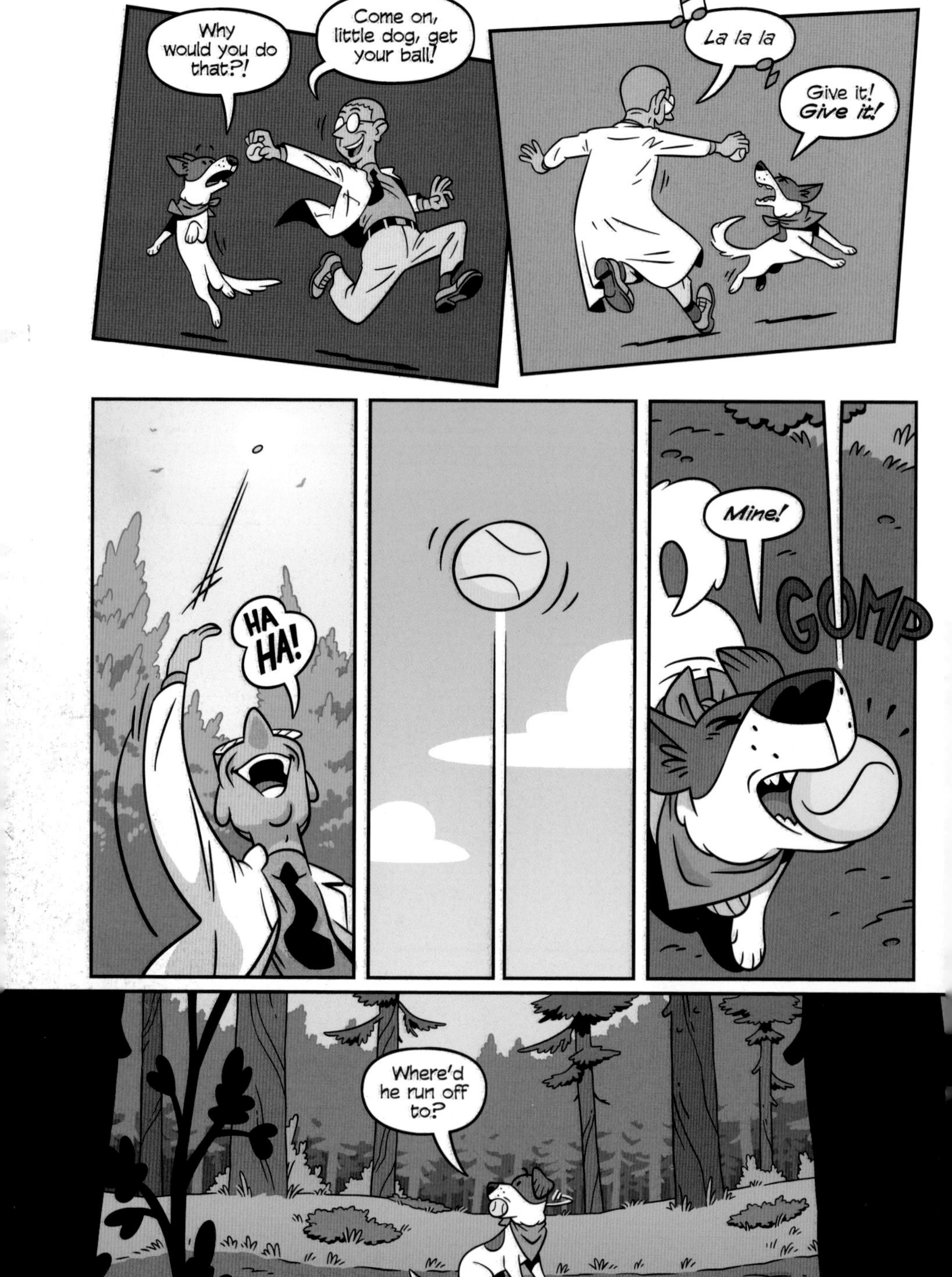
Why would you do that?!
Come on, little dog, get your ball!
La la la
Give it! Give it!
HA HA!
Mine!
GOMP
Where'd he run off to?

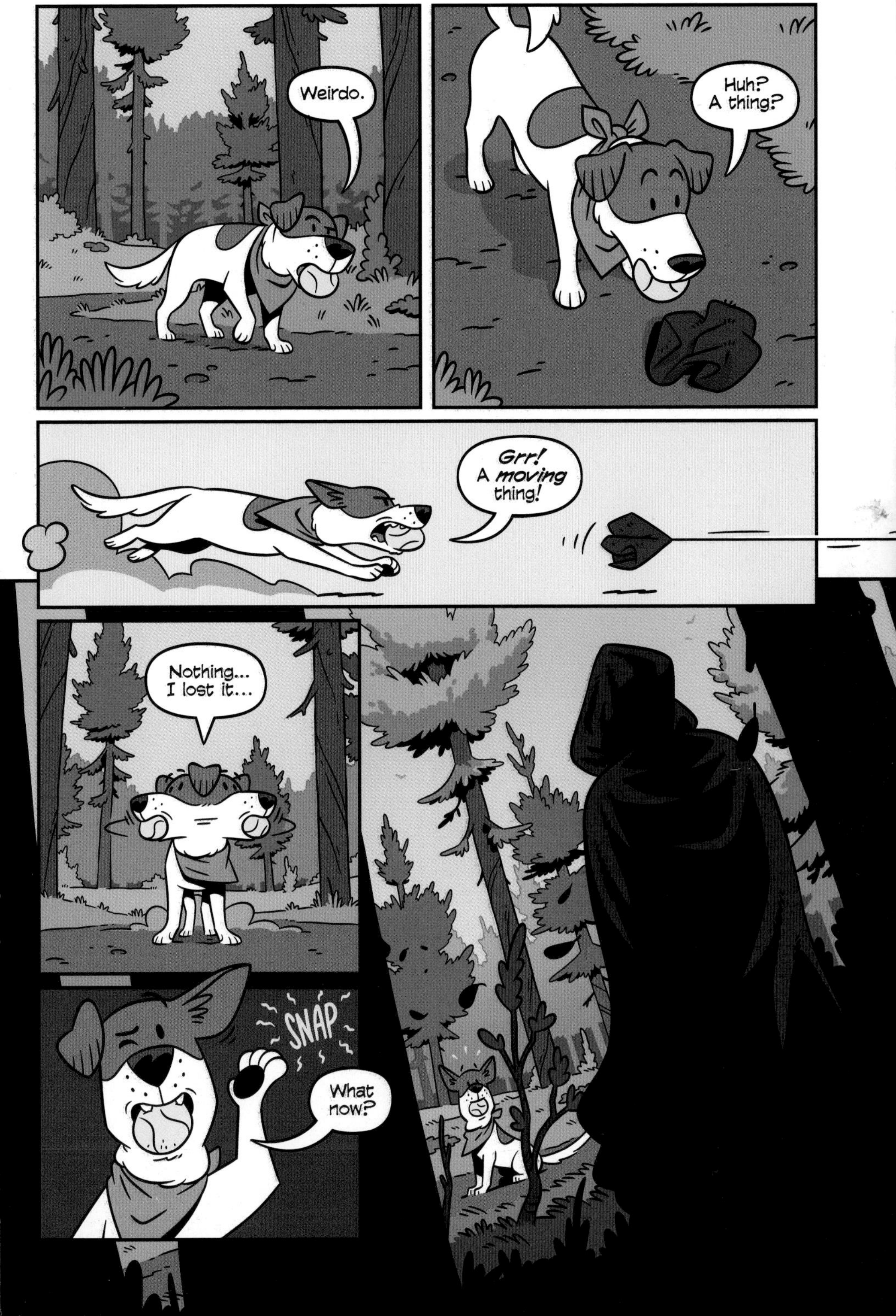
Weirdo.
Huh? A thing?
Grr! A *moving* thing!
Nothing... I lost it...
SNAP
What now?

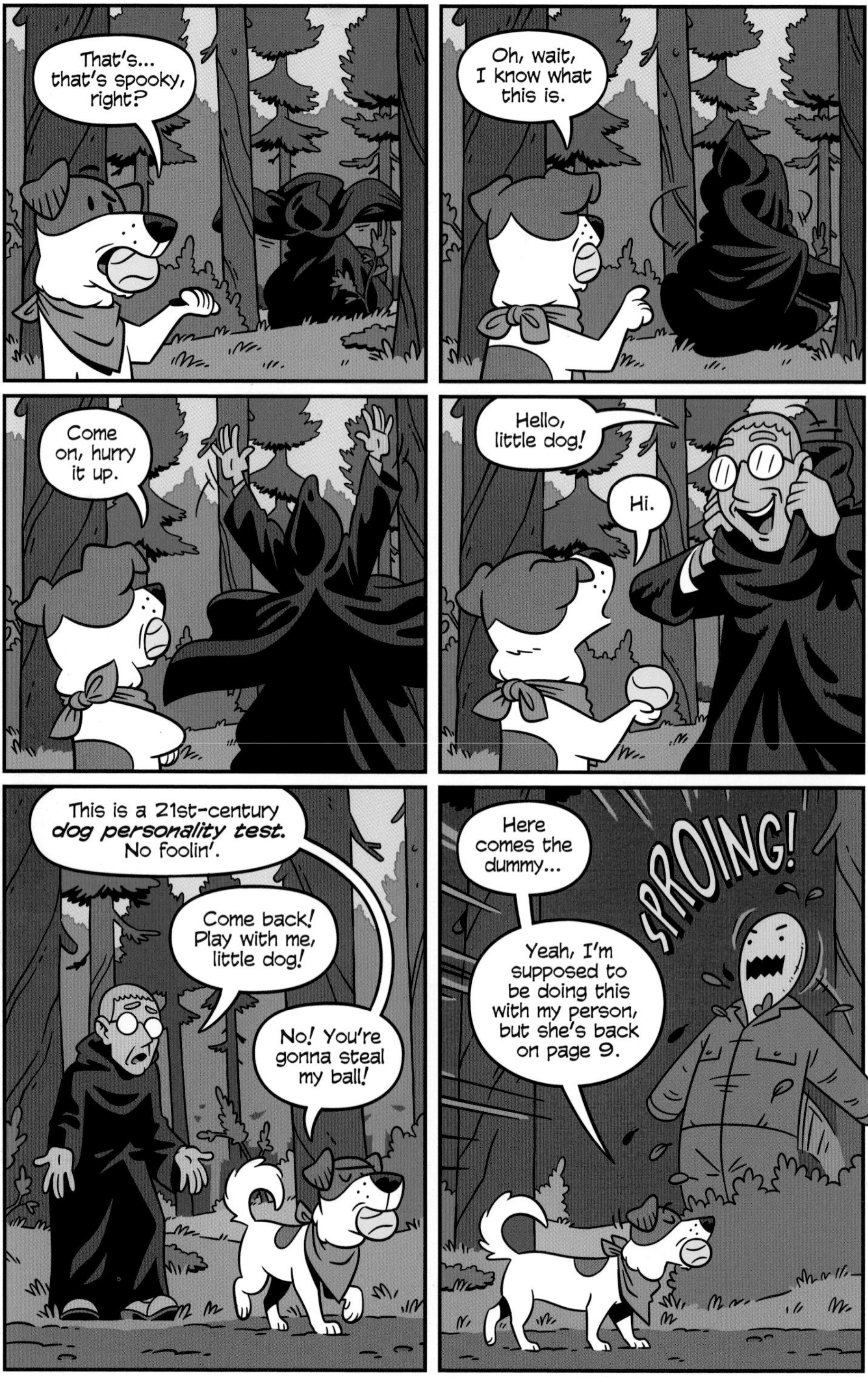
That's... that's spooky, right?
Oh, wait, I know what this is.
Come on, hurry it up.
Hello, little dog!
Hi.
This is a 21st-century ***dog personality test.*** No foolin'.
Come back! Play with me, little dog!
No! You're gonna steal my ball!
Here comes the dummy...
SPROING!
Yeah, I'm supposed to be doing this with my person, but she's back on page 9.

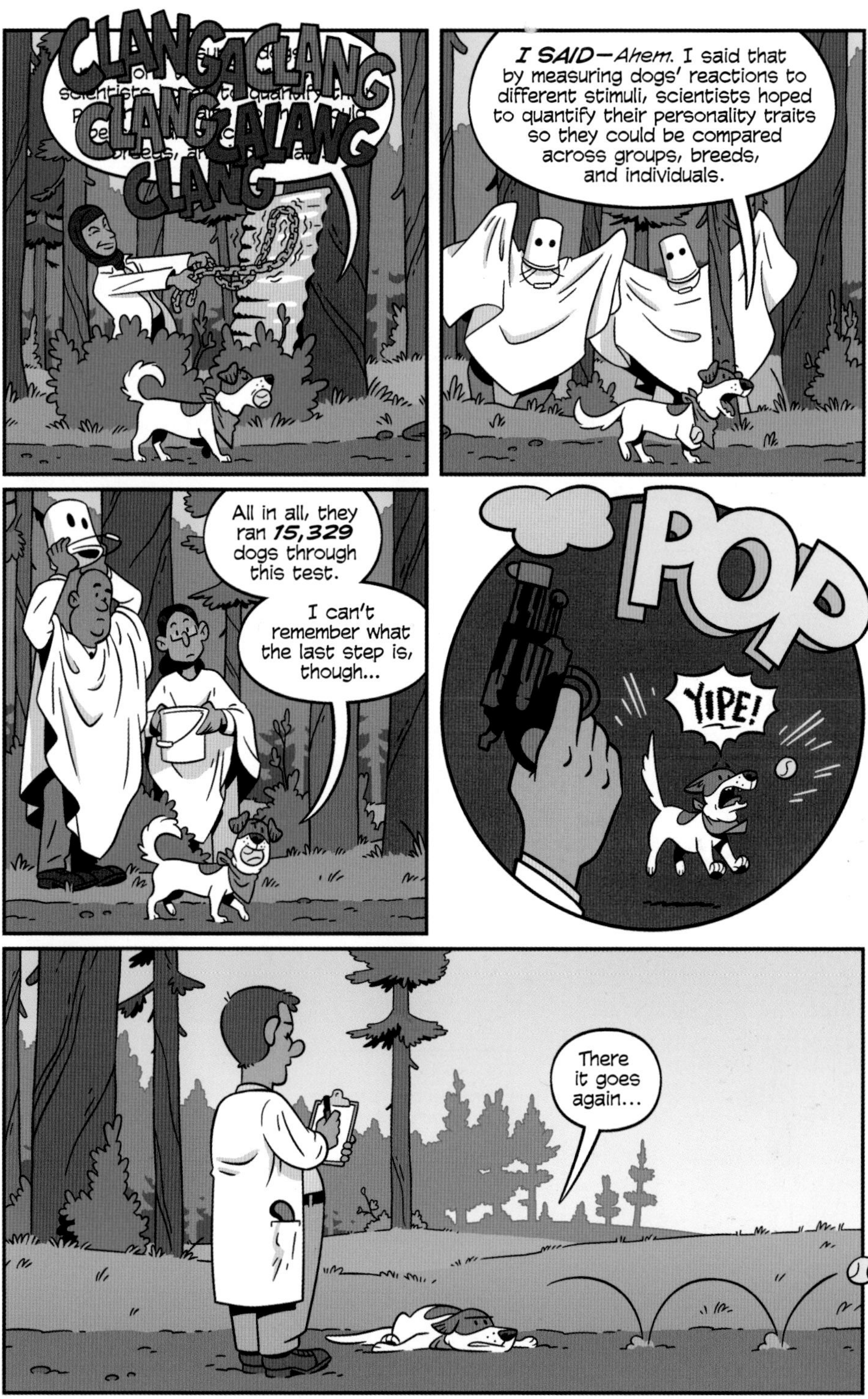
CLANGACLANG CLANGALANG CLANG
I SAID—Ahem. I said that by measuring dogs' reactions to different stimuli, scientists hoped to quantify their personality traits so they could be compared across groups, breeds, and individuals.
All in all, they ran 15,329 dogs through this test.
I can't remember what the last step is, though...
POP
YIPE!
There it goes again...

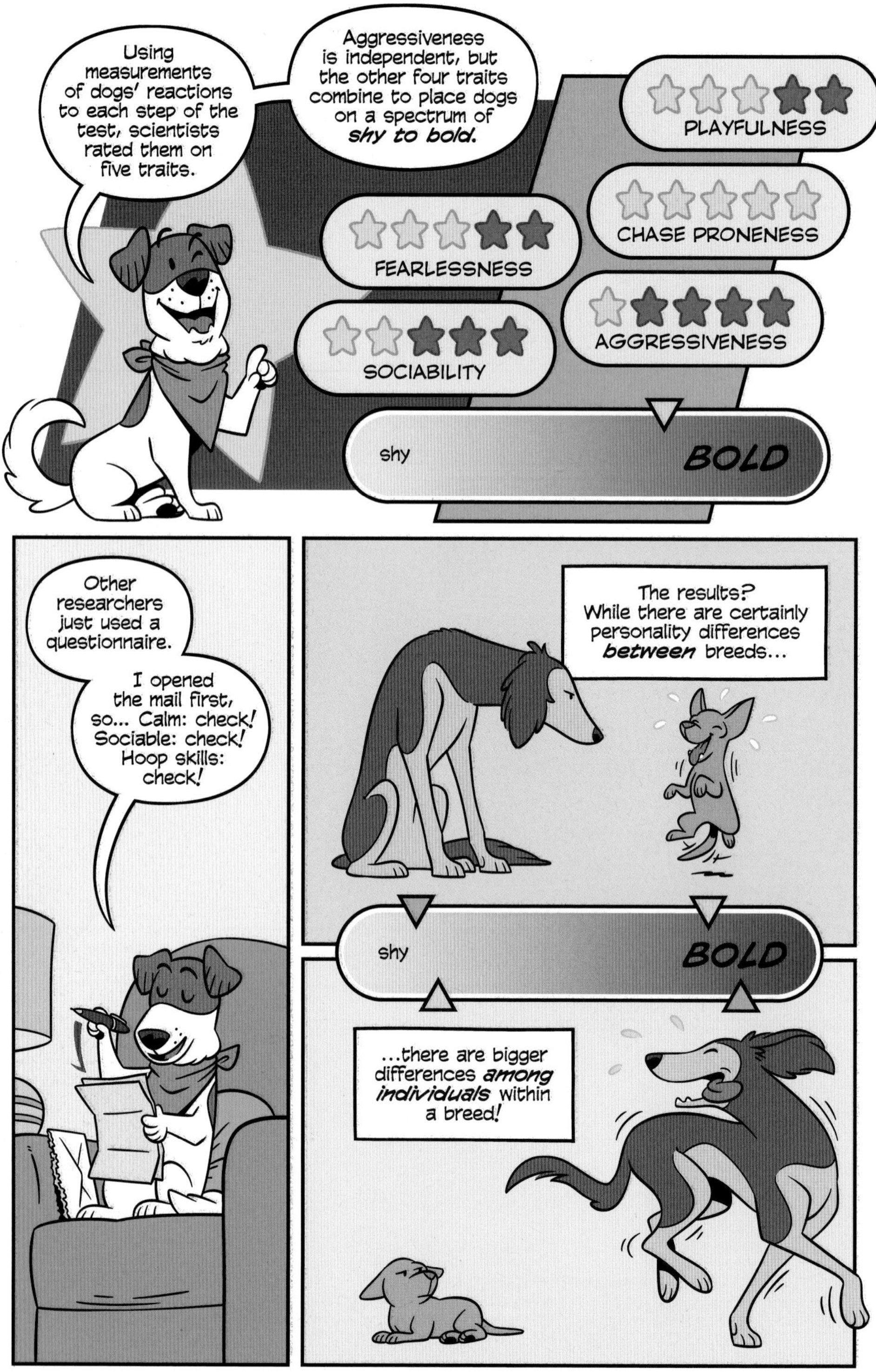

Using measurements of dogs' reactions to each step of the test, scientists rated them on five traits.
Aggressiveness is independent, but the other four traits combine to place dogs on a spectrum of *shy to bold.*
PLAYFULNESS
CHASE PRONENESS
FEARLESSNESS
AGGRESSIVENESS
SOCIABILITY
shy
BOLD
Other researchers just used a questionnaire.
I opened the mail first, so... Calm: check! Sociable: check! Hoop skills: check!
The results? While there are certainly personality differences *between* breeds...
shy
BOLD
...there are bigger differences *among individuals* within a breed!

Some of a dog's personality traits can be estimated based on their ***genetic group!*** This is a way of organizing breeds based on genetic relatedness and common ancestry.

Let me tell you, this page would have to be a whole lot bigger to fit ***all*** the breeds!

Scientists arrived at these groups through ***genetic testing,*** which involves mapping a dog's genome by writing out the order of As, Ts, Cs, and Gs.

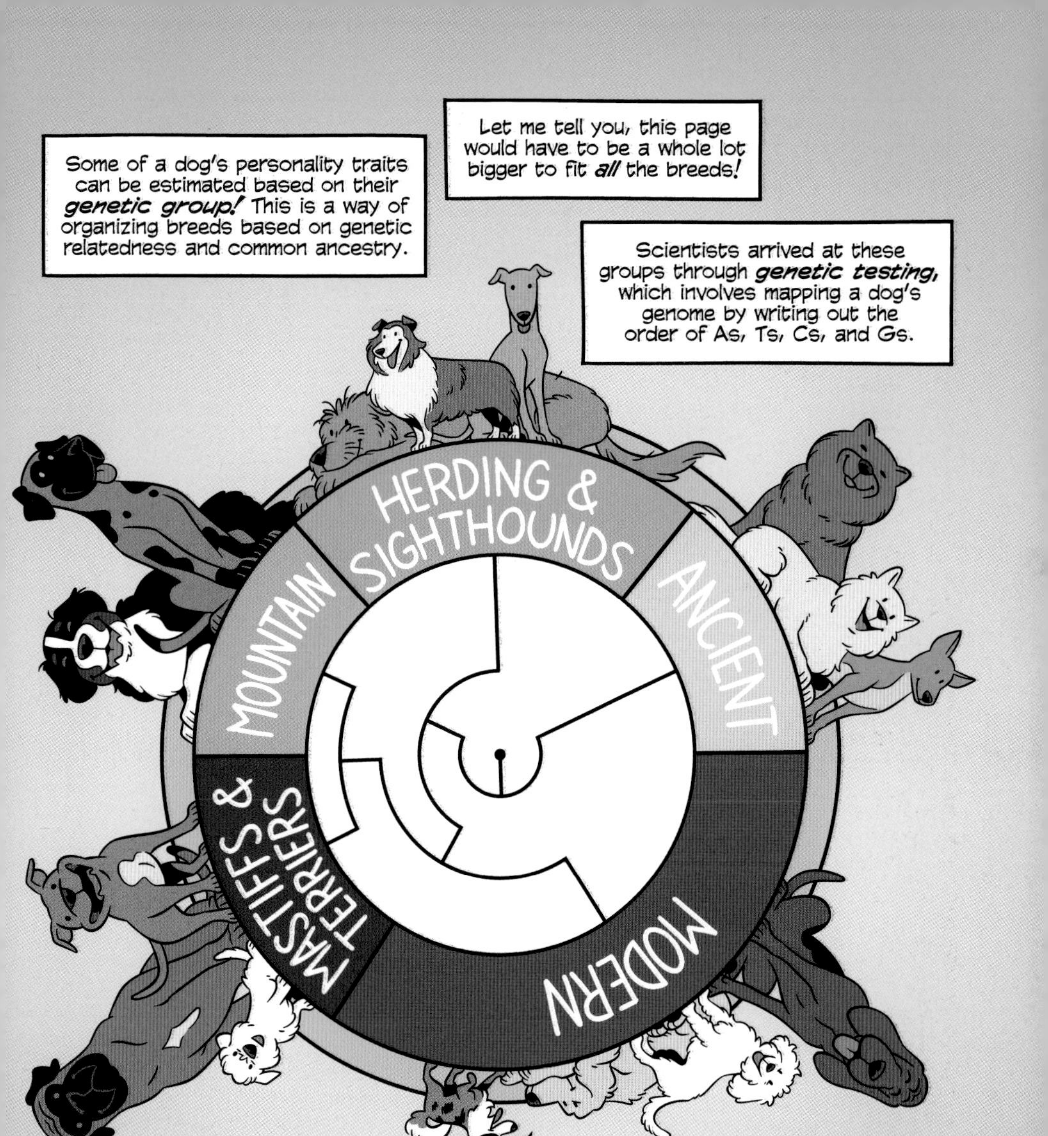

HERDING & SIGHTHOUNDS
ANCIENT
MODERN
MASTIFFS & TERRIERS
MOUNTAIN

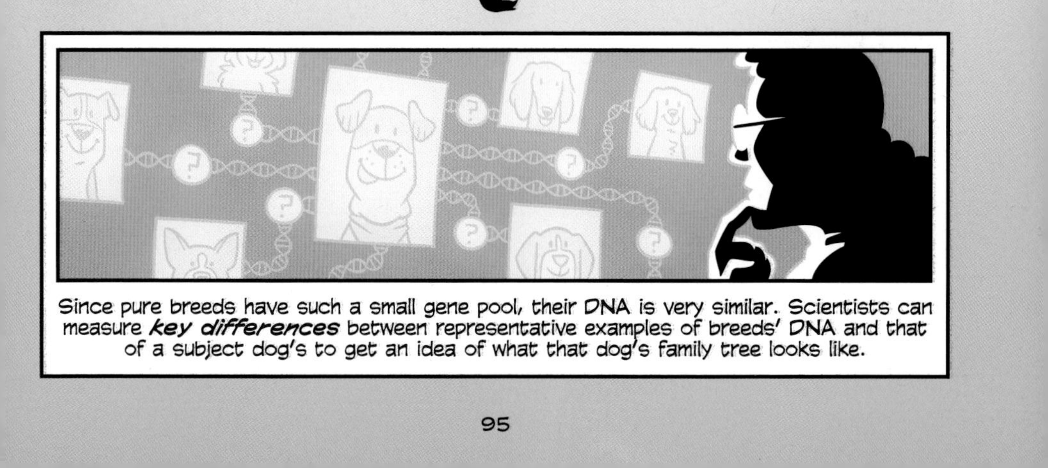

Since pure breeds have such a small gene pool, their DNA is very similar. Scientists can measure ***key differences*** between representative examples of breeds' DNA and that of a subject dog's to get an idea of what that dog's family tree looks like.

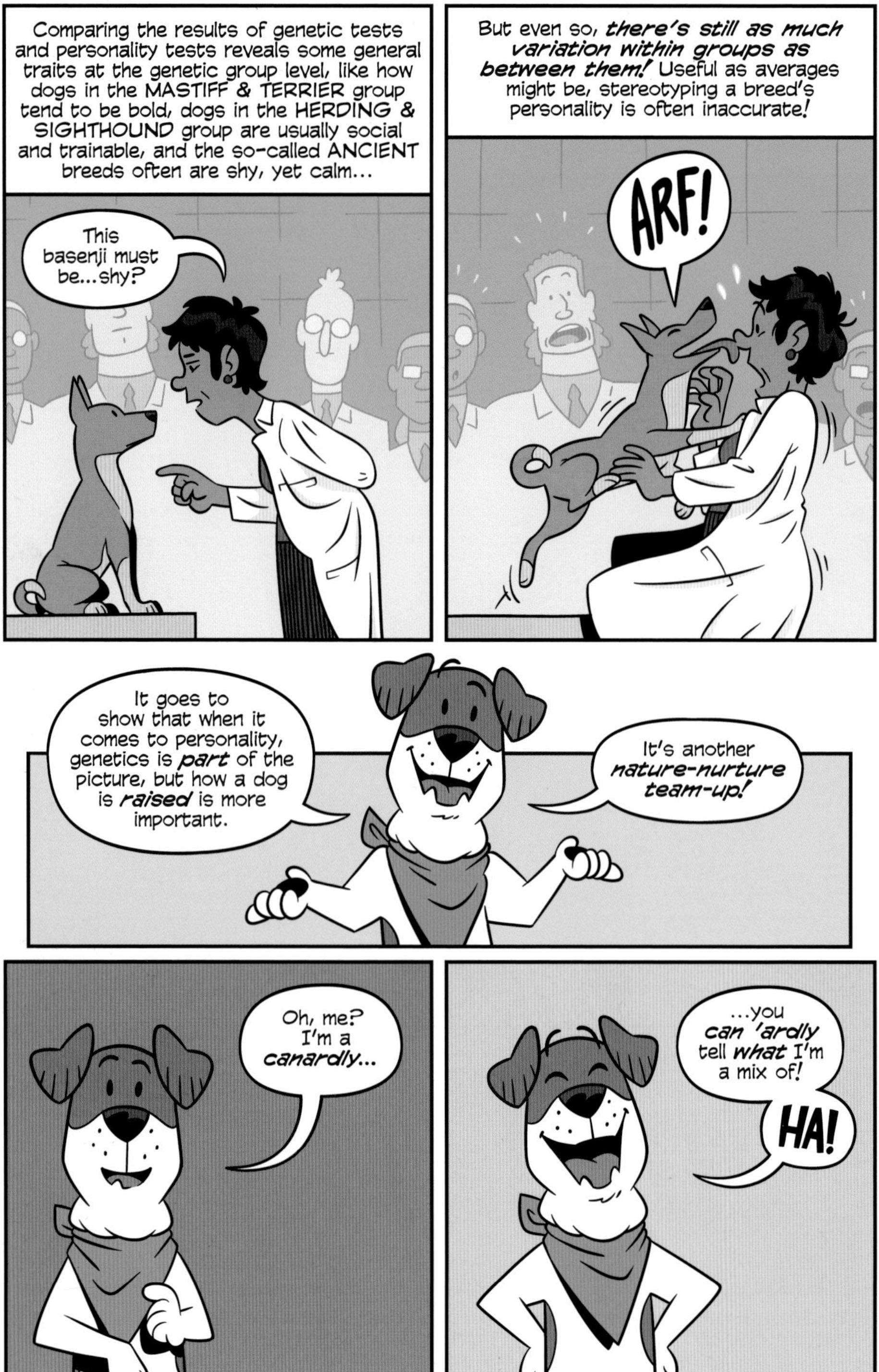
Comparing the results of genetic tests and personality tests reveals some general traits at the genetic group level, like how dogs in the MASTIFF & TERRIER group tend to be bold, dogs in the HERDING & SIGHTHOUND group are usually social and trainable, and the so-called ANCIENT breeds often are shy, yet calm...
This basenji must be...shy?
But even so, *there's still as much variation within groups as between them!* Useful as averages might be, stereotyping a breed's personality is often inaccurate!
ARF!
It goes to show that when it comes to personality, genetics is *part* of the picture, but how a dog is *raised* is more important.
It's another *nature-nurture team-up!*
Oh, me? I'm a *canardly*...
...you *can 'ardly* tell *what* I'm a mix of!
HA!

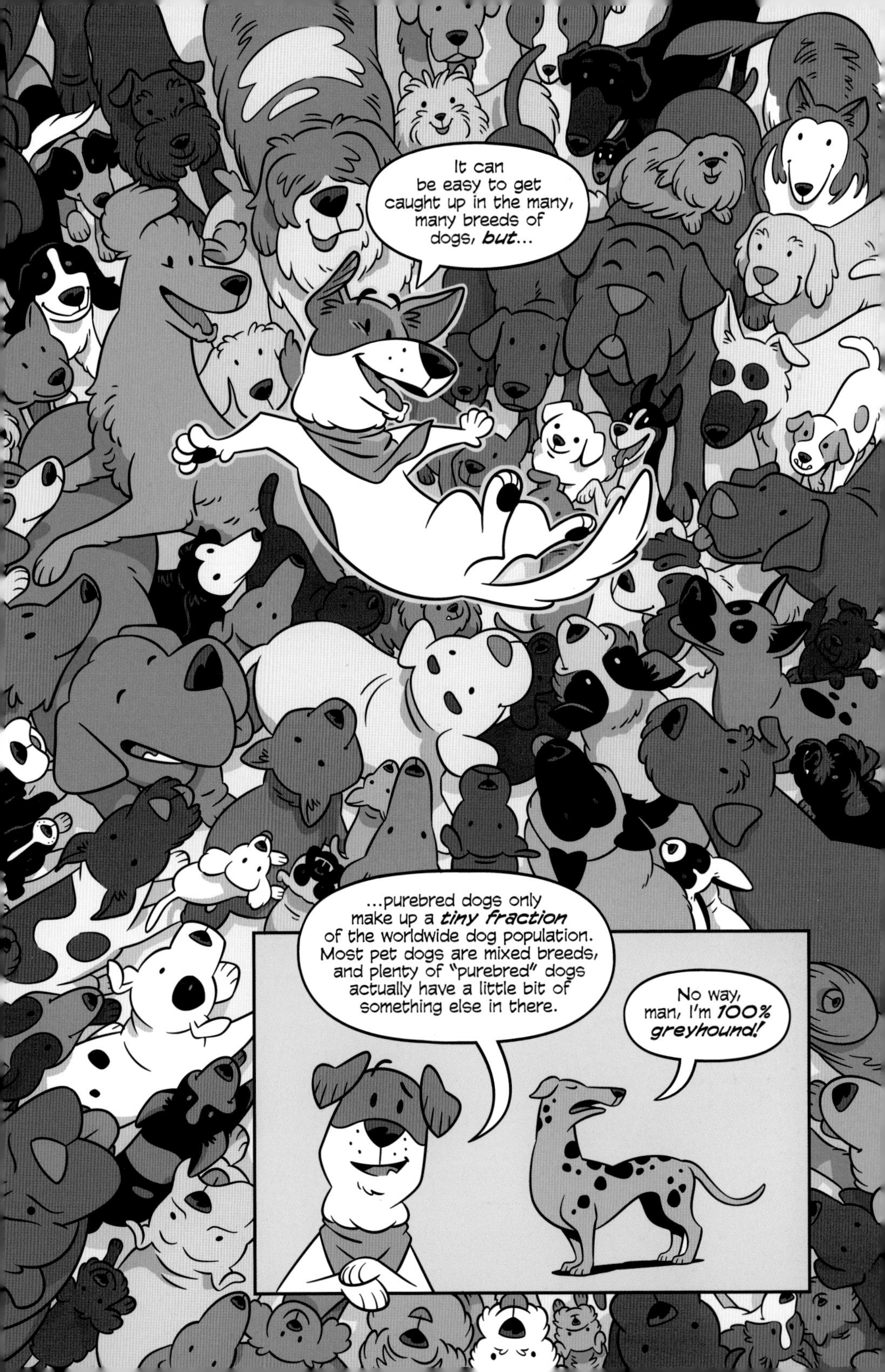
It can be easy to get caught up in the many, many breeds of dogs, *but*...
...purebred dogs only make up a *tiny fraction* of the worldwide dog population. Most pet dogs are mixed breeds, and plenty of "purebred" dogs actually have a little bit of something else in there.
No way, man, I'm *100% greyhound!*

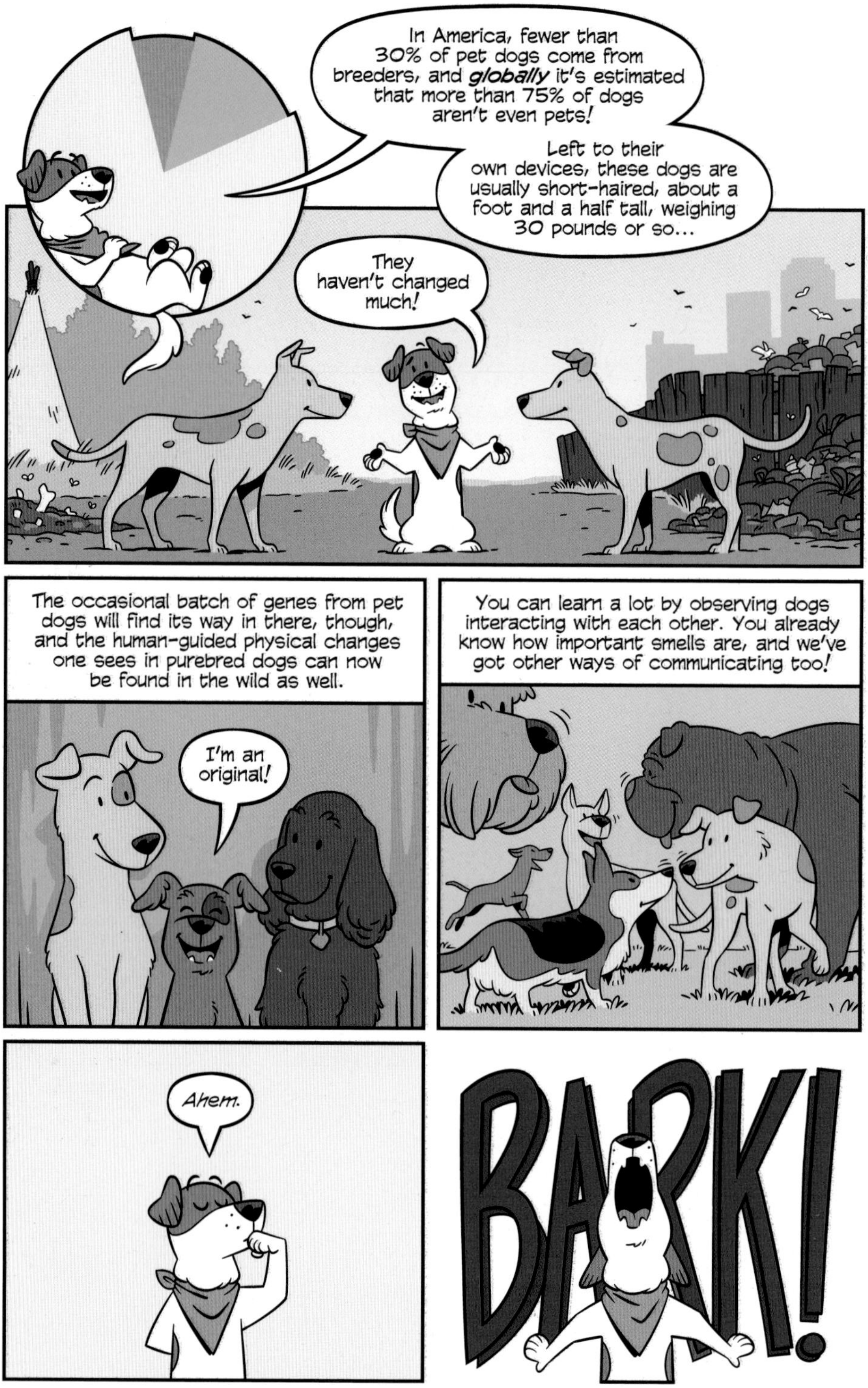

In America, fewer than 30% of pet dogs come from breeders, and *globally* it's estimated that more than 75% of dogs aren't even pets!
Left to their own devices, these dogs are usually short-haired, about a foot and a half tall, weighing 30 pounds or so...
They haven't changed much!
The occasional batch of genes from pet dogs will find its way in there, though, and the human-guided physical changes one sees in purebred dogs can now be found in the wild as well.
I'm an original!
You can learn a lot by observing dogs interacting with each other. You already know how important smells are, and we've got other ways of communicating too!
Ahem.
BARK!

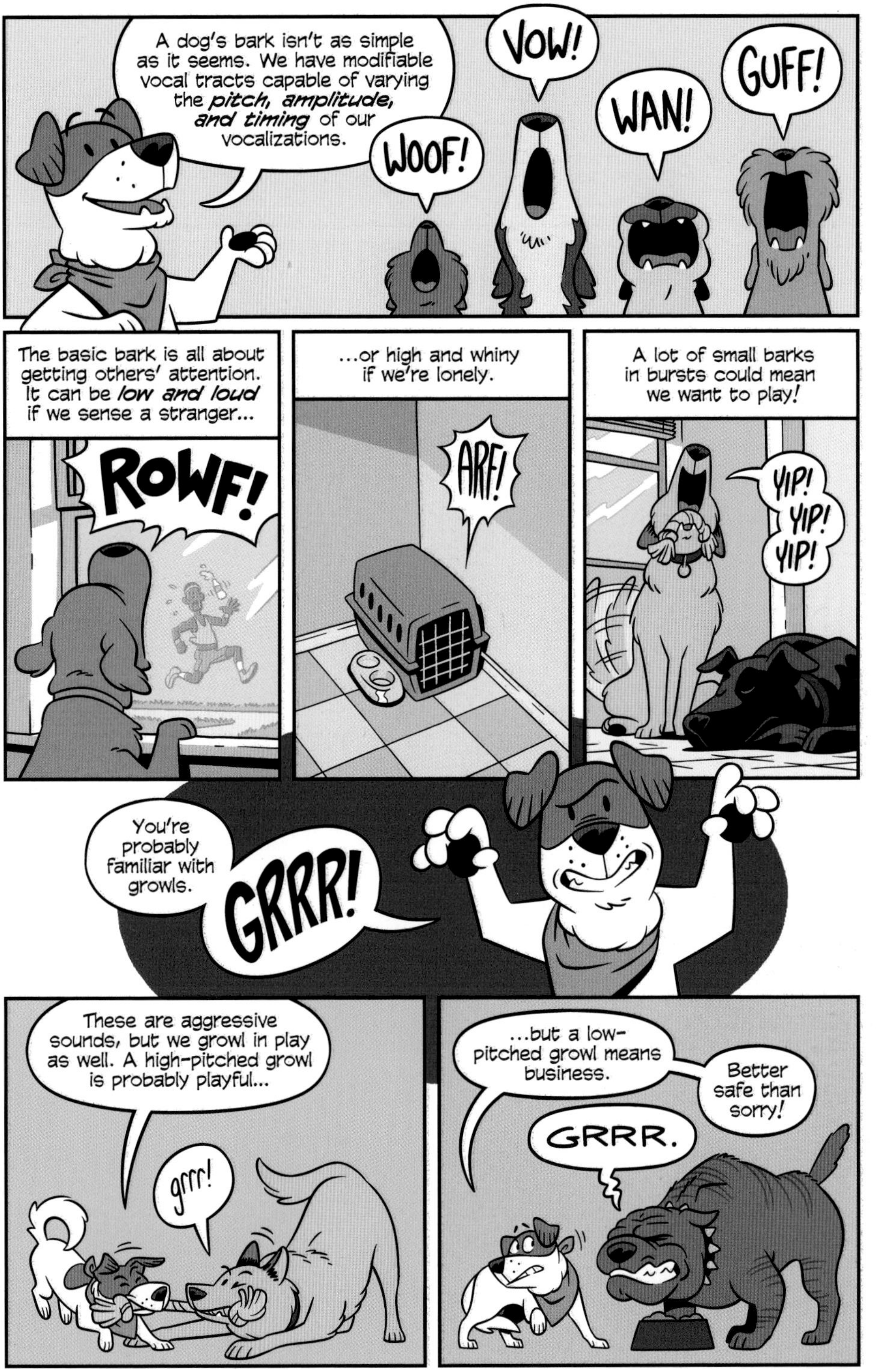
A dog's bark isn't as simple as it seems. We have modifiable vocal tracts capable of varying the *pitch, amplitude, and timing* of our vocalizations.
WOOF!
VOW!
WAN!
GUFF!
The basic bark is all about getting others' attention. It can be *low and loud* if we sense a stranger...
ROWF!
...or high and whiny if we're lonely.
ARF!
A lot of small barks in bursts could mean we want to play!
YIP! YIP! YIP!
You're probably familiar with growls.
GRRR!
These are aggressive sounds, but we growl in play as well. A high-pitched growl is probably playful...
grrr!
...but a low-pitched growl means business.
Better safe than sorry!
GRRR.

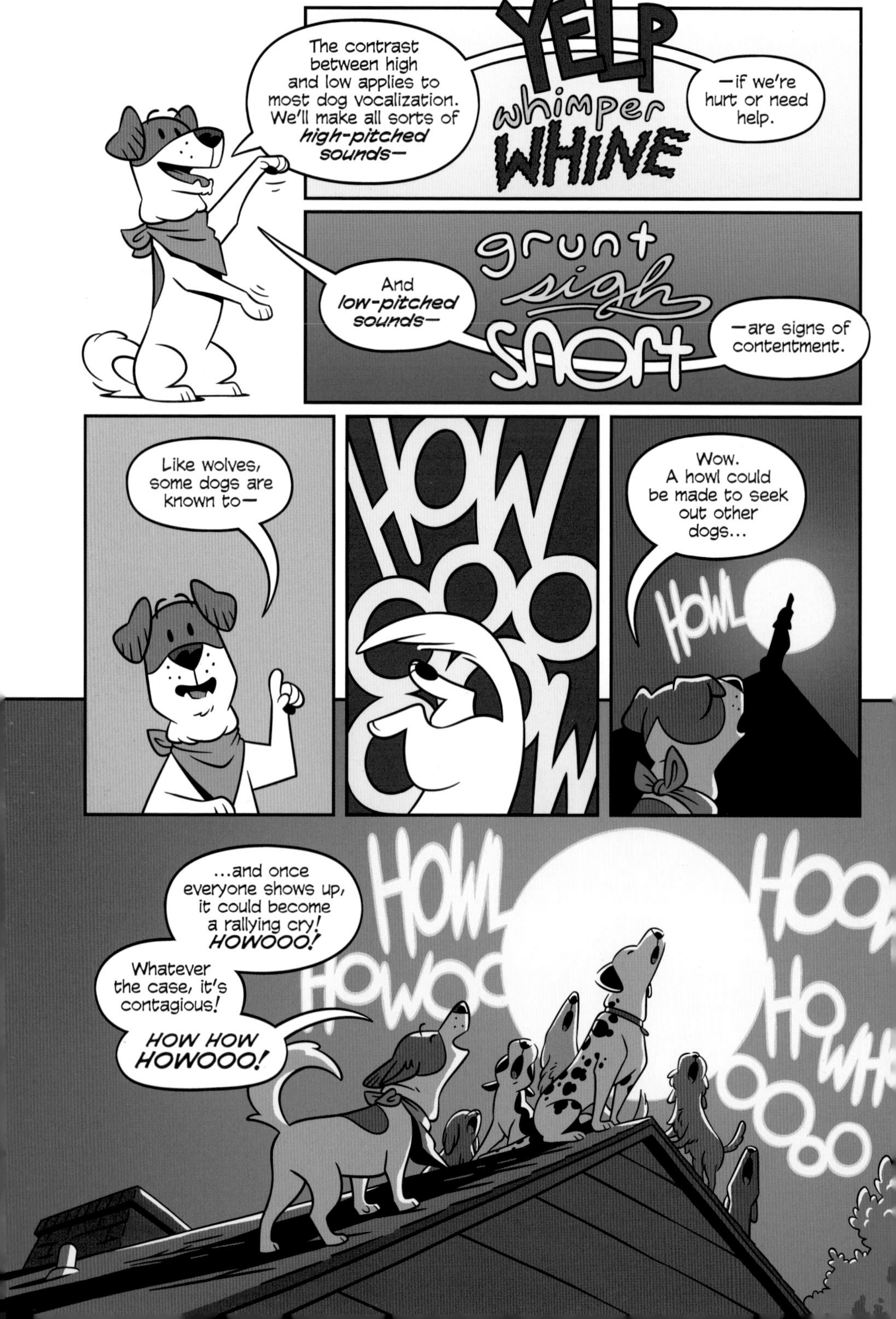

The contrast between high and low applies to most dog vocalization. We'll make all sorts of *high-pitched sounds*—
YELP
whimper
WHINE
—if we're hurt or need help.
And *low-pitched sounds*—
grunt
sigh
snort
—are signs of contentment.
Like wolves, some dogs are known to—
HOWOOOOW
Wow. A howl could be made to seek out other dogs...
HOWL
...and once everyone shows up, it could become a rallying cry! ***HOWOOO!***
HOWL
HOWOO
Whatever the case, it's contagious!
HOW HOW HOWOOO!
HOO
HO
HOWHOOOOO

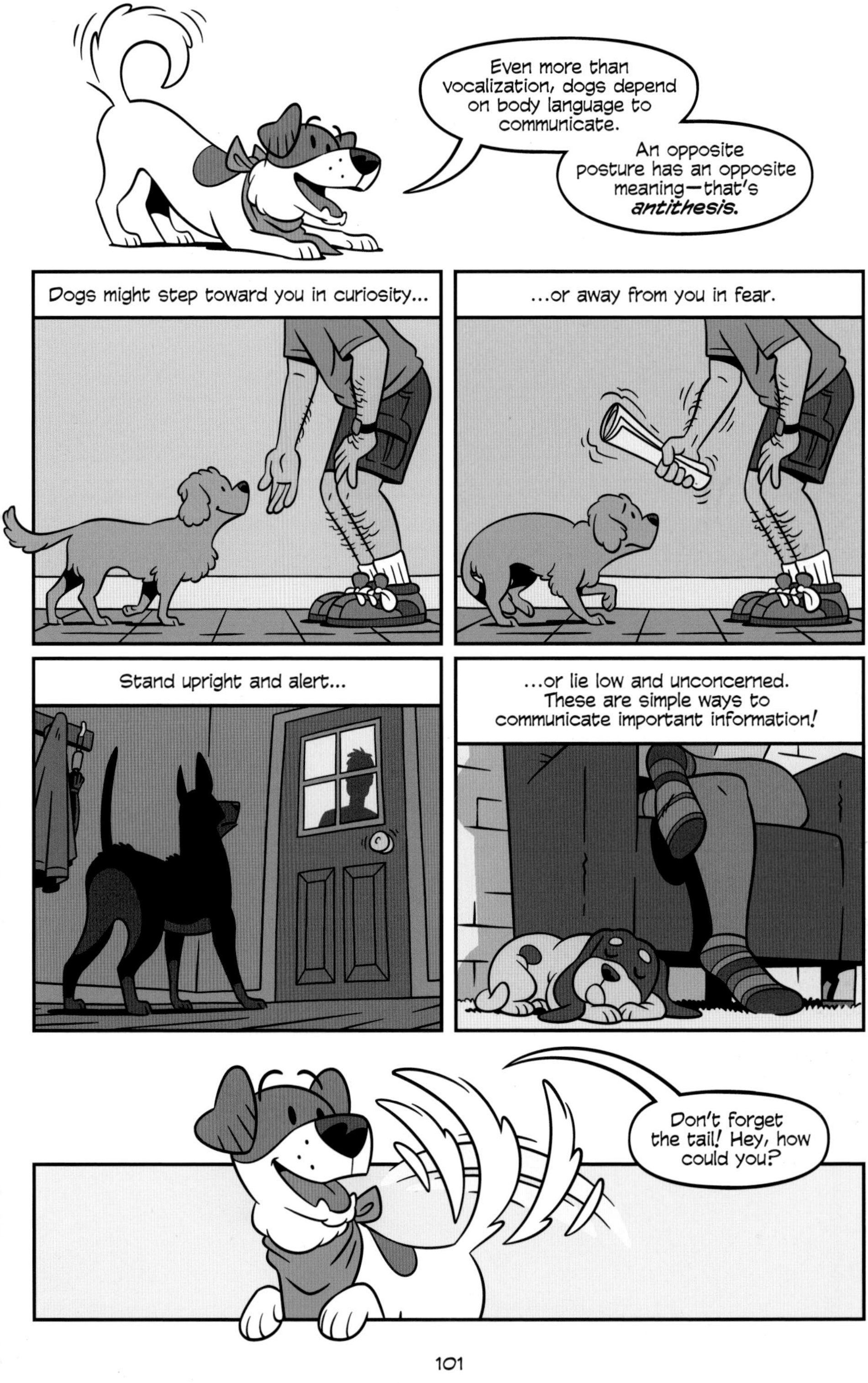
Even more than vocalization, dogs depend on body language to communicate.
An opposite posture has an opposite meaning—that's *antithesis.*
Dogs might step toward you in curiosity...
...or away from you in fear.
Stand upright and alert...
...or lie low and unconcerned. These are simple ways to communicate important information!
Don't forget the tail! Hey, how could you?

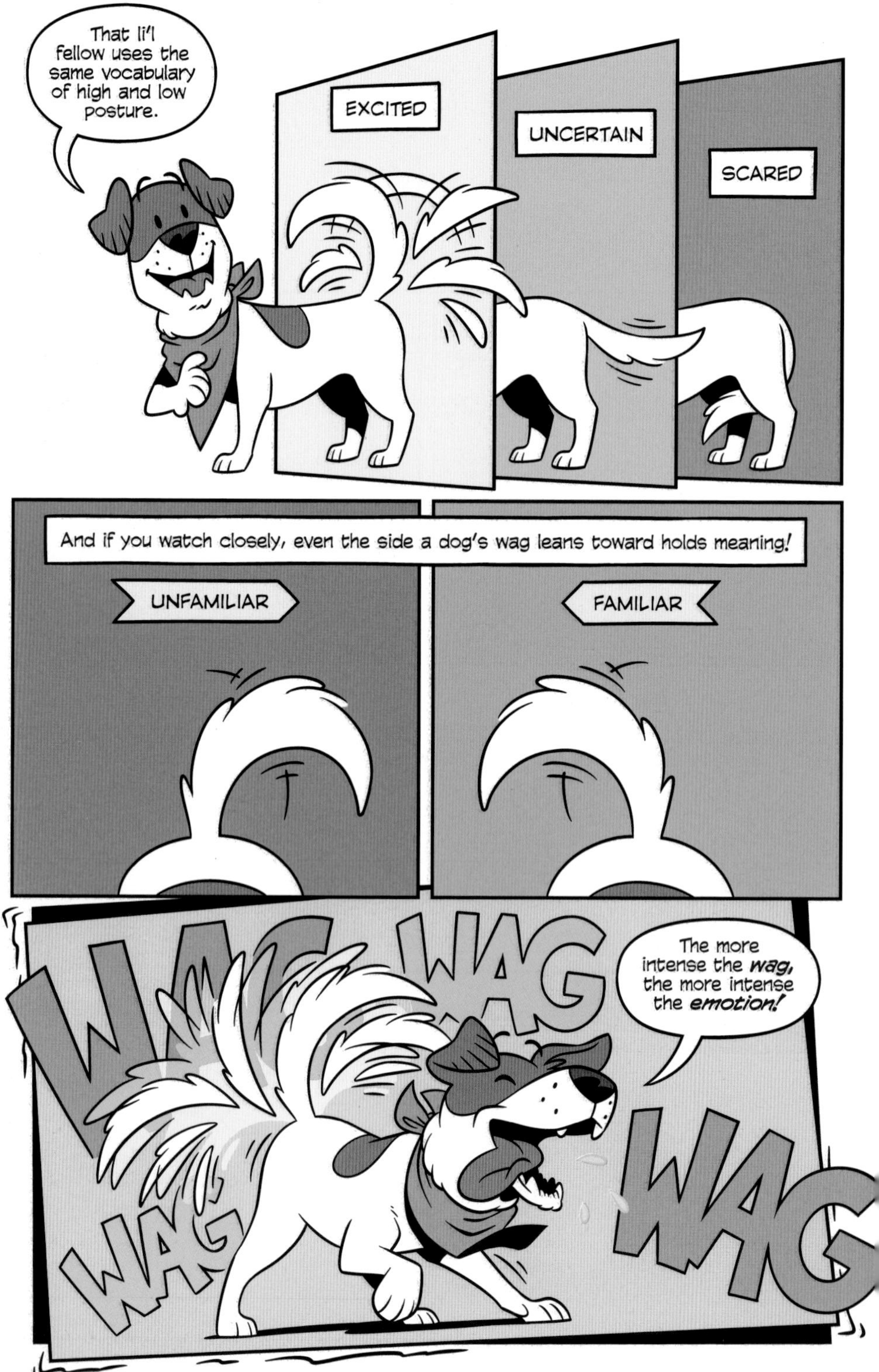
That li'l fellow uses the same vocabulary of high and low posture.
EXCITED
UNCERTAIN
SCARED
And if you watch closely, even the side a dog's wag leans toward holds meaning!
UNFAMILIAR
FAMILIAR
WAG
WAG
The more intense the *wag*, the more intense the *emotion!*
WAG
WAG

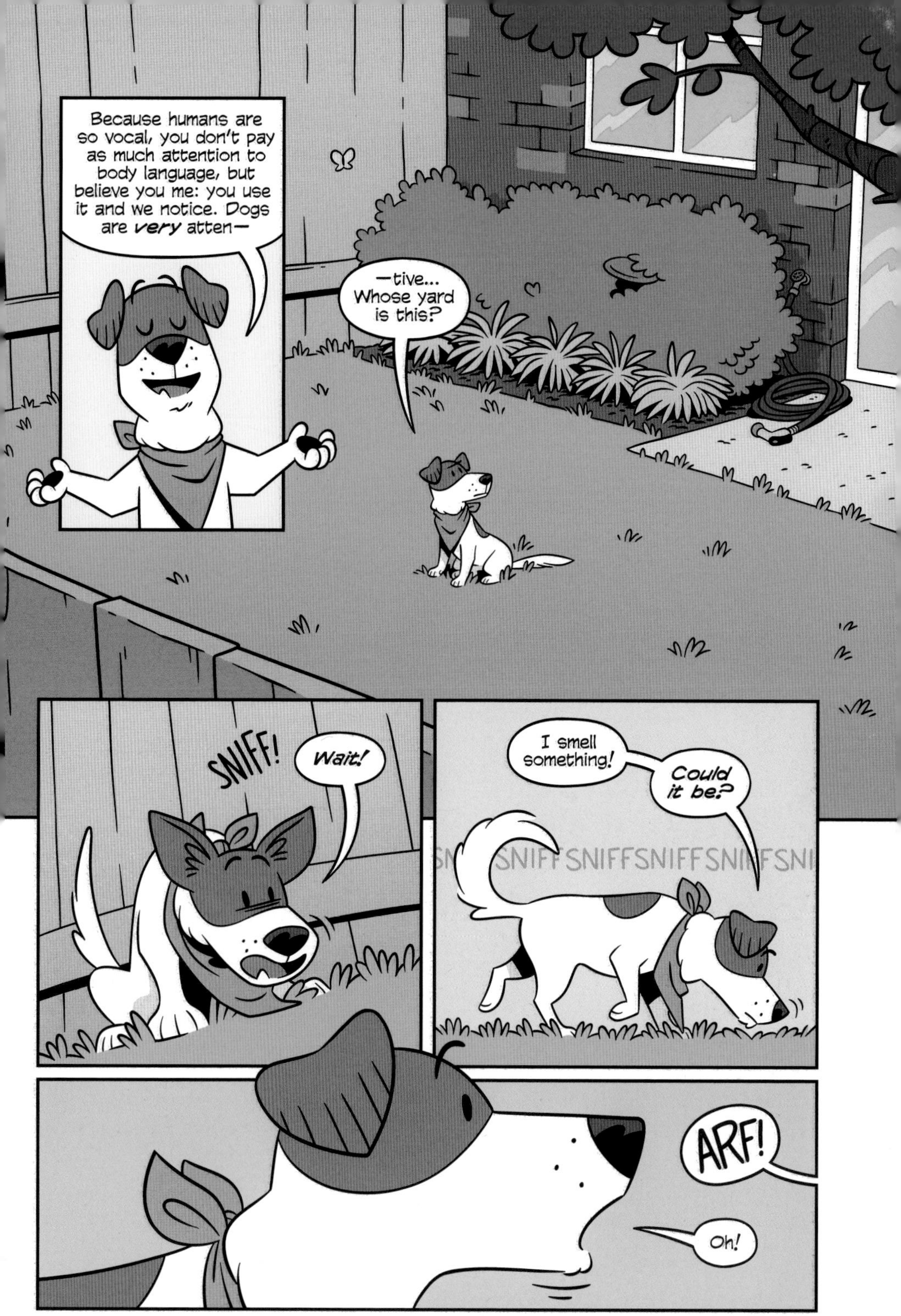
Because humans are so vocal, you don't pay as much attention to body language, but believe you me: you use it and we notice. Dogs are *very* atten—
—tive... Whose yard is this?
SNIFF!
Wait!
I smell something!
Could it be?
SNIFFSNIFFSNIFFSNIFFSNIFFSNI
ARF!
Oh!

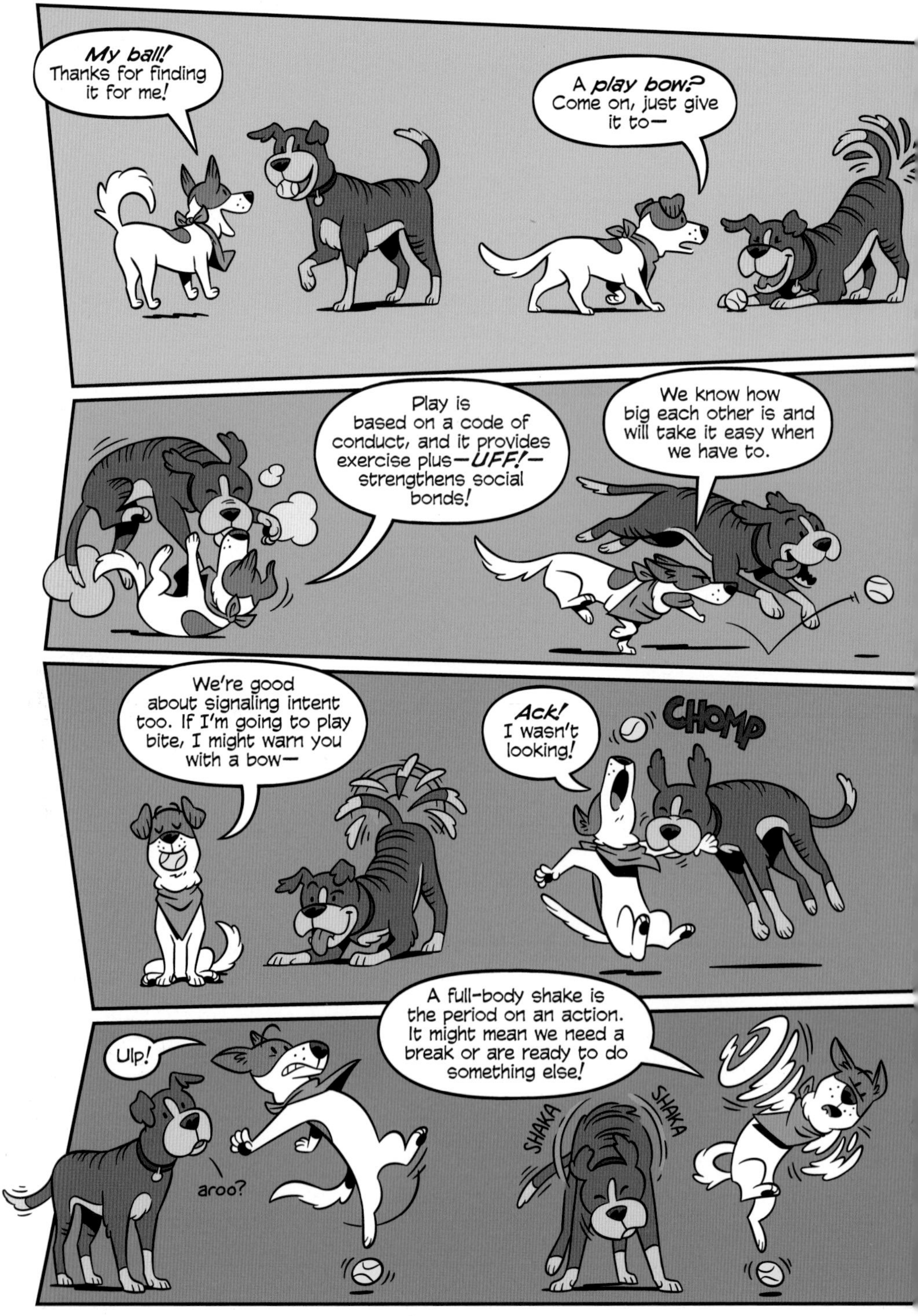
My ball! Thanks for finding it for me!
A play bow? Come on, just give it to—
Play is based on a code of conduct, and it provides exercise plus—UFF!—strengthens social bonds!
We know how big each other is and will take it easy when we have to.
We're good about signaling intent too. If I'm going to play bite, I might warn you with a bow—
Ack! I wasn't looking!
CHOMP
Ulp!
aroo?
A full-body shake is the period on an action. It might mean we need a break or are ready to do something else!
SHAKA
SHAKA

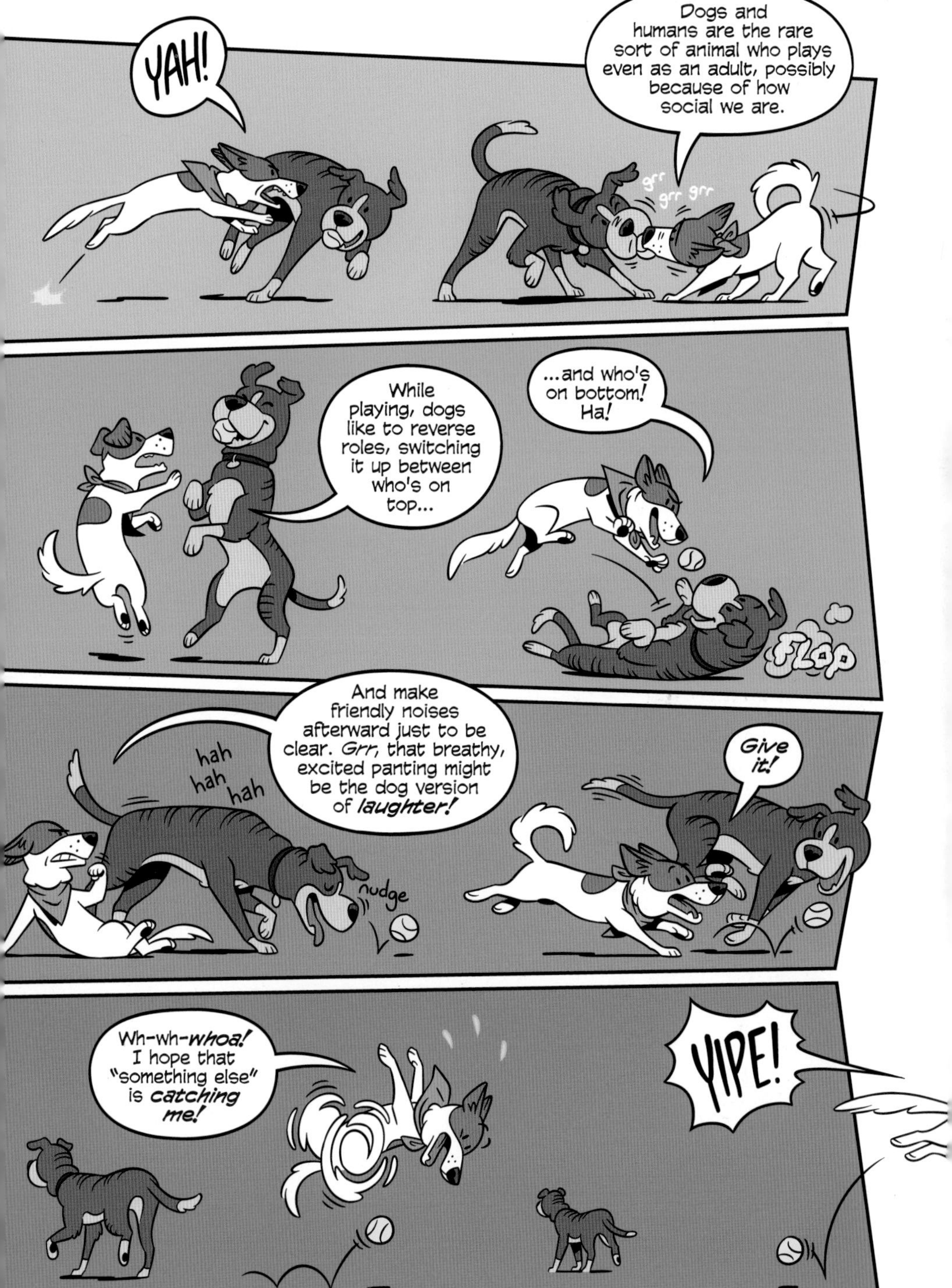
YAH!
Dogs and humans are the rare sort of animal who plays even as an adult, possibly because of how social we are.
grr grr grr
While playing, dogs like to reverse roles, switching it up between who's on top...
...and who's on bottom! Ha!
FLOP
And make friendly noises afterward just to be clear. Grrr, that breathy, excited panting might be the dog version of *laughter!*
hah hah hah
nudge
Give it!
Wh-wh-*whoa!* I hope that "something else" is *catching me!*
YIPE!

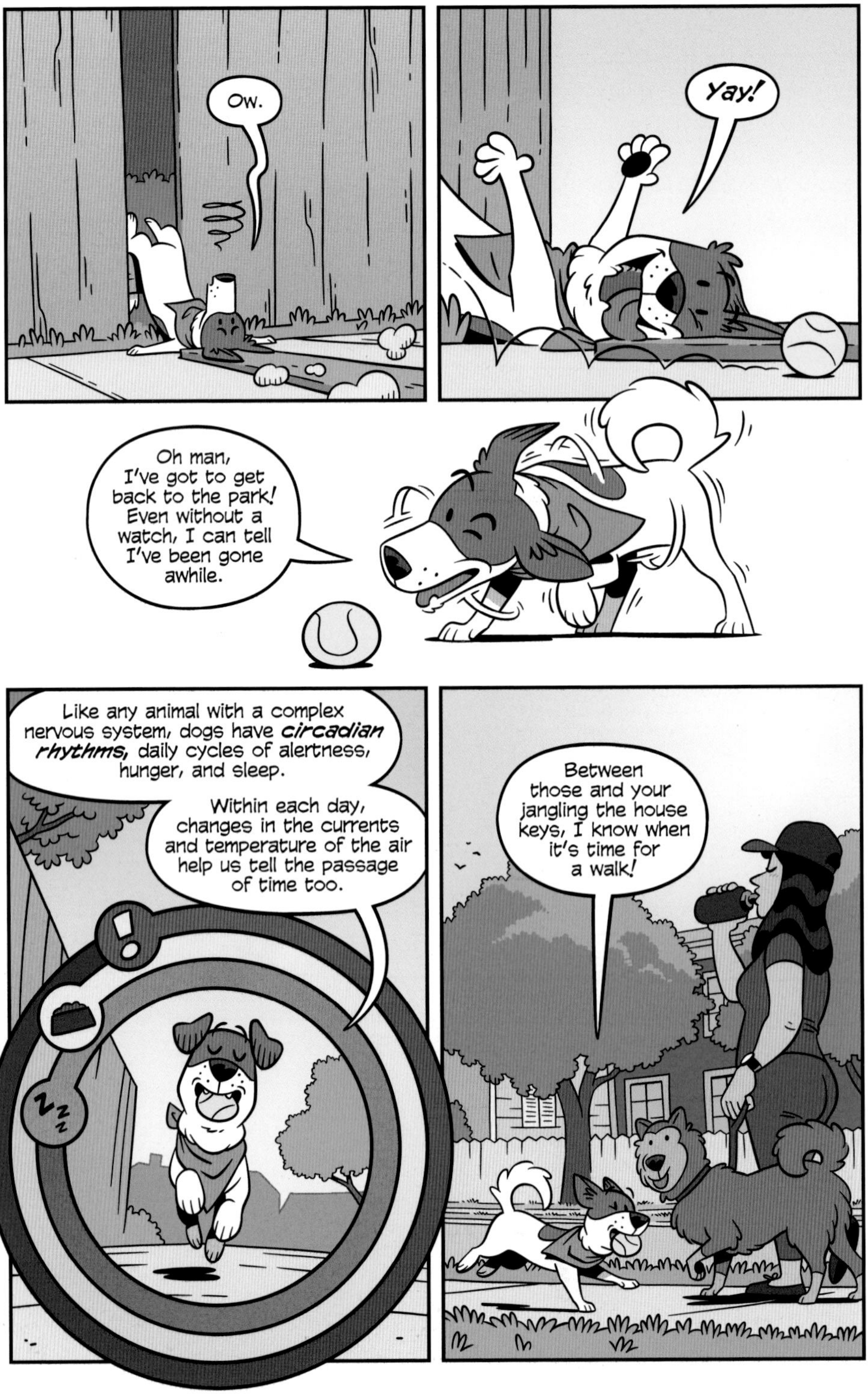
Ow.
Yay!
Oh man, I've got to get back to the park! Even without a watch, I can tell I've been gone awhile.
Like any animal with a complex nervous system, dogs have ***circadian rhythms,*** daily cycles of alertness, hunger, and sleep.
Within each day, changes in the currents and temperature of the air help us tell the passage of time too.
Between those and your jangling the house keys, I know when it's time for a walk!

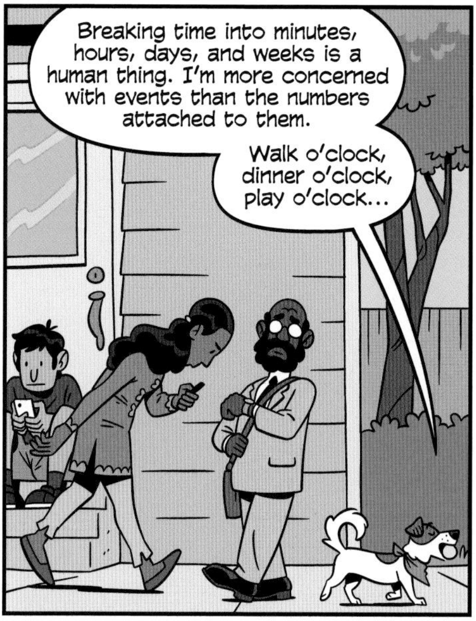
Breaking time into minutes, hours, days, and weeks is a human thing. I'm more concerned with events than the numbers attached to them.
Walk o'clock, dinner o'clock, play o'clock...

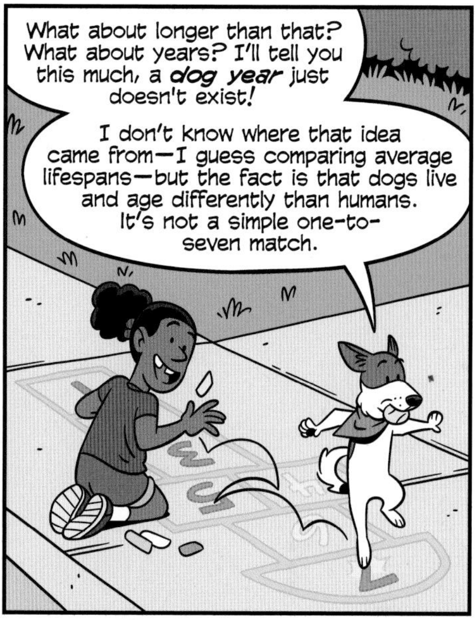
What about longer than that? What about years? I'll tell you this much, a **dog year** just doesn't exist!
I don't know where that idea came from—I guess comparing average lifespans—but the fact is that dogs live and age differently than humans. It's not a simple one-to-seven match.

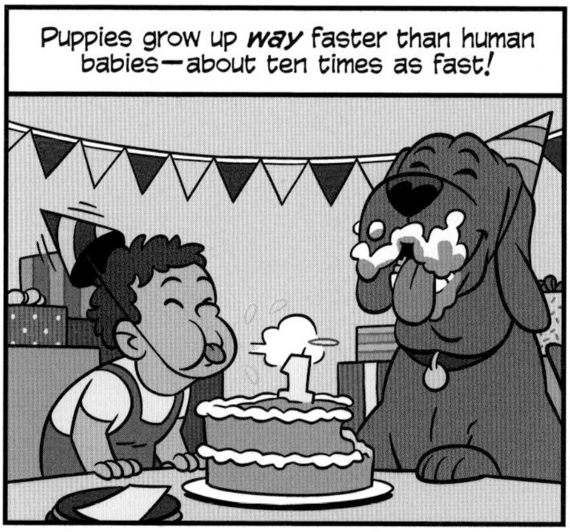
Puppies grow up ***way*** faster than human babies—about ten times as fast!

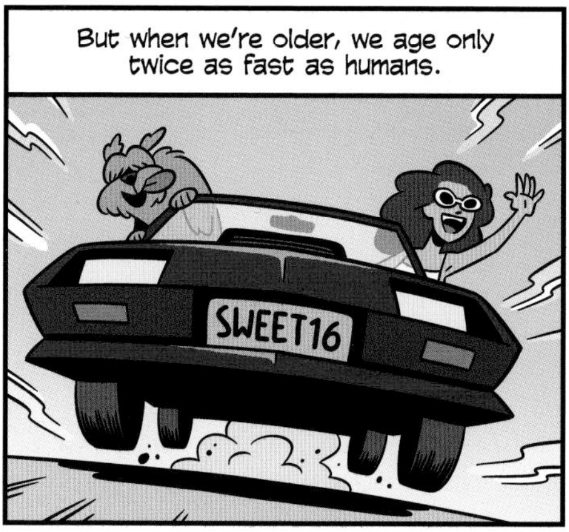
But when we're older, we age only twice as fast as humans.
SWEET16

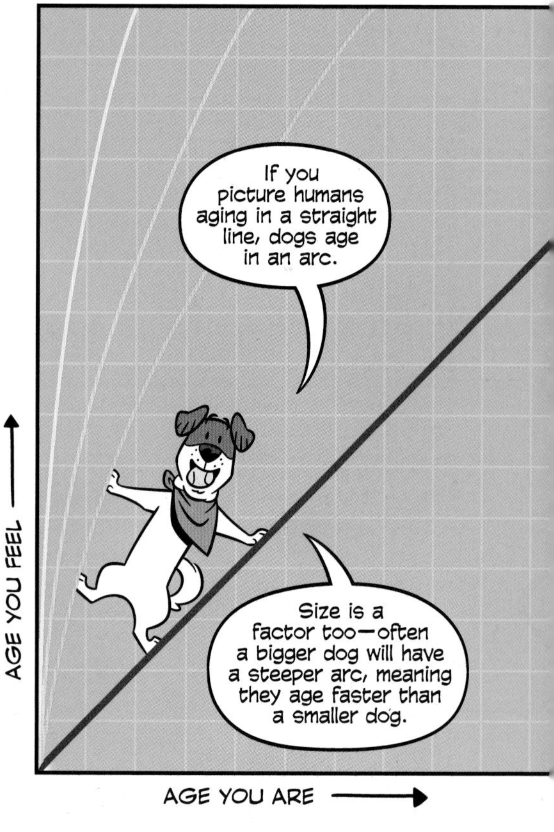
If you picture humans aging in a straight line, dogs age in an arc.
Size is a factor too—often a bigger dog will have a steeper arc, meaning they age faster than a smaller dog.
AGE YOU FEEL
AGE YOU ARE

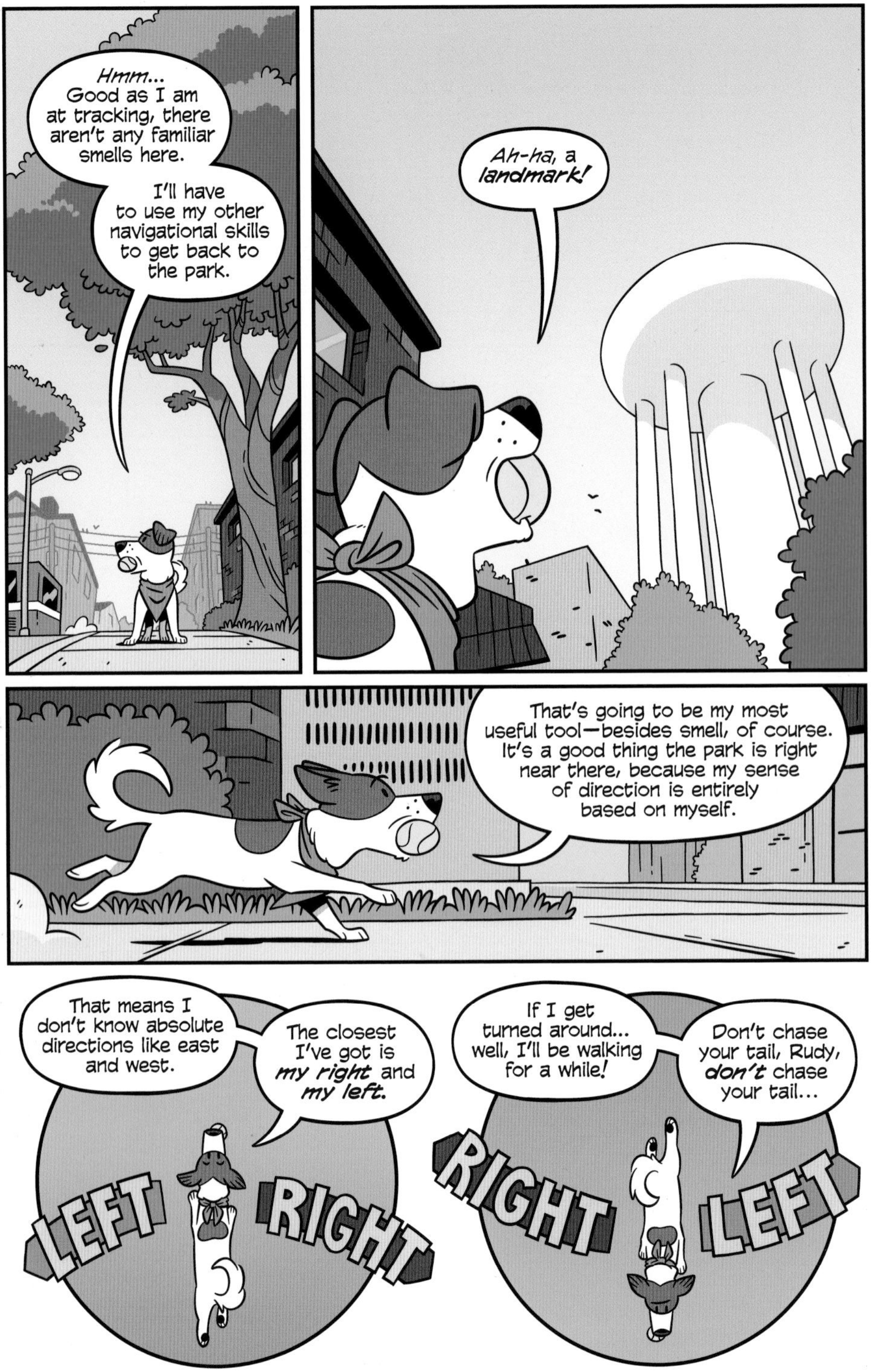

Hmmm... Good as I am at tracking, there aren't any familiar smells here.
I'll have to use my other navigational skills to get back to the park.
Ah-ha, a landmark!
That's going to be my most useful tool—besides smell, of course. It's a good thing the park is right near there, because my sense of direction is entirely based on myself.
That means I don't know absolute directions like east and west.
The closest I've got is my right and my left.
LEFT
RIGHT
If I get turned around... well, I'll be walking for a while!
Don't chase your tail, Rudy, don't chase your tail...
RIGHT
LEFT

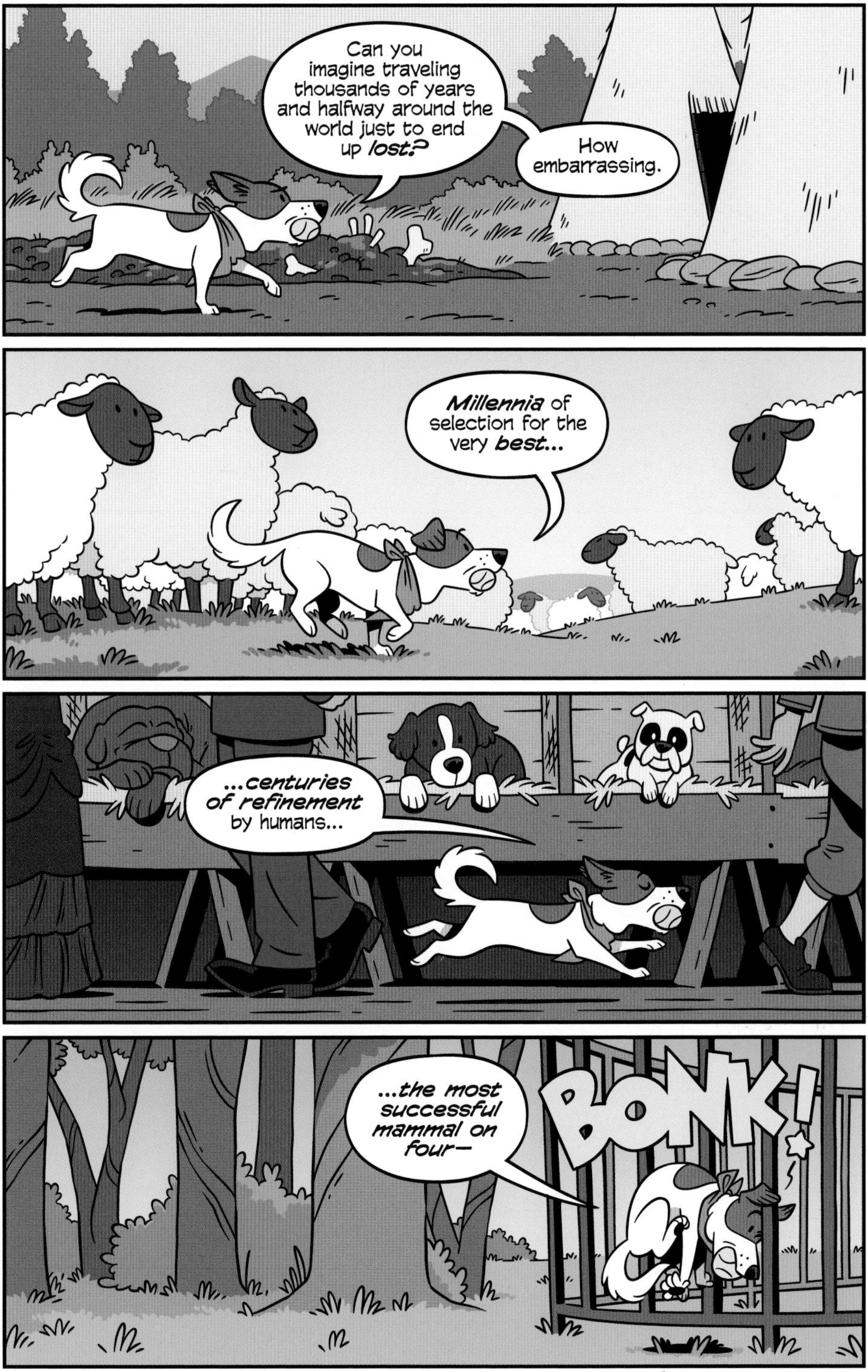
Can you imagine traveling thousands of years and halfway around the world just to end up *lost?*
How embarrassing.
Millennia of selection for the very *best...*
...centuries of refinement by humans...
...the most successful mammal on four—
BONK!

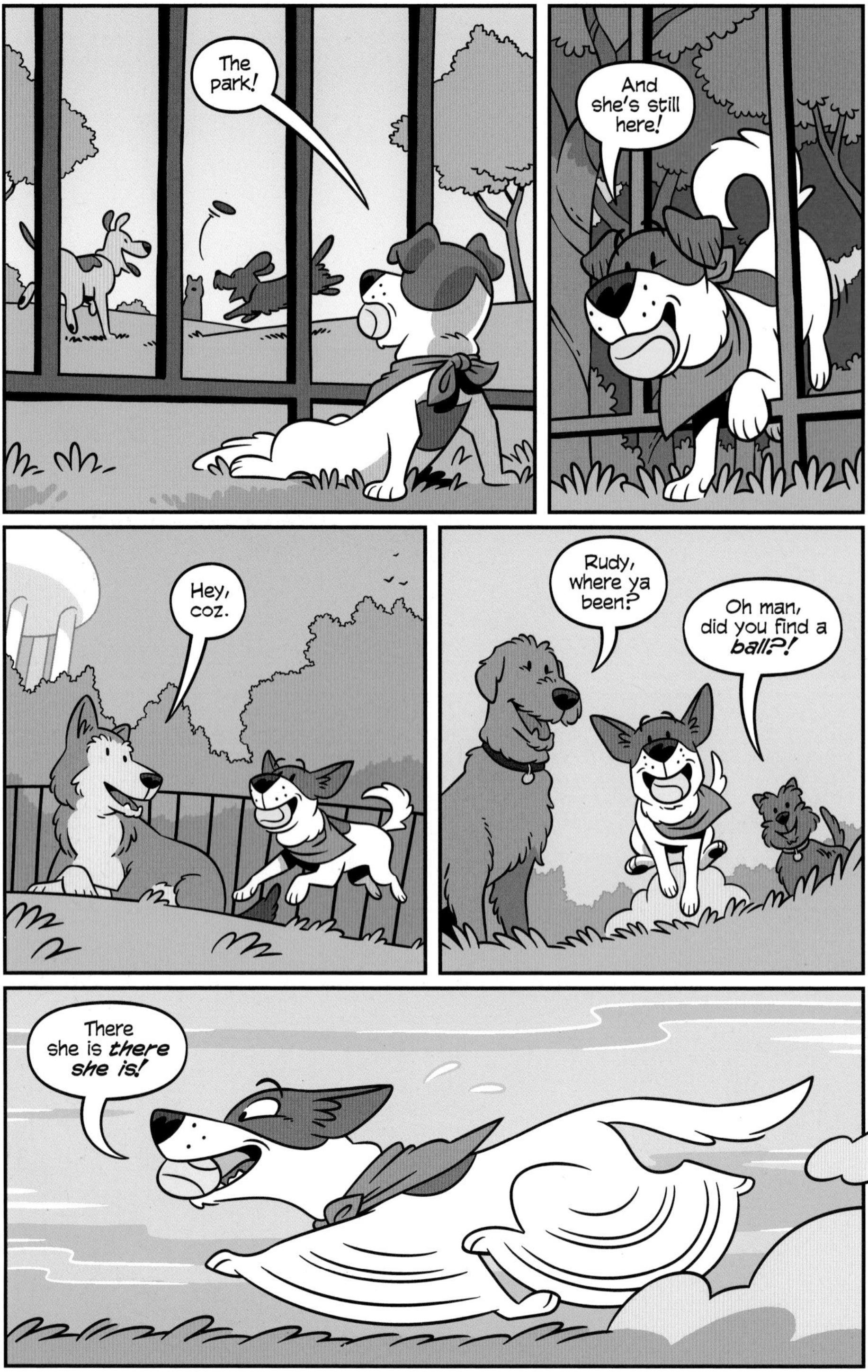
The park!
And she's still here!
Hey, coz.
Rudy, where ya been?
Oh man, did you find a ***ball?!***
There she is ***there she is!***

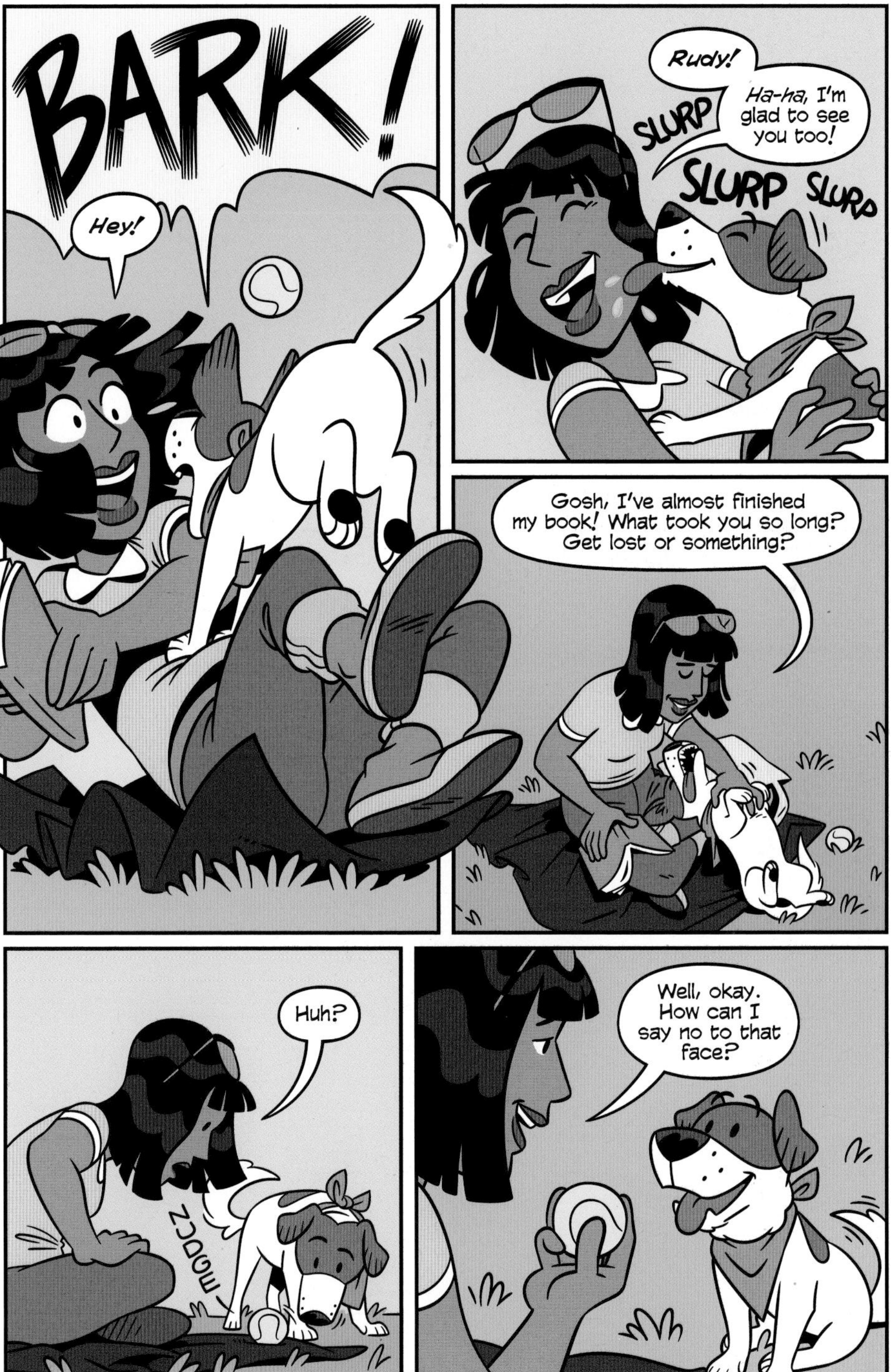
BARK!
Hey!
Rudy!
SLURP
Ha-ha, I'm glad to see you too!
SLURP
SLURP
Gosh, I've almost finished my book! What took you so long? Get lost or something?
Huh?
NUDGE
Well, okay. How can I say no to that face?

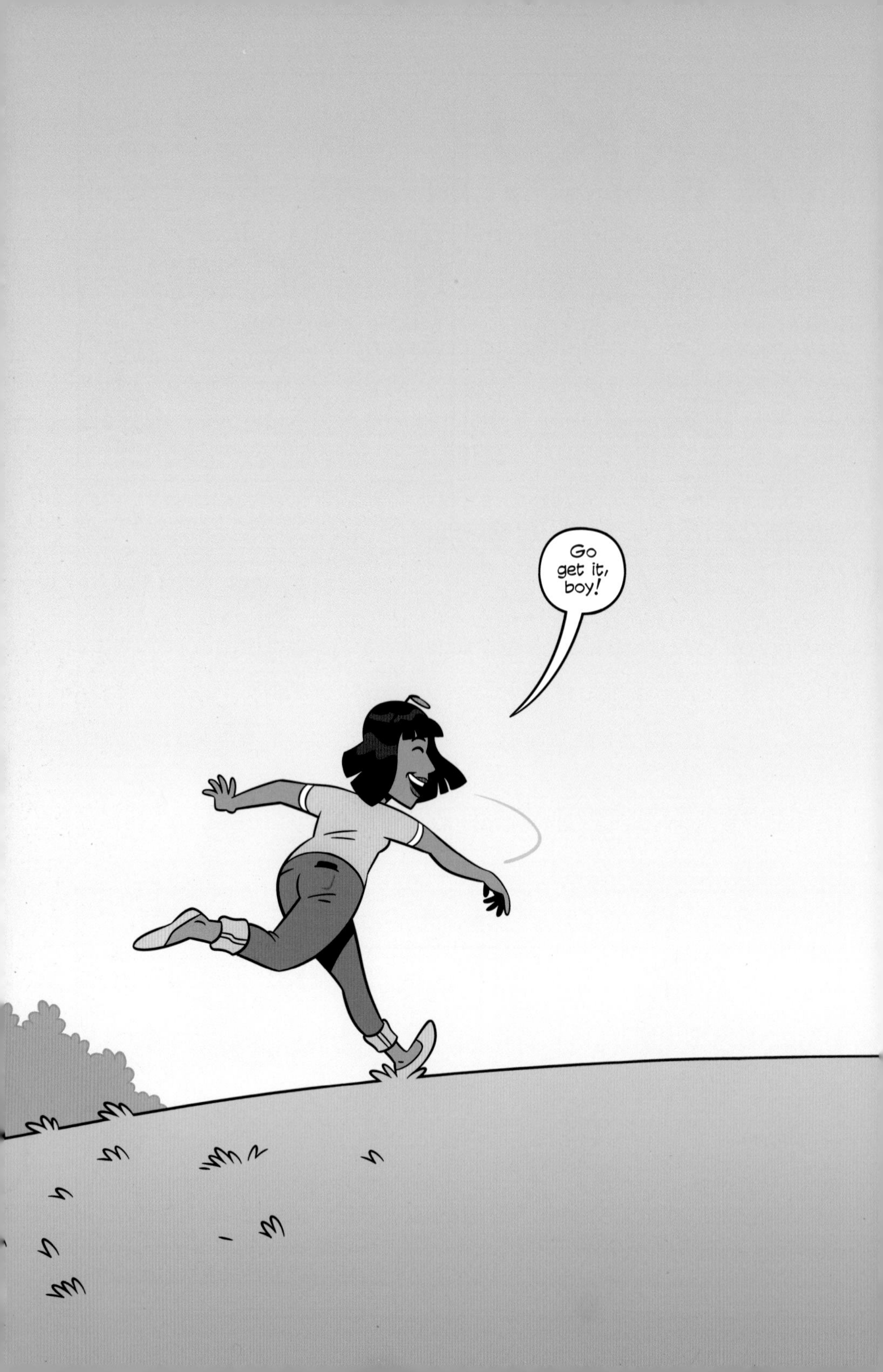
Go get it, boy!

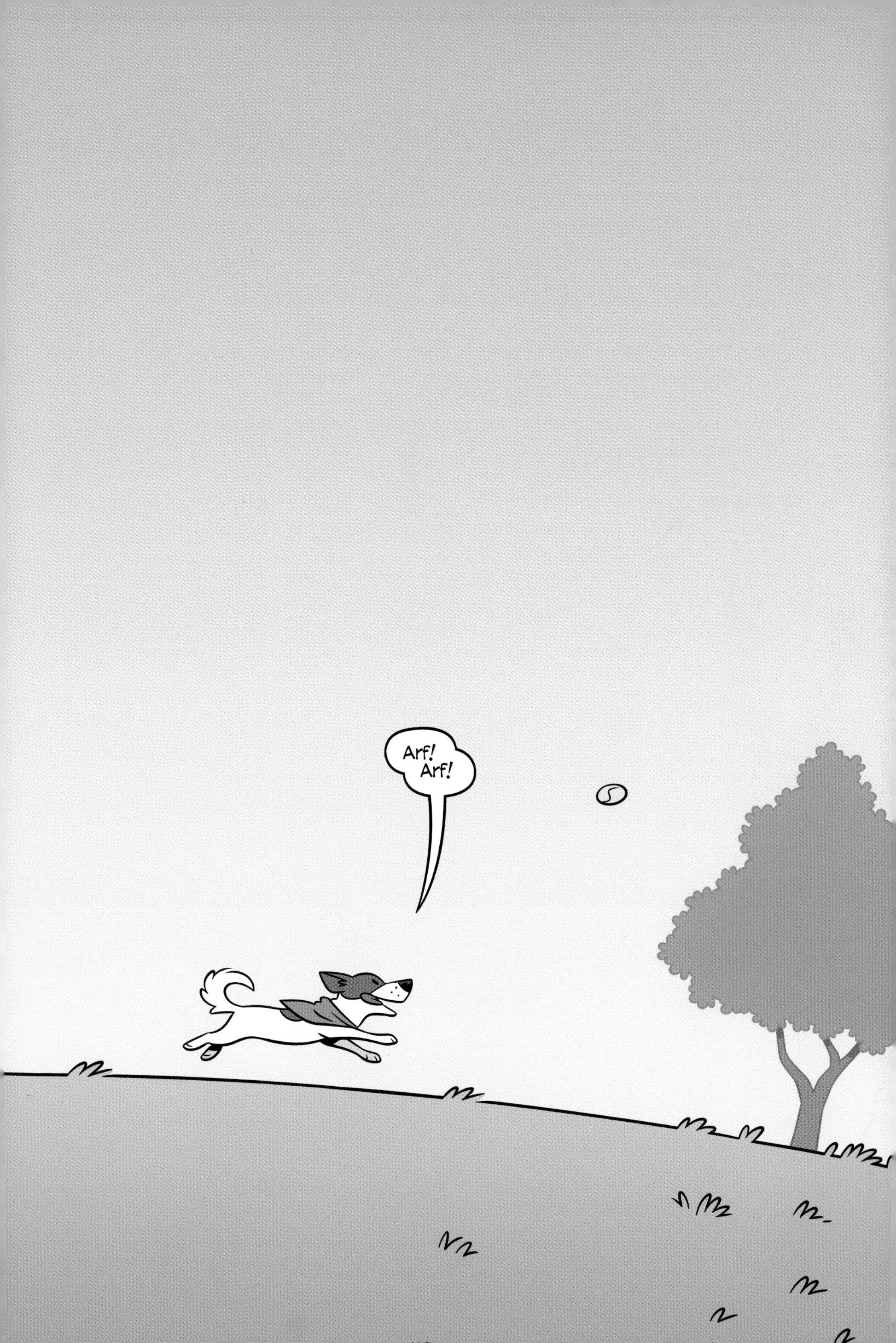
Arf!
Arf!

—GLOSSARY—

Adaptation

> A functional trait evolved by natural selection. Adaptations make an animal more fit for its environment.

Allele

> A version of a gene. There are two alleles, one from each parent, at each location in the genome.
>> *Completely dominant:* A pair of alleles in which only the dominant allele is expressed, and the recessive allele is completely masked.
>> *Codominant:* A pair of alleles in which both are expressed.
>> *Incompletely dominant:* A pair of alleles that produces a blend or intermediate of both.

Antithesis

> In behavior, the idea that opposite postures and sounds communicate opposite information.

Breed

> A distinct type of dog, selected for by people, that is different from any other in measurable ways. Members of the breed are expected to look and act a certain way, according to the written description given by the "breed standard" document.

Canine

> Any member of the genus *Canis*. Dogs, wolves, coyotes, and jackals are all canines.

Chromosome

> A strand of DNA inherited from an organism's parents. They are arranged in pairs, of which dogs have 39.

DNA

A complex molecule made up of adenine, thymine, guanine, and cytosine. DNA is the recipe for an organism and determines how it will develop and function.

Domestication

The process of adapting a species to a human environment.

Evolution

Changes in a species's traits over time, allowing the members of the species to adapt to and diversify within their environment.

Artificial selection: The process by which only organisms displaying traits selected for by humans are allowed to reproduce.

Natural selection: The process by which organisms most fit to their environment survive, thrive, and reproduce at rates higher than those less fit.

Fossil

The preserved remains or traces of organisms from long ago.

Gamete

A cell containing half of the genetic information for an organism. During reproduction, two gametes combine to create a new offspring cell.

Gene

A section of DNA with instructions for one piece of an organism. Genes are the basic units of heredity.

Genotype

The genetic makeup of an organism, it can contain code for traits that are not displayed.

—GLOSSARY CONTINUED—

Genotype

The genetic makeup of an organism; it contains codes for traits both displayed (phenotype) and not displayed.

Heterozygous

A gene with a non-matching pair of alleles.

Homozygous

A gene with a matching pair of alleles.

Inheritance

The process of passing on genes from one generation to the next.

Meiosis

Cell division for reproduction, this process results in gametes.

Phenotype

The observable form of an organism, including both appearance and behavior.

Pure breed

A breed of dog that has reproduced only within its breed for generations.

Species

Traditionally, a group of populations capable of successfully interbreeding with one another and producing offspring that are also fertile.

Taxonomy

The practice of naming and classification.

Vomeronasal organ

A pheromone-detecting secondary sense organ located above the roof of the mouth and deep in a dog's snout.

—FURTHER READING—

BOOKS

Coppinger, Raymond, Lee Spector, and Lynn Miller. "What, if anything, is a Wolf?" *The World of Wolves: New Perspectives on Ecology, Behaviour and Management,* edited by M. Musiani, L. Boitani, and P. Paquet. University of Calgary Press, 2009.

Coppinger, Raymond and Lorna. *Dogs: A Startling New Understanding of Canine Origin, Behavior & Evolution.* Scribner, 2001.

Francis, Richard C. *Domesticated: Evolution in a Man-Made World.* Norton, 2015.

Hare, Brian, and Vanessa Woods. *The Genius of Dogs: How Dogs Are Smarter Than You Think.* Dutton, 2013.

Horowitz, Alexandra. *Inside of a Dog: What Dogs See, Smell, and Know.* Scribner, 2009.

McConnell, Patricia B. *The Other End of the Leash: Why We Do What We Do Around Dogs.* Ballantine Books, 2002.

Miklósi, Ádám. *Dog Behaviour, Evolution, and Cognition.* Oxford University Press, 2009.

Morris, Desmond. *Dogs: The Ultimate Dictionary of Over 1,000 Breeds.* Trafalgar Square, 2001.

Serpell, James A., and Deborah L. Duffy. "Dogs Breeds and Their Behavior." *Domestic Dog Cognition and Behavior: The Scientific Study of Canis Familiaris,* edited by A. Horowitz. Springer, 2014.

—FURTHER READING CONTINUED—

JOURNALS

Parker, Heidi G. "Genomic Aanalyses of Modern Dog Breeds." *Mammalian Genome* 23 (2012): 19–27.

Svartberg, Kenth, and Björn Forkman. "Personality Traits in the Domestic Dog (*Canis familiaris*)." *Applied Animal Behaviour Scienc*e 79 (2002): 133–55.

Svartberg, Kenth. "Breed-Typical Behaviour in Dogs—Historical Remnants or Recent Constructs?" *Applied Animal Behaviour Science* 96 (2006): 293–313.

Turscán, Borbála, et al. "Trainability and Boldness Traits Differ Between Dog Breed Clusters Based on Conventional Breed Categories and Genetic Relatedness." *Applied Animal Behaviour Science* 132 (2011): 61–70.

vonHoldt, Bridgett M., et al. "Genome-wide SNP and Haplotype Analyses Reveal a Rich History Underlying Dog Domestication." *Nature* 464 (2010): 898–902

WEB

"Understanding Evolution," University of California Museum of Paleontology, accessed August 24, 2016, evolution.berkeley.edu.

Liou, Stephanie, "An Introduction to DNA and Chromosomes," Stanford University, last modified February 5, 2011, accessed August 24, 2016, web.stanford.edu/group/hopes/cgi-bin/hopes_test/an-introduction-to-dna-and-chromosomes-text-and-audio/.

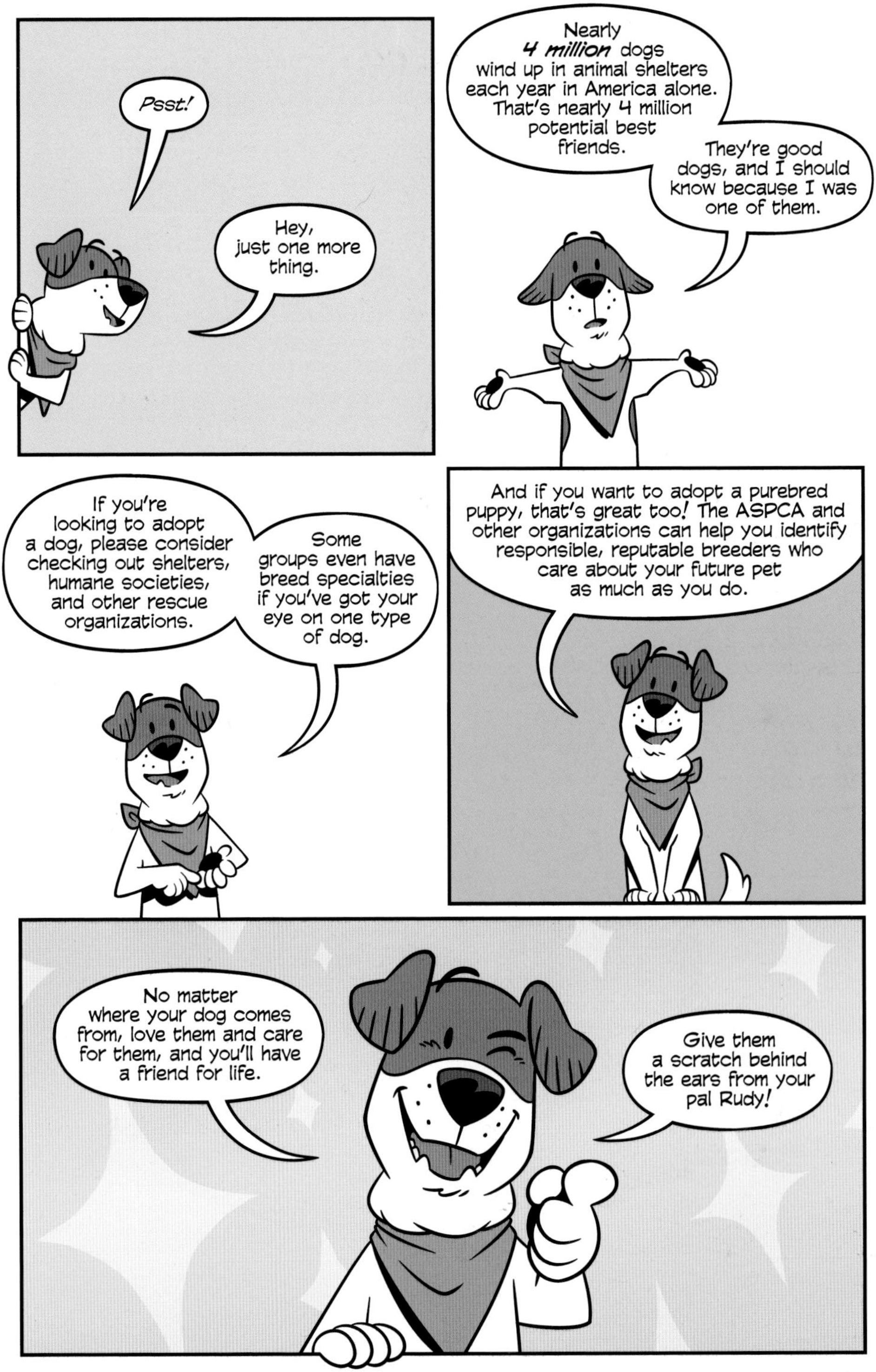
Psst!
Hey, just one more thing.
Nearly *4 million* dogs wind up in animal shelters each year in America alone. That's nearly 4 million potential best friends.
They're good dogs, and I should know because I was one of them.
If you're looking to adopt a dog, please consider checking out shelters, humane societies, and other rescue organizations.
Some groups even have breed specialties if you've got your eye on one type of dog.
And if you want to adopt a purebred puppy, that's great too! The ASPCA and other organizations can help you identify responsible, reputable breeders who care about your future pet as much as you do.
No matter where your dog comes from, love them and care for them, and you'll have a friend for life.
Give them a scratch behind the ears from your pal Rudy!

Special thanks to Richardson Humane Society,
Plano Public Library System, and TexShare.